# World Wisd
## The Library of Perennial Philosophy

The Library of Perennial Philosophy is dedicated to the exposition of the timeless Truth underlying the diverse religions. This Truth, often referred to as the *Sophia Perennis*—or Perennial Wisdom—finds its expression in the revealed Scriptures as well as the writings of the great sages and the artistic creations of the traditional worlds.

*The Shin Buddhist Classical Tradition: A Reader in Pure Land Teaching, Vol. 2* appears as one of our selections in the Treasures of the World's Religions series.

## The Treasures of the World's Religions Series

This series of anthologies presents scriptures and the writings of the great spiritual authorities of the past on fundamental themes. Some titles are devoted to a single spiritual tradition, while others have a unifying topic that touches upon traditions from both the East and the West, such as prayer and virtue. Some titles have a companion volume within the Perennial Philosophy series.

# The Shin Buddhist Classical Tradition

## A Reader in Pure Land Teaching

### VOLUME 2

Edited by

## Alfred Bloom

Foreword by

## Kenneth K. Tanaka

World Wisdom

The Shin Buddhist Classical Tradition:
A Reader in Pure Land Teaching, Vol. 2
© 2014 World Wisdom, Inc.

Library of Congress Cataloging-in-Publication Data

The Shin Buddhist classical tradition : a reader in Pure Land teaching / Edited by
Alfred Bloom ; Foreword by Kenneth K. Tanaka.
     pages cm. -- (The treasures of the world's religions series)
Includes bibliographical references and index.
ISBN 978-1-936597-27-7 (pbk. : alk. paper)  1. Shin (Sect)--Doctrines. I. Bloom,
Alfred.
BQ8718.3.S46 2013
294.3'42046--dc23

                                    2013026871

Printed on acid-free paper in the United States of America.

For information address World Wisdom, Inc.
P.O. Box 2682, Bloomington, Indiana 47402-2682
www.worldwisdom.com

# CONTENTS

## VOLUME 2

# Acknowledgements

I am very grateful to Professor Hisao Inagaki, Dr. Joji Atone, and Mr. Wayne S. Yokoyama for personally permitting the use of their translations, as well as all the publisher permissions to reprint passages from the following scholars' translations which have contributed to this text, as follows:

Joji Atone and Yoko Hayashi, trans. *The Promise of Amida Buddha: Honen's Path to Bliss.* Boston: Wisdom Publications, 2011.

Yoshito Hakeda, trans. *The Awakening of Faith.* New York: Columbia University Press, 1967.

Dennis Hirota, trans. *No Abode: The Record of Ippen.* Honolulu: The University of Hawai'i Press, 1997.

Julian F. Pas. *Visions of Sukhavati: Shan-tao's Commentary on the Kuan-wu-liang-shou-Fo Ching.* Albany: State University of New York Press, 1995.

Kenneth K. Tanaka. *The Dawn of Chinese Pure Land Doctrine: Ching-ying Hui-yuan's Commentary on the Visualization Sutra.* Albany: State University of New York Press, 1990.

I want to thank Dr. Kenneth K. Tanaka for graciously writing the two Forewords for both volumes of *The Shin Buddhist Classical Tradition: A Reader in Pure Land Teaching.* I am also grateful to Ms. Kenya Lee Province for her editorial help, and Mr. Esho Shimazu and Dr. Tsuneichi Takeshita for their assistance.

Finally, I must express my deep appreciation to Ms. Mary-Kathryne Steele and her staff at World Wisdom for their limitless patience as I dealt with various health issues in the course of producing this book. Also I am thankful for my family, who supported my effort to complete the work. The author takes responsibility for any errors, omissions, or misunderstandings.

# Foreword

In Volume Two, Dr. Bloom focuses on practice in the Pure Land tradition by placing Pure Land practices in the context of general Buddhism from its very beginnings. Pure Land practices emerged within the early development of Mahayana Buddhism and included rigorous meditative disciplines. These meditative disciplines were designed to attain visualization of the Buddhas, the *bodhisattvas*, and the features of the Pure Land. And when these meditative disciplines were fully realized, they served as confirmation of the practitioners' birth in the Pure Land at the end of their lives and the eventual realization of Buddhahood in the Pure Land.

Dr. Bloom highlights the fact that in the course of this history, particularly starting in China, the Amida-centered Pure Land teaching raised the hope for birth in that Land for the masses by interpreting the central practice of the eighteenth Vow of Amida as the recitation of the Buddha's Name, rather than as the more difficult visualization practices alluded to above. While it has sometimes been noted that doctrine and belief are not central issues of Buddhism, as they are in Western religions, the popular development of Pure Land teaching included belief in the efficacy of the recitation of the Name of Amida (*nembutsu*) along with the belief in a realistic Pure Land, which was portrayed with detailed descriptions in the sutras. The popularity of Pure Land teaching and practice were also encouraged by the belief in the decline of Buddhism in the theory of "the last age in the demise of the *Dharma*" (*mappo*). In the last age, as an alternative to the difficult monastic disciplines, the *nembutsu* was easily available for all people, regardless of their spiritual abilities. Consequently, Pure Land Buddhist practices came to be incorporated by many Buddhist traditions in East Asia, for not only the lay followers but even for the monks and nuns.

As Dr. Bloom points out, there were two significant features in the further development of Pure Land Buddhism when transmitted to Japan. The one was Honen's establishment, in 1175, of Pure Land Buddhism as an independent sect based strictly on Pure Land sutras and treatises. The other development was seen in Honen's disciple Shinran's reinterpretation of Pure Land Buddhism. Shinran placed much greater emphasis on entrusting to Amida's vow, endowed by the Buddha, and transformed the meaning of the recitation of his Name from an efficacious act to gain birth and Buddhahood to that of an expression of gratitude for the endowed vow of Amida.

Honen declared the universal applicability of the exclusive practice of *nembutsu*. In the last age of the *Dharma* only the *nembutsu* could save monk and layperson alike. In following his teacher's lead, Shinran stressed that all people are assured of birth in the Pure Land through entrusting to Amida's vow and not by self-striving practice. In so doing, he focused particularly on the inner dimension and experience of trust in the vow to a greater degree than his teacher. Given this focus on the inner spiritual dimension, in more recent times, Shinran's interpretation has raised the question of just what constitutes practice in Jodo Shinshu Buddhism. This concern has become especially acute within the Western context, where practice-centered traditions, particularly meditation, mingle and compete as the authentic form of Buddhism.

It is noteworthy that Honen and Shinran also declare that the *nembutsu* offers vast benefits and frees believers from depending on gods and other Buddhas. These benefits are not material, worldly, or magical but include protection of the Buddha's light that symbolizes the overall spiritual well-being of the faithful. Such protection is the natural result of faith [-425-]. However, as Honen states: "An illness which one contracts in daily life cannot be overcome by prayers to various Buddhas and deities. If prayer healed and prolonged life there would be no illness or death" [-419-]. Faith in Amida offsets our residual karma, enabling us to be born in the Pure Land.

In addition to considerations of *nembutsu* practice, the volume also covers topics that have relevance for contemporary Buddhism. The ideals of sharing the *Dharma*, the Good Teacher, and the *Bodhisattva* returning to this world from the Pure Land, indicate that one's commitment to and pursuit of the Pure Land teaching is not a self-centered concern. Equality and non-discrimination, and the practice of compassion, provide the basis for positive and wholesome human relations. Concern for society and ethics are also taken up, as well as dealing with mourners and those facing death. The philosophical section, thus, reflects the deeper foundations of Pure Land thought rooted in the ideals of Mahayana Buddhism. We see from these assembled passages that Pure Land teaching covers a broad range of issues, inviting us to deeper study.

Dr. Kenneth Kenshin Tanaka
Professor, Musashino University
President, International Association of Shin Buddhist Studies

# Introduction

Volume 2 of our presentation of Pure Land tradition focuses on practice. Practice has always been a central issue in the history of Buddhism. The concern for practice began with Gautama, Sakyamuni Buddha. He left his five companions over a difference in practice. These companions wanted to practice asceticism and Gautama initially followed them. There are images showing him as gaunt and half-starved in meditation. However, Gautama found this style of practice fruitless. He rejected extreme asceticism and sought his own path of intensive meditation, while caring for the needs of the body, following the path of a sound mind in a sound body and moderation in all things, the Middle Path. As legend informs us, he simply sat in the lotus position on a seat of straw, without any yogic postures developed in Indian religion. Determined to attain enlightenment, Gautama remained there for several days, receiving nourishment from porridge given to him by a young woman named Sujata. Finally, he had a breakthrough, becoming enlightened.

Gautama's enlightenment experience was crystallized in the First Sermon at Benares, known as the *Turning of the Dharma Wheel Sutta*, which summarizes important principles that became central to Buddhism thereafter. Theravada Buddhism highlights the ideal of the *Arhat*, who pursues his individual goal of enlightenment, carrying on the style of practice initiated by Gautama, the pioneer and model of practice.

History does not stop. Change is fundamental to reality. As Buddhism continued to develop, the appearance of Mahayana Buddhism, which advocates the *Bodhisattva* ideal of shared enlightenment, also gave rise to changes in practice, largely in China. Chinese monasteries initially followed the traditional Theravada-style monastic discipline in rules transmitted from India. Later, *Bodhisattva* precepts emerged as more consistent with Mahayana ideals. The *Bodhisattva* has the mission to guide all beings to enlightenment, as well as himself, thereby also giving rise to modification of the discipline.

Inspired by the Mahayana *Bodhisattva* ideal, proponents of the Pure Land teaching, such as T'an-luan, opened the door to lay people, outside the monastery. He promoted the teaching of the decline of Buddhism (*mappo*), as explained in Volume 1, indicating that we live in an age distant in time from the Buddha, when the power of his example has waned. This situation later led to the reinterpretation of the eighteenth vow of Amida Buddha in the Mahayana *Larger Pure Land Sutra* as advocating the recitation of Amida's Name.

Early Pure Land teachers changed the reading of the vow from its original teaching of *thinking* on the Buddha, understood as meditation, to the recognition of the vocal *recitation* of the Name of Amida Buddha with faith as a valid means for birth into the Pure Land by lay people. This opened a path, more easily attained by ordinary people, to their ultimate attainment of enlightenment. Shan-tao is chiefly credited with advancing this interpretation. Amida's eighteenth vow was read: "To *recite* the Name of Amida at least ten times." This understanding continues to this day in the Pure Land tradition.

However, Pure Land teachers continued to maintain monastic-meditative practice for capable people, while also propagating the recitation of Amida's Name for ordinary people, suitable as the practice authorized by the eighteenth vow. Later, in Japan, Honen went further, holding that *nembutsu* recitation was the only means for people, monks as well as lay people, to gain birth in the Pure Land in the last age, establishing the basis for the independent sect of Pure Land teaching. His declaration of the supremacy of *nembutsu* recitation involves a trenchant social critique. He rejected all forms of elitism, whether social status and wealth, intellectual abilities, religious proficiency, or moral capacity. He observed that with such elitism, the spiritual realm would be closed to the multitudes of poor and incapable people [-127-].

Over this history, the assumption governing meditation or recitation remained the same. All practices yielded merit which advanced the person's spiritual status. The Pure Land teaching, with its universal availability, became an aspect of all Mahayana traditions. It was assumed that Buddhist practices, particularly incessant recitation of the vocal *nembutsu*, increased and strengthened an individual's spiritual potential to attain enlightenment through several lives and rebirths.

However, Shinran, a disciple of Honen, initiated the next major turn in the understanding of *nembutsu*. Shinran declared that the *nembutsu* was neither a practice nor a good deed [-405-]. He rejected the meritorious character of *nembutsu* recitation. It was not a monastic-meditation practice such as monks might use to gain enlightenment, nor was it a good deed which lay people might employ to gain merits for birth in the Pure Land, or worldly benefits such as health, wealth, or spiritual protection. It was not a mantra to dispel disasters or ward off evil as practiced in other sects. While many earlier teachers are recorded as reciting *nembutsu* as many as 70,000 times a day as a badge of their virtue, there is no record of Shinran's reciting it in that manner. There is no set time or number for reciting [-399-]. For him the only reason to recite it is to express gratitude for the deliverance we have already been assured.

For Shinran, the *nembutsu* was a sign and expression that Amida's vow had been fulfilled, and the urge to recite the Name meant that one had already been embraced by Amida's compassion, never to be abandoned. It was a witness of spiritual emancipation already given and liberation from all types of spiritual anxieties and fears that attended many other forms of religious practice. In the Jodo Shinshu Buddhist tradition, following Shinran, *nembutsu* expressed gratitude for salvation already given and was not a means to gain a salvation lying in the future.

In the context of Shinran's rejection of the instrumental use of *nembutsu*, it has been traditionally taught that there is no practice or transfer of merit in Jodo Shinshu Buddhism from the side of the devotee [-396-]. Rather, all living becomes a sphere for practice in a broad sense as we reflect on our lives and deepen our awareness of Amida's compassion, responding with grateful *nembutsu*. The liberation that his compassion affords increases our sense of responsibility to share and communicate that compassion. As the brighter the light, the sharper the shadows, we become more cognizant of our egoism and how it distorts others' lives beside our own. Buddhist practice here is to confront our egoism in the continuing process of entrusting ourselves to Amida's vow.

Shinran's reinterpretation of the meaning of *nembutsu* as faith or true entrusting in the vow, which is the true cause of deliverance, brought about a transformation in self-understanding and the meaning of religion. It is neither self-serving nor ego-aggrandizing, but gratitude and dedication. *Nen* (thought), viewed as trust in the vow, is inspired and awakened in the devotee through the working of Amida Buddha in our heart-minds. It is also seen as the fulfillment of Buddha nature, as the essence of our reality, and focused on the welfare of all beings. There are social implications embodied in the teaching which only now have begun to work themselves out in the context of social and political freedom in Japan and the West.

As a consequence of his distinctive interpretation, Shinran stated that the recitation does not produce trust, but it is trust that gratefully produces the Name. He transformed the traditional recitation from a plea for the Buddha to save, "Please save me!" to, in effect, "I am grateful to Amida Buddha's vow that saves me." It is trust that evokes the Name in recognition of Amida's compassionate working. This perspective maintains the primacy of the spiritual meaning of *nembutsu* recitation against its ritualistic, magical, or pragmatic use. It opens to deeper human relations and highlights the dedication implicit in one's grateful response as he declared in the *Ondokusan* ("Dedication") verses:

Such is the benevolence of Amida's great compassion,
That we must strive to return it, even to the breaking of our bodies;

Such is the benevolence of the masters and true teachers,
That we must endeavor to repay it, even to our bones becoming dust.
[-433-]

Despite the limitations of Japanese social and political history, Shinran's interpretation became a hallmark of Jodo Shinshu Buddhism. It has been transmitted over the centuries through Shinran's writings and particularly Rennyo's letters, which constantly exhort his followers to a life of gratitude and dedication [-286-; -287-; -294-; -295-; -435-]. Though he called for great care in sharing Shinran's radical teaching with others, his liberating message spread rapidly, giving birth to a major religious and social movement in Japanese history. Buffeted by the waves of history and changing society, as well as movement from East to West, the message of spiritual and personal liberation remains embodied within the Pure Land tradition, becoming more universally available for wider study and inspiration through modern means of communication.

Alfred Bloom

# Conventions

- The terms *nembutsu* and *bombu* will be used throughout in their untranslated form.

- The term *shinjin*, interpreted as "true entrusting," remains in its untranslated form throughout because of the pervasiveness of its use and its importance as a key term for Shinran. However, its meaning in the writings of earlier teachers does not imply its special use made by Shinran.

- The more commonly used Wade-Giles system is used for Chinese Romanization.

- No diacritical marks will be used.

- In the interest of uniformity and comprehension, all titles, textual references, and technical terms in other languages will be given in their Japanese form where possible.

- Abbreviations: *CWS* refers to *The Collected Works of Shinran*.

# II. Teachings of the Pure Land Tradition (Cont.)

## H. Pure Land Practice

1. General Approach to Practice
Asvaghosha
-317- Next, suppose there is a man who learns this teaching for the first time and wishes to seek the correct faith but lacks courage and strength. Because he lives in this world of suffering, he fears that he will not always be able to meet the Buddhas and honor them personally, and that, faith being difficult to perfect, he will be inclined to fall back. He should know that the *Tathagatas* have an excellent expedient means by which they can protect his faith: that is, through the strength of wholehearted meditation on the Buddha, he will in fulfillment of his wishes be able to be born in the Buddha-land beyond, to see the Buddha always, and to be forever separated from the evil states of existence. It is as the sutra says: "If a man meditates wholly on Amida Buddha in the world of the Western Paradise and wishes to be born in that world, directing all the goodness he has cultivated [toward that goal], then he will be born there." Because he will see the Buddha at all times, he will never fall back. If he meditates on the *Dharmakaya*, the Suchness of the Buddha, and with diligence keeps practicing [the meditation], he will be able to be born there in the end because he abides in the correct *samadhi*. (Yoshito Hakeda, trans., *Awakening of Faith* [New York: Columbia University Press, 1967], p. 102)

Nagarjuna
-318- To the practicers of Mahayana, the Buddha said: "To make vows and seek the Path to Buddhahood is a task harder than lifting the whole universe."

You say that the Stage of Non-retrogression is extremely difficult to enter, requiring a long period of practice, and ask me if there is a path of easy practice whereby you can attain this stage quickly. These are words of a cowardly and contemptible man, and not those of a brave man with a strong aspiration. If, however, you insist on hearing from me about this method of practice, I will explain it to you.

There are innumerable modes of entry into the Buddha's teaching. Just as there are in the world difficult and easy paths—travelling on foot by land is full of hardship and travelling in a boat by sea is pleasant—so it is among the paths of the *bodhisattvas*. Some exert themselves diligently, while others quickly enter Non-retrogression by the easy practice based on faith. (Hisao Inagaki, *Discourse on the Ten Stages, Easy Practice Section*, http://www12.canvas.ne.jp/horai/igyohon.htm; see also *CWS, Kyogyoshinsho*, I, p. 22, II:15)

Nagarjuna

-319- In the Buddha's teaching there are countless gates. Just as there are difficult and easy among the paths of this world—for journeying overland is full of hardship while sailing on board of a boat is pleasant—so it is with the paths of *bodhisattvas*. Some engage in rigorous practice and endeavor; others quickly reach the stage of non-retrogression through the easy practice of entrusting as the means [for attaining it]. . . .

> If a person desires quickly to attain
> The stage of non-retrogression,
> He or she should, with a reverent heart,
> Say the Name, holding steadfast to it.
> (*Commentary on the Ten Bodhisattva Stages, CWS, Kyogyoshinsho*, I, #15, p. 22, II:15)

Vasubandhu

-320- Again, there are five gates, which in order produce five kinds of merit. One should realize the implication of this. What are the five gates? They are: (1) the gate of approach, (2) the gate of great assemblage, (3) the gate of residence, (4) the gate of chamber, and (5) the gate of playing ground.

Of the five gates, the first four produce the merit in the phase of "going in" and the fifth produces the merit in the phase of "going out."

The first gate in the phase of "going in" is to worship Amida Buddha in order to be born in his Land; by this one attains birth in the Land of Peace and Bliss, and so it is called the first gate in the phase of "going in."

The second gate in the phase of "going in" is to praise Amida Buddha, while reciting his Name in compliance with its meaning and practicing in compliance with his light of wisdom; by this one joins the great assemblage. This is called the second gate in the phase of "going in."

The third gate in the phase of "going in" is to aspire single-mindedly and wholeheartedly to be born there and to perform the practice of *shamatha*, the *samadhi* of tranquility; by this one can reach the Land of Lotus-Treasury. This is called the third gate in the phase of "going in."

The fourth gate in the phase of "going in" is to contemplate wholeheartedly those glorious adornments and so practice *vipashyana*; by this one can reach that Land, where one will enjoy various flavors of the *Dharma*. This is called the fourth gate of "going in."

The fifth gate in the phase of "going out" is to observe with great compassion all suffering beings, manifest accommodated and transformed bodies, and enter the garden of birth-and-death and the forest of evil passions, where [*bodhisattvas*] play about, exercising transcendent powers; they thus dwell in the stage of teaching others through [Amida's] transference of merit by their Primal Vow-Power. This is called the fifth gate in the phase of "going out."

*Bodhisattvas* accomplish the practice for their own benefit with the four gates in the phase of "going in." One should realize the implication of this.

Through the fifth gate of "going out" *bodhisattvas* accomplish the practice of benefiting others by transference of merit. One should realize the implication of this.

Thus, by performing the five mindful practices, *bodhisattvas* accomplish both self-benefit and benefit for others, and so quickly attain *anuttara-samyak-sambodhi*. (Hisao Inagaki, *Discourse on the Pure Land* [*Jodoron*], http://www12.canvas.ne.jp/horai/jodoron.htm; see also Hisao Inagaki, trans., *T'an-Luan's Commentary on Vasubandhu's Discourse on the Pure Land* [*Ojoronchu*] [Kyoto: Nagata Bunshodo, 1998], pp. 281-285)

T'an-luan

-321- When I reverently read Nagarjuna's *Discourse on the Ten Stages*, I find the following passage:

"There are two paths by which *Bodhisattvas* reach the stage of Non-retrogression: The path of difficult practice and the path of easy practice.

The path of difficult practice is a way of trying to reach the Stage of Non-retrogression in the period of the five defilements when no Buddha dwells in the world. It is difficult to follow this path and there are reasons for this. In order to clarify this, I shall outline five reasons as follows:

1. Non-Buddhist ways of doing what seems to be good are at variance with the *Bodhisattva's* practice.

2. The *shravaka's* pursuit of self-benefit obstructs the *Bodhisattva's* acts of great compassion.

3. Evil-doers, who have no regard for consequences, destroy the superior merit of others.

4. The results of good deeds based on deluded thinking offer a distraction from sacred practices.

5. Relying solely on our own power, we miss the support of the Other-Power.

These facts are seen everywhere. The path of difficult practice is, therefore, like an overland journey painstakingly made, on foot.

The path of easy practice is followed by aspiring to be born in the Pure Land through faith in Amida Buddha and attaining birth in his Pure Land by the power of his vows. In the Pure Land we are sustained by the Buddha's power and join those who are rightly established in the Mahayana Path. 'Rightly established' refers to the stage of non-retrogression. The path of easy practice is, therefore, like a pleasant journey on water."

The *Upadesa on the Amitayus Sutra* is indeed the ultimate teaching of Mahayana, a ship sailing before the favorable wind of non-retrogression. (Hisao Inagaki, trans., *T'an-Luan's Commentary on Vasubandhu's Discourse on the Pure Land* [*Ojoronchu*] [Kyoto: Nagata Bunshodo, 1998], p. 121)

T'an-luan
-322- 1. The section on the power of the five mindful practices:
In presenting the five gates of mindful practice, [Vasubandhu] says: "What are the five gates of mindful practices? They are: (1) worship; (2) praise; (3) aspiration; (4) contemplation; and (5) merit-transference."

"Gate" is "that through which one comes in and goes out."

If one has a gate, one, can freely come in and go out through it.

The first four mindful practices are the gate through which one enters the Land of Peace and Bliss. The last one is the gate through which one goes out to perform the beneficial act of teaching people the Buddha *Dharma*. (Hisao Inagaki, trans., *T'an-Luan's Commentary on Vasubandhu's Discourse on the Pure Land* [*Ojoronchu*] [Kyoto: Nagata Bunshodo, 1998], pp. 205-207)

Shan-tao
-323- Those who are mindful of Amida continuously until the end of their lives as stated above will be born in the Pure Land, ten out of ten and a hundred out of a hundred. The reason is that they are free of miscellaneous influences from outside, they have attained the right mindfulness, they are in accord with the Buddha's Primal Vow, they do not disagree with the Buddha's teachings, and they accord with the Buddha's words.

Those who set aside the exclusive practice and seek to perform miscellaneous acts will rarely attain birth, perhaps one or two out of a hundred or three or five out of a thousand. The reason is that miscellaneous influences arise in confusion and disrupt one's right-mindfulness. Such practitioners are not in accord with the Buddha's Primal Vow, they are in disagreement with the Buddha's teachings, they do not accord with the Buddha's words, their mindfulness does not continue, their recollecting thoughts are intermittent, their aspiration for birth by transferring their merits towards it is not deep-rooted and sincere, evil passions such as greed, anger, and various wrong views arise to interrupt their mindfulness, and they lack the mind of repentance. (Hisao Inagaki, trans., *Shan-tao's Liturgy for Birth* [*Ojoraisan*], http://www12.canvas.ne.jp/horai/raisan.htm)

Shan-tao
-324- I reverently advise you, all the aspirants of birth, to consider your capacities. If you wish to attain birth, you should necessarily strive, mind

and body, day and night, without abolishing the practice, whether walking, stopping, sitting or lying down, until the end of your lives.

To keep practicing all through life appears somewhat painful, but the moment life ends, the next moment you will be born in that land, where you will everlastingly enjoy the *Dharma*-bliss of No-action and will no longer be subject to birth-and-death until you attain Buddhahood. Is this not wonderful? You should be aware of this. (Hisao Inagaki, trans., *Shan-tao's Liturgy for Birth* [*Ojoraisan*], http://www12.canvas.ne.jp/horai/raisan.htm)

Shan-tao

-325- I take refuge in and prostrate myself with sincerity of heart to Amida Buddha in the Western Quarter.

The upper grade of aspirants are those of superior capacity who perform superior practices;

Aspiring to be born in the Pure Land, they sever their greed and anger.

According to different types of practice performed, aspirants are divided into three levels.

(The upper grade of aspirants) continuously perform the five (mindful) practices to strengthen the three causes.

By single-minded diligent practice for one to seven days,

When they die, they mount lotus-daises and leave the world of the six objects of sensation.

How joyful! I have encountered what is difficult to encounter.

I shall eternally realize the body of *Dharma*-nature and No-action.

I wish to be born in the Land of Peace and Bliss together with all sentient beings.

I take refuge in and prostrate myself with sincerity of heart to Amida Buddha in the Western Quarter.

The middle grade of aspirants are those of medium capacity who perform the middle level of practices;

They observe the precepts of abstinence for one day and so will go to the West enclosed in gold lotus-flowers.

They are taught to transfer the merit of their loving care for their parents to the Pure Land,

So that it may become the cause of bliss to be enjoyed in the Western Land.

The Buddha, together with hosts of *shravakas*, will come to welcome them,

Enabling them to go immediately near Amida's lotus throne.

Enclosed in the hundred-jeweled flowers, they will spend seven days;

When the flowers for the three grades of aspirants open, they will realize

Hinayana truth.

I wish to be born in the Land of Peace and Bliss together with all sentient beings.

I take refuge in and prostrate myself with sincerity of heart to Amida Buddha in the Western Quarter.

The lower grade of aspirants are those of inferior capacity who do evil acts;

They commit acts of greed and anger, such as the ten evil acts and the five gravest offenses,

And also violate the four major prohibitions, steal monks' property and abuse the right *Dharma*,

Without ever repenting their offenses committed.

At the end of their lives, visions of torture surround them like clouds,

And fierce fires of hell appear before those sinners.

At that moment, they may suddenly meet good teachers of the way to birth,

Who lose no time in urging them to recite the Buddha's Name with singleness of heart.

Responding to the voice, transformed Buddhas and *bodhisattvas* come to them.

With a single thought of mindfulness at the time of death, they will enter the jeweled pond.

Owing to their heavy hindrances committed with three kinds of acts, their flowers will not open until after many *kalpas*.

When the flowers open, they will, for the first time, awaken the cause of *Bodhi*.

I wish to be born in the Land of Peace and Bliss together with all sentient beings.

(Hisao Inagaki, trans., *Shan-tao's Liturgy for Birth* [*Ojoraisan*], 1-3, http://www12.canvas.ne.jp/horai/raisan.htm)

Shan-tao

-326- . . . those who have a compassionate mind and do not kill [other beings]. Now there are many actions by which one may kill: killing through words, through deeds, through thoughts. (1) Killing through words: [e.g.,] to condemn to execution or to approve of it. (2) Killing through deeds, [i.e.,] through one's physical actions. (3) Killing through thoughts, [e.g.,] to conceive convenient mental plots.

Speaking about the action of killing, no matter whether it refers to [any of] the four forms of life, they all cause sin[ful karma] and hinder rebirth in the Land of Purity. On the other hand, those who produce a compassionate mind toward all forms of life bestow the peace and happiness of longevity upon all sentient beings, which also is the supreme and most excellent precept, and corresponds with the "Worldly Merits." It consists of a twofold goodness: desisting and acting. Not to harm others oneself is called "desisting goodness"; to teach others not to harm is called "acting goodness." [Or explaining the terms in another way] if oneself and others start to desist [from killing], it is called "desisting goodness"; if one till the end forever eliminates [killing], it is called "acting goodness." Although there is a twofold goodness, desisting and upholding, they [both] ultimately indicate the completion of the inferior practice of compassion. (Julian F. Pas, *Visions of Sukhavati: Shan-Tao's Commentary on the Kuan-wu-Liang-Shou-Fo Ching* [Albany, NY: State University of New York Press, 1995], p. 231)

Honen

-327- Next, there are also two classifications of the non-contemplative practices. One is the three [types of] beneficial practices and the other, the practices for the nine levels [of people].

First, regarding the three [types of] beneficial practice, the *Contemplation Sutra* says: first of these is filial piety toward one's father and mother, reverence for one's teachers and elders, the compassionate heart that avoids any kind of killing, and performance of the ten good acts. The second is to hold fast to the three refuges, to observe the various precepts, and not to violate the rules of proper conduct. The third is to awaken the *bodhicitta*, to have deep faith in [karmic] causality, to read and recite the Mahayana sutras, and to encourage other practitioners.

There are two kinds of "filial piety toward one's father and mother": one is secular filial piety, and the other is religious filial piety. Secular filial piety is as described in the *Book of Filial Piety* and elsewhere. Religious filial piety is as described in the *vinaya* that speaks of the prescribed method of serving the parents responsible for one's birth.

There are also two kinds of "reverence for one's teachers and elders": one is reverence for one's secular teachers and elders; the other is reverence for one's religious teachers and elders. Secular teachers teach benevolence, righteousness, courtesy, wisdom, trustworthiness, and the like. Religious teachers teach the gateways of the Holy Path and the Pure Land, and the like. Even though the other practices are lacking, filial piety and reverence for one's parents and teachers can be the karmic action for birth in the Pure Land. (*Senchakushu* English Translation Project, *Honen's Senchakushu: Passages on the Selection of the Nembutsu in the Original Vow* [*Senchaku Hongan Nembutsu Shu*] [Honolulu, HI: University of Hawaii Press, 1998], p. 127)

Ippen

**-328-** *Precepts for the Nembutsu Practicer*

With wholeness of heart
Revere the luminous majesty of the gods;
Do not slight the virtue of their original source.
With wholeness of heart
Think on Buddha, *Dharma*, and *Sangha*;
Do not overlook the power in the interaction between Buddha's compassion and our aspiration.
With wholeness of heart
Perform the practice of saying the Name;
Do not endeavor in sundry practices.
With wholeness of heart
Entrust yourself to the *Dharma* you revere;
Do not denounce the teachings followed by others.
With wholeness of heart
Waken the realization of sameness;
Do not engage in discriminative thinking.
With wholeness of heart
Give rise to compassion;
Do not be forgetful of others' sorrow.
With wholeness of heart
Disclose a gentle countenance;
Do not manifest marks of anger and intolerance.
With wholeness of heart
Dwell firmly in humility's insights;
Do not arouse a spirit of arrogance.
With wholeness of heart
Discern the sources of impurity;
Do not generate a mind that cherishes attachments.
With wholeness of heart
Contemplate the reality of impermanence;
Do not awaken thoughts of greed and desire.
With wholeness of heart
Rectify your own faults;
Do not revile others for their transgressions.
With wholeness of heart
Sport in the activity of transforming others;
Do not be negligent in practice for self-benefit.
With wholeness of heart
Fear the three low paths;
Do not indulge in evil acts.

With wholeness of heart
Aspire for the Land of Peace;
Do not disregard the pain in the three dark courses.
With wholeness of heart
Be settled in contemplation of birth;
Do not become lax in the practice of saying the Name.
With wholeness of heart
Hold the West in mindfulness;
Do not divide your thoughts among the other nine regions.
With wholeness of heart
Endeavor in the practice leading to enlightenment;
Do not keep company with those given to amusement and pleasure.
With wholeness of heart
Follow the guidance of your good teacher;
Do not leave matters to your self-will.
To the end of the last age,
Disciples who survive me
Should strictly uphold what is written here.
Exert all your powers, and never neglect
[The Name that is] the embodiment of practice pervading the three
    modes of action.
*Namu-amida-butsu*
(Dennis Hirota, trans., *No Abode: The Record of Ippen* [Honolulu: University of Hawaii Press, rev. 1997], pp. 17-19; see also -107-; -230-)


## 2. Devotion to Amida and All Buddhas
Nagarjuna
-329- Amida Buddha's Primal Vow is as follows: If anyone contemplates me, recites my name, and takes refuge in me, he will instantly enter the Stage of Assurance and subsequently attain the highest perfect *bodhi*. For this reason, you should always be mindful of him. I will now praise him in verse. The Buddha of Infinite Light and Wisdom, whose body is like a mountain of genuine gold,
    I worship with my body, speech, and heart by joining hands and bowing
        down toward him.
His glorious golden radiance reaches all the worlds,
Manifesting its forms in accordance with the beings whom he saves.
So I bow down and worship him.
If anyone, after the end of his life, obtains birth in Amida's land,
He will be instantly endowed with immeasurable merit.
So I take refuge in Amida.
If anyone is mindful of that Buddha's infinite power and merit,

9

He will instantly enter the stage of assurance.

So I am always mindful of Amida.

Even though people of his land may be subject to various sufferings after death,

They will not fall into the evil realm of hell.

So I take refuge in him and worship him.

If anyone is born in that land, he will never again fall into the three evil realms or the realm of *asuras*.

So I now take refuge in him and worship him.

Those born in his land are free from attachment to "myself" and "mine."

They do not produce discriminative thoughts.

So I bow down and worship him.

There are innumerable *shravakas* [in his land], who have attained release from the prison of the Three Worlds;

Their eyes are like lotus-petals.

So I bow down and worship him.

All the sentient beings of his land have a gentle nature,

And spontaneously perform the ten good deeds.

So I bow down to the King of Sages.

They shine brightly and purely through performing good deeds;

Their number is infinite and incalculable.

They are the most distinguished of all humans.

So I take refuge in him.

If anyone, aspiring to become a Buddha, contemplates Amida in his heart,

Amida will instantly manifest himself before him.

So I take refuge in him.

By the power of the Buddha's Primal Vow, *bodhisattvas* of the ten directions

Come to make offerings to him and hear the *Dharma*.

So I bow down to him. . . .

The Buddha's sermons destroy the roots of evil;

They are beautifully worded and bring great benefit.

So I bow down and worship him.

With these beautifully worded sermons, he cures people's addiction to pleasures;

He saved beings in the past and is saving beings now; all gods kneel down and worship him.

He is the most honored of all human and heavenly beings; all gods kneel down and worship him,

With their crowns made of seven treasures touching his feet.

So I take refuge in him. . . .

All wise and holy sages and multitudes of human and heavenly beings
Together take refuge in him. . . .
Like those Buddhas, I have praised his boundless virtue.
By this act, I pray that the Buddha may always think of me.
With whatever merit I have acquired in this and previous lives,
I wish to be in the presence of the Buddha and attain eternal purity of
    heart.
May the supreme merit I have acquired by this meritorious act
Be shared with all other sentient beings.

(Hisao Inagaki, trans., *Path of Easy Practice: The Ninth Chapter of the Discourse on the Ten Stages* [*Igyohon*], http://www12.canvas.ne.jp/horai/igyohan.html)

Nagarjuna
-330- *The Twelve Personal Dedications*
The Buddha said to Ananda: The *Bhiksu* Dharmakara, having thus proclaimed those vows, spoke the following verses:

1. With reverence I bow my head to Amida, the Sage,
The Most Honored One, who is revered by humans and *devas*.
You dwell in the wonderful Land of Peace and Bliss,
Surrounded by innumerable children of the Buddhas.
2. Your spotless golden body is like Sumeru, the king of mountains;
Your steps while you are absorbed in *shamatha* are like an elephant's;
Your eyes are as pure as blue lotus-flowers.
Hence, I prostrate myself to the ground and worship Amida, the Holy
    One.
3. Your face is in perfect shape and serene like the full moon;
Your majestic light shines like a thousand suns and moons put together;
Your voice sounds like a heavenly drum or a cuckoo.
Hence, I prostrate myself to the ground and worship Amida, the Holy
    One.
4. You reside in the crown which Kannon wears on his head;
Your excellent features are adorned with jewel-ornaments;
You destroy anti-Buddhist views, devilish thoughts and conceited ideas.
Hence, I prostrate myself to the ground and worship Amida, the Holy
    One.
5. Incomparable, spotless, broad, and pure
Is your virtue; it is serene and clear like space.
You have attained freedom in giving benefit to beings.
Hence, I prostrate myself to the ground and worship Amida, the Holy
    One.

6. *Bodhisattvas* in your Land, renowned everywhere in the ten directions,
Are always glorified even by innumerable maras;
You dwell with the Vow-Power for the sake of all sentient beings.
Hence, I prostrate myself to the ground and worship Amida, the Holy
   One.
7. In the jewel-pond strewn with gold sands grows a lotus;
The excellent throne on its dais has been produced by your acts of merit;
On the throne you are seated like the king of mountains.
Hence, I prostrate myself to the ground and worship Amida, the Holy
   One.
8. From the ten directions the Buddhas' children come in flocks;
Manifesting supernatural powers, they reach the Land of Peace and
   Bliss.
They look up at your august face adoringly and worship you without
   interruption.
Hence, I prostrate myself to the ground and worship Amida, the Holy
   One.
9. All things are impermanent and selfless,
Like an image of the moon in the water, lightning, or morning dew.
Your sermons to the multitudes are, in reality, wordless.
Hence, I prostrate myself to the ground and worship Amida, the Holy
   One.
10. In the Revered Buddha's Land exist no evil names,
Nor are there beings in the female form, nor fear of evil realms.
All worship the Honored One in sincerity of heart.
Hence, I prostrate myself to the ground and worship Amida, the Holy
   One.
11. In the Buddha's Land accomplished with innumerable skillful
   devices,
There are no samsaric realms, nor evil teachers;
Upon attaining birth there, one reaches *bodhi* without falling back.
Hence, I prostrate myself to the ground and worship Amida, the Holy
   One.
12. I have extolled the Buddha's excellent virtue,
Thereby acquiring boundless merit like the ocean.
The roots of pure good I have thus acquired
I wish to share with other beings, aspiring together to be born in his
   Land.
(Hisao Inagaki, trans., *Nagarjuna's Junirai Twelve Adorations*, http://
www12.canvas.ne.jp/horai/larger-sutra-1.htm; see also *CWS, Kyogyoshinsho,*
I, pp. 23-24, II:15)

T'an-luan

-331- *Gathas in Praise of Amida Buddha* states:

*Namu-amida-butsu.*

Interpreting the title, I call this work *An Appended Scripture on the Buddha of Immeasurable Life.*

In praising Amida, it also refers to the land of peace.

Since attainment of Buddhahood, ten *kalpas* have passed;

The Buddha's life indeed has no measure.

*Dharma*-body's wheel of light pervades the *dharma*-realm,

Shining on the blind and ignorant of the world; hence, I bow in homage.

The light that is wisdom cannot be measured;

Hence, the Buddha is called "immeasurable light."

All limited beings receive this dawn-light;

Thus, I pay homage to the true and real light.

Infinite is the wheel-like light that brings emancipation;

Hence, the Buddha is called "boundless light."

All touched by it are freed from being and nonbeing;

Thus, I pay homage to the enlightenment of nondiscrimination.

The cloud of light is unhindered, like boundless space;

Hence, the Buddha is called "unhindered light."

It benefits all beings caught in hindrances;

Thus, I bow in homage to the one beyond conception.

The light of purity is beyond compare;

Hence, the Buddha is called "unequaled light."

Those who encounter it are rid of karmic bonds;

Thus, I pay homage to the ultimate shelter.

The Buddha-light, shining in splendor, is supreme;

Hence, the Buddha is called "lord of blazing light."

The pitch darkness of the three lower courses receives it and is dispelled;

Thus, I bow in homage to the great one worthy of offerings.

*Bodhi's* effulgence, in its brilliance, transcends all colors;

Hence, the Buddha is called "light of purity."

Once shone upon, beings are freed from evil's defilements

And all gain emancipation; thus, I bow in homage.

The light of compassion reaches far, bestowing happiness;

Hence, the Buddha is called "light of joy."

Wherever it shines, joy of *dharma* is attained;

Thus, I pay homage to the great consolation.

The Buddha-light rends the darkness of ignorance;

Hence, the Buddha is called "light of wisdom."

All Buddhas and sages of the three vehicles

Together offer praise; thus, I pay homage.

The light, at all times, shines everywhere;
Hence, the Buddha is called "uninterrupted light."
Because beings hear this light-power, their thoughts uninterrupted,
They all attain birth; thus, I bow in homage.
None, excepting the Buddhas, can fathom this light;
Hence, the Buddha is called "inconceivable light."
The Buddhas of the ten quarters all extol birth
And praise Amida's virtue; thus, I pay homage.
The majestic light transcends forms; it cannot be named.
Hence, the Buddha is called "inexpressible light."
With this light as cause, Buddhahood was attained; its resplendence
Is praised by all Buddhas. Thus, I bow in homage.
The light, in its luminosity, surpasses sun and moon;
Hence, the Buddha is called "light that surpasses sun and moon."
Even Sakyamuni Buddha's praise is not exhaustive;
Thus, I pay homage to the unequaled. . . .
The great master, Nagarjuna Mahasattva, manifested form,
And first corrected distortions [of the teaching].
He closed off wrong views and opened the right path;
He is the eye for all beings of this Jambudvipa continent.
Reverently accepting the Honored-one's words, he reached the stage of
    joy,
Took refuge in Amida, and was born in the land of happiness.
I have been wandering in the three realms since the beginningless past,
Turning on the wheel of falsity.
The karma I commit every moment, every instant,
Is a step bound to the six courses, so that I stay in the three paths.
May the compassionate light protect me
And keep me from losing the mind aspiring for enlightenment.
I praise the voice of the Buddha's wisdom and virtue.
May all beings of the ten quarters having ties with the teaching be
    brought to hear it,
And may those who aspire for birth in the land of happiness
All, everywhere, have their hindrances dispersed as they desire.
My merits, whether great or small,
I give to all beings, so that all be born together.
Entrusting to the inconceivable light,
I single-heartedly take refuge and pay homage.
Those throughout the ten quarters and three times who awaken immea-
    surable wisdom
All alike accord with oneness and are called "perfectly enlightened."
In them the two wisdoms—real and accommodated—are perfectly ful-

filled; their awakening is of equality.

Their grasping and guiding beings, according to conditions, is truly immense.

My taking refuge in Amida Buddha's Pure Land

Is taking refuge in all the Buddhas' lands;

Single-heartedly I extol one Buddha;

May it extend to the unhindered ones throughout the ten quarters.

To each of the innumerable Buddhas of the ten quarters,

With all my heart, I bow in homage.

(*CWS, Kyogyoshinsho*, I, pp. 194-197, V:29)


Shan-tao

-**332**- (10) I take refuge in the Buddha of Immeasurable Light in the Western Land of Utmost Bliss.

May I take refuge in him together with all sentient beings.

Hence, I prostrate myself in worship to him, aspiring for birth in his land.

I take refuge in the Buddha of Boundless Light in the Western Land of Utmost Bliss.

May I take refuge in him together with all sentient beings.

Hence, I prostrate myself in worship to him, aspiring for birth in his land.

I take refuge in the Buddha of Unhindered Light in the Western Land of Utmost Bliss.

May I take refuge in him together with all sentient beings.

Hence, I prostrate myself in worship to him, aspiring for birth in his land.

I take refuge in the Buddha of Unequaled Light in the Western Land of Utmost Bliss.

May I take refuge in him together with all sentient beings.

Hence, I prostrate myself in worship to him, aspiring for birth in his land.

I take refuge in the Buddha of King of Flame-Light in the Western Land of Utmost Bliss.

May I take refuge in him together with all sentient beings.

Hence, I prostrate myself in worship to him, aspiring for birth in his land.

I take refuge in the Buddha of Pure Light in the Western Land of Utmost Bliss.

May I take refuge in him together with all sentient beings.

Hence, I prostrate myself in worship to him, aspiring for birth in his land.

I take refuge in the Buddha of Joyful Light in the Western Land of Utmost Bliss.

May I take refuge in him together with all sentient beings.

Hence, I prostrate myself in worship to him, aspiring for birth in his land.

I take refuge in the Buddha of Wisdom-Light in the Western Land of Utmost Bliss.

May I take refuge in him together with all sentient beings.

Hence, I prostrate myself in worship to him, aspiring for birth in his land.

I take refuge in the Buddha of Uninterrupted Light in the Western Land of Utmost Bliss.

May I take refuge in him together with all sentient beings.

Hence, I prostrate myself in worship to him, aspiring for birth in his land.

I take refuge in the Buddha of Inconceivable Light in the Western Land of Utmost Bliss.

May I take refuge in him together with all sentient beings.

Hence, I prostrate myself in worship to him, aspiring for birth in his land.

I take refuge in the Buddha of Ineffable Light in the Western Land of Utmost Bliss.

May I take refuge in him together with all sentient beings.

Hence, I prostrate myself in worship to him, aspiring for birth in his land.

I take refuge in the Buddha of Light Outshining the Sun and Moon in the Western Land of Utmost Bliss.

May I take refuge in him together with all sentient beings.

Hence, I prostrate myself in worship to him, aspiring for birth in his land.

(11) I take refuge in Amida Buddha in the Western Land of Utmost Bliss;

May the Buddha enfold and protect me with compassion

And let me multiply the seeds of the *Dharma*;

In this life and in the life to come,

May the Buddha always embrace me.

May I take refuge in him together with all sentient beings.

Hence, I prostrate myself in worship to him, aspiring for birth in his land.

I take refuge in Avalokiteshvara *Bodhisattva* in the Western Land of Utmost Bliss;

May I take refuge in him together with all sentient beings.

Hence, I prostrate myself in worship to him, aspiring for birth in that land.

I take refuge in Mahasthamaprapta *Bodhisattva* in the Western Land of Utmost Bliss;

May I take refuge in him together with all sentient beings.

Hence, I prostrate myself in worship to him, aspiring for birth in that land.

At the end of the lives of all sentient beings, these two *bodhisattvas* bring flower-seats and give them to the practitioners. Amida Buddha sends forth great floods of light which illumine their bodies. Furthermore, innumerable transformed Buddhas, *bodhisattvas*, and *shravaka* monks extend their hands to them all at the same time, and so, in the time it takes to snap one's fingers, they attain birth. To repay my indebtedness to the Buddha, I offer him an act of worship with sincerity of heart.

I take refuge in the great ocean of hosts of pure sages, the *bodhisattvas* in the Western Land of Utmost Bliss.

May I take refuge in the Buddha together with all sentient beings.

Hence, I prostrate myself in worship to him, aspiring for birth in that land.

May all these *bodhisattvas* follow the Buddha to welcome the practitioners.

To repay my indebtedness to him, I offer an act of worship with sincerity of heart.

(12) I take refuge in the Buddha and repent before him so that my teacher, parents, good friends of the Way, and sentient beings of the universe may destroy the three karmic hindrances and together attain birth in the land of Amida Buddha. . . .

(23) I take refuge in and prostrate myself with sincerity of heart to Amida Buddha in the Western Quarter.

The ocean of Amida's Wisdom and Vow

Is deep, broad, and boundless;

Those who hear the Name and aspire to be born

All, without exception, reach that land.

I wish to be born in the Land of Peace and Bliss together with all sentient beings.

. . . I take refuge in and prostrate myself with sincerity of heart to Amida Buddha in the Western Quarter

One who has met Buddhas in the past

Can accept this teaching.

Such a person respectfully worships, hears

And upholds it, and rejoices so greatly as to dance.

I wish to be born in the Land of Peace and Bliss together with all sentient beings.

(24) I take refuge in and prostrate myself with sincerity of heart to Amida Buddha in the Western Quarter.
Those who have been able to hear
The Name of Amida Buddha
And rejoice even with one thought of mindfulness
Will all attain birth in that land.
I wish to be born in the Land of Peace and Bliss together with all sentient beings. . . .
I take refuge in and prostrate myself with sincerity of heart to Amida Buddha in the Western Quarter.
Even if the whole world is on fire,
Be sure to pass through it to hear the Buddha's Name;
Those who, having heard the Name, rejoice and praise him
Will all attain birth in that land.
I wish to be born in the Land of Peace and Bliss together with all sentient beings. . . .
I take refuge in and prostrate myself with sincerity of heart to Amida Buddha in the Western Quarter.
It is extremely difficult to encounter an age in which a Buddha appears in the world;
It is also difficult for the people to realize the wisdom of faith;
To be able to hear the rare *Dharma*
Is among the most difficult.
I wish to be born in the Land of Peace and Bliss together with all sentient beings. . . .
I take refuge in and prostrate myself with sincerity of heart to Amida Buddha in the Western Quarter.
To accept it in faith and teach others to believe in it
Is the difficulty among all the difficulties;
To spread the great compassion everywhere and guide others
Is truly to repay the Buddha's benevolence.
I wish to be born in the Land of Peace and Bliss together with all sentient beings.
I take refuge in and prostrate myself with sincerity of heart to Amida Buddha in the Western Quarter.
May the Buddha enfold and protect me with compassion
And let me multiply the seeds of the *Dharma*.
In this life and in the life to come,
May the Buddha always embrace me.
I wish to be born in the Land of Peace and Bliss together with all sentient beings.
I take refuge in and prostrate myself with sincerity of heart to Avalok-

iteshvara *Bodhisattva* in the Western Land of Utmost Bliss.

I wish to be born in the Land of Peace and Bliss together with all sentient beings.

I take refuge in and prostrate myself with sincerity of heart to Mahasthamaprapta *Bodhisattva* in the Western Land of Utmost Bliss.

I wish to be born in the Land of Peace and Bliss together with all sentient beings. . . .

(26) I take refuge in the Buddha and repent before him so that my teacher, parents, good friends of the Way, and sentient beings of the universe may destroy the three karmic hindrances and together attain birth in the land of Amida Buddha. . . .

(27) . . . Reverently based on Nagarjuna *Bodhisattva's Hymns of Worship and Praise Aspiring for Birth*, I prostrate myself in worship sixteen times at midnight accompanied by repentance as specified before and afterwards. . . .

(28) I take refuge in and prostrate myself with sincerity of heart to Amida Buddha in the Western Quarter.

With reverence I bow my head to Amida, the Sage,

The Most Honored One, who is revered by humans and *devas*.

You dwell in the wonderful Land of Peace and Bliss,

Surrounded by innumerable children of the Buddhas.

I wish to be born in the Land of Peace and Bliss together with all sentient beings. . . .

All things are impermanent and selfless,

Like an image of the moon in the water, lightning, or morning dew.

Your sermons to the multitudes are, in reality, wordless.

Hence, I prostrate myself in worship to Amida, the Holy One.

I wish to be born in the Land of Peace and Bliss together with all sentient beings.

I take refuge in and prostrate myself with sincerity of heart to Amida Buddha in the Western Quarter.

In the Revered Buddha's Land exist no evil names,

Nor are there beings in the female form, nor fear of evil realms.

All worship the Honored One in sincerity of heart.

Hence, I prostrate myself in worship to Amida, the Holy One.

I wish to be born in the Land of Peace and Bliss together with all sentient beings.

I take refuge in and prostrate myself with sincerity of heart to Amida Buddha in the Western Quarter.

In the Buddha's Land accomplished with innumerable skillful devices,

There are no samsaric realms, nor evil teachers;

Upon attaining birth there, one reaches *bodhi* without falling back.

Hence, I prostrate myself in worship to Amida, the Holy One.

I wish to be born in the Land of Peace and Bliss together with all sentient beings.

I take refuge in and prostrate myself with sincerity of heart to Amida Buddha in the Western Quarter.

I have extolled the Buddha's excellent virtue,

Thereby acquiring boundless merit like the ocean.

The roots of pure good I have thus acquired

I wish to share with other beings, aspiring together to be born in his Land.

I wish to be born in the Land of Peace and Bliss together with all sentient beings. . . .

(29) I take refuge in and prostrate myself with sincerity of heart to Amida Buddha in the Western Quarter.

May the Buddha enfold and protect me with compassion;

Let the seeds of the *Dharma* multiply;

In this life and in the life to come,

May the Buddha always embrace me.

I wish to be born in the Land of Peace and Bliss together with all sentient beings.

I take refuge in and prostrate myself with sincerity of heart to Avalok-iteshvara *Bodhisattva* in the Land of Utmost Bliss of the Western Quarter.

I wish to be born in the Land of Peace and Bliss together with all sentient beings.

I take refuge in and prostrate myself with sincerity of heart to Mahast-hamaprapta *Bodhisattva* in the Land of Utmost Bliss of the Western Quarter.

I wish to be born in the Land of Peace and Bliss together with all sentient beings. . . .

(30) I take refuge in the Buddha and repent before him so that my teacher, parents, good friends of the Way, and sentient beings of the universe may destroy the three karmic hindrances and together attain birth in the land of Amida Buddha.

(Hisao Inagaki, trans., *Shan-tao's Liturgy for Birth* [*Ojoraisan*], http://www12.canvas.ne.jp/horai/raisan.htm)

## Kakunyo
### —Object of Worship

-333- Instead, holding to what Vasubandhu, the Treatise master, in the passage on the "Gate of Obeisance," referred to as, *Kimyo jinjippo mugeko nyorai*, "I pay obeisance to the *Tathagata* of Unimpeded Light (*Mugeko*

*Nyorai*) whose Light shines unimpeded in the ten directions," he (Shinran) reverenced this as Shinshu's object of worship. (W.S. Yokoyama, *Setting the Claims Straight* [Kakunyo's *Gaijasho*], #2, unpublished translation)

Kakunyo
-334- Generally speaking, Shinshu's main object of worship is *jippo mugeko nyorai*, "The *Tathagata* of unimpeded light shining in every direction"; the Pure Land where this object of worship dwells is the realm of the ultimate, like the empty sky. Embracing this view, the Founding Master (Shinran)'s *Kyogyoshinsho* says, "The Buddha is this Buddha of Inconceivable Light, the Land is the land of Infinite Light"; so be it. (W.S. Yokoyama, *Setting the Claims Straight* [Kakunyo's *Gaijasho*], #12, unpublished translation)

3. Aspiration for Birth in the Pure Land
Vasubandhu
-335- (1) O World-Honored One, with singleness of mind,
　　I take refuge in the *Tathagata* of Unhindered Light
　　Shining throughout the Ten Directions,
　　And aspire to be born in the Land of Peace and Bliss.
　　(2) Depending on the sutras' exposition
　　Of the manifestation of true merit,
　　I compose verses of aspiration in condensed form,
　　Thereby conforming to the Buddha *Dharma*.
　　(Hisao Inagaki, trans., *Vasubandhu's Discourse on the Pure Land* [*Jodoron*]; see also *T'an-Luan's Commentary on Vasubandhu's Discourse on the Pure Land* [*Ojoronchu*] [Kyoto: Nagata Bunshodo, 1998], pp. 127-133)

T'an-luan
-336- In the *Amitayus Sutra* preached at Rajagrha, I find in the section on the three grades of aspirants that although their practices differ according to their superior or inferior qualities, they all, without fail, awaken the aspiration for the highest *bodhi*. This aspiration is the resolve to become a Buddha. The aspiration to become a Buddha is the resolve to save all sentient beings. The aspiration to save sentient beings is the resolve to embrace sentient beings and lead them to attain birth in a Buddha-land. It follows that those who wish to be born in the Pure Land of Peace and Bliss should awaken the aspiration for the highest *bodhi*. If there is anyone who does not awaken the aspiration for the highest *bodhi* but, having heard of the endless pleasures to be enjoyed in that land, desires to be born there simply because of such pleasures, he will not attain birth. (Hisao Inagaki, trans., *T'an-Luan's Commentary on Vasubandhu's Discourse on the Pure Land* [*Ojoronchu*] [Kyoto: Nagata Bunshodo, 1998], p. 271)

Shan-tao

-337- 1. All Buddhists of the present, both monks and lay-people, and those of the future should each awaken the highest aspiration.

Birth-and-death is extremely difficult to abhor, and the Buddha *Dharma* hard to seek.

2. Together you should make the diamond-hard resolution and leap over the four violent streams;

Take refuge in and worship Amida with joined hands wishing to enter Amida's Land.

3. O World-Honored One, with singleness of heart, I take refuge in the ocean of True Suchness,

*Dharma* Nature, Recompensed and Transformed Buddhas throughout the ten directions,

4. Also in each and every *bodhisattva*, who is attended by innumerable retinues;

I pay homage to *bodhisattvas* who have bodies of glory and transformation, those of the ten stages and three sagacities,

5. Those who have reached the end of the time of practice as well as those who have not, those who have perfected wisdom and practice as well as those who have not,

Those who have destroyed passions as well as those who have not, those who have exhausted their residues as well as those who have not,

6. Those who still require effort as well as those who do not, those who have realized perfect wisdom as well as those who have not,

The Supremely Enlightened Ones and those of Equal Enlightenment, and also those, having attained the Adamantine Mind

7. And come in accord with True Suchness in a flash of thought, have realized the fruition of *Nirvana*.

Let us take refuge in all the Honored Ones possessed of the three kinds of Buddha-bodies.

8. We seek your divine protection with unobstructed supernatural powers; please take us in your embrace.

We all take refuge in the sages of the three vehicles who have learned the Buddha's great compassion

9. And forever dwell in the state of non-retrogression.

We seek their endowment of power to enable us to see the Buddhas in every thought-moment.

10. After floundering in *samsara* since long, distant past, we ignorant beings

Have encountered the declining *Dharma* bequeathed by Shakyamuni Buddha,

11. And met with the Primal Vow of Amida, the main gateway to the

Land of Utmost Bliss.

By transferring the merit of both meditative and non-meditative good toward it, I wish to attain quickly the body of no-birth.

12. Based on the One-Vehicle teaching for quick emancipation in the *Bodhisattva-Pitaka*,

I have composed a verse of the three refuges in accord with the Buddha's Mind.

13. May Buddhas in the ten directions, as numerous as the sand-grains of the Ganges, look upon me with their six supernatural powers!

I will widely open the Pure Land gate in accordance with the teachings of the two Buddhas, Amida and Shakyamuni.

14. I wish to share the merit of writing this work equally with all beings,

So that we may all awaken aspiration for *Bodhi* and together attain birth in the Land of Peace and Bliss.

(Hisao Inagaki, *Shan-tao's Three Refuges* [*Kisamboge*], http://www12. canvas.ne.jp/horai/kisamboge.htm)

Shan-tao

-338- I take refuge in Shakyamuni and all the other Buddhas, their *Dharmas*, and *Sanghas*. I bow to them in worship, aspiring to be born in the Land of the Buddha of Infinite Life by transferring the merits of this act towards it.

This Buddha is the Master of priests and laypeople of the present age. The three treasures are the field of immeasurable merits. To bow to them in worship even once is to repay the Master's benevolence and accomplish one's own practice. By transferring the merit of this single act, I aspire to attain birth.

I take refuge in all the three treasures of the ten quarters in the three periods, existing in the lands, as numerous as the dust-motes, throughout the universe even to the extreme limit of the open space. I bow in worship to them, aspiring to be born in the Land of the Buddha of Infinite Life by transferring the merit of this act towards it.

Since the open space extending throughout the ten quarters is bound-less, the three treasures therein are inexhaustible. Even one act of worship offered to them yields immeasurable virtues and inexhaustible merits. By offering an act of worship to them with sincerity of heart, one will acquire the roots of good for emancipation in one's bodily, verbal, and mental acts from each Buddha, each *Dharma*, each *bodhisattva*, each holy sage, and each Buddha's relics. These merits will come and benefit the practitioner, and fulfill one's required practices. By transferring the merit of this single act, I aspire to attain birth. (Hisao Inagaki, trans., *Shan-tao's Liturgy for Birth* [*Ojoraisan*], http://www12.canvas.ne.jp/horai/raisan.htm)

Shan-tao

-339- (13) Next, recite the following hymns (from the *Discourse on the Jewel-Nature*) and make an aspiration:

With all the merits of worship and repentance, at the time of death, I wish to see the body of immeasurable merits of the Buddha of Infinite Life. May I and other aspirants behold the Buddha, acquire the eye of non-defilement, be born in the Land of Peace and Bliss, and realize the supreme enlightenment.

(14) Having worshiped and repented, I take refuge in all the three treasures.

I take refuge in the Buddha. I will attain the *bodhi*-mind and will not regress from it at any time.

May I attain birth in the Land of the Buddha of Infinite Life together with all sentient beings by transferring all the merits towards it.

I take refuge in the *Dharma*. I will realize omniscience and attain the great *dharani* gate.

May I attain birth in the Land of the Buddha of Infinite Life together with all sentient beings by transferring all the merits towards it.

I take refuge in the *Sangha*. I will stop idle discussions and join the ocean of unity and harmony.

May I attain birth in the Land of the Buddha of Infinite Life, together with all sentient beings, by transferring all the merits towards it.

May all sentient beings purify their three kinds of action, uphold Buddhism, and revere all the sages.

May I attain birth in the Land of the Buddha of Infinite Life together with all sentient beings by transferring all the merits towards it.

(15) All of you, please listen. I will recite the following hymns on impermanence for the sunset service.

Alas, people are busily engaged in secular matters,

Taking no notice of their lives wearing away by day and by night,

Like a lamp in the wind—how long can it last?

In the six realms of the vast *samsara* there is no fixed abode.

Until we are emancipated from the sea of suffering,

How can we rest peacefully? Why should we not be terrified?

Let each one of us hear the *Dharma* while young and strong;

Let us strive and diligently seek the path to Eternity. . . .

(16) Having recited these hymns, make an aspiration in mind and utter it with your mouth.

I wish that my disciples, at the time of their death, hold their minds unperverted, undistracted, and mindful and that their minds and bodies be free of pain and affliction and dwell in happiness as when one is in meditation. I wish that holy sages appear before them and, riding the

Buddha's Primal Vow, they attain the upper grade of birth in the Land of Amida Buddha. Having reached it, they will acquire the six supernatural powers, with which they enter worlds of the ten quarters and save and embrace suffering beings until the universe throughout the open space comes to an end. My vow shall be like this. Having thus made a vow, I take refuge in Amida Buddha with sincerity of heart.

(17) The hymn for the service at the first watch of the night (based on the *Meditation Samadhi Sutra*):

Deep and bottomless are our blind passions;
Boundless is the sea of birth-and-death.
Until we board the ship to cross the sea of suffering,
How can we enjoy sleep?
Let us make courageous efforts
And keep our thoughts absorbed in meditation.

(18) The hymn for the midnight service (based on the *Great Wisdom Discourse*):

You should not lay your foul-smelling bodies in bed.
An aggregate of impurities is temporarily called a "person."
When you are attacked by a serious illness, it is like an arrow penetrating the body;
All sorts of pain will assemble to torment you. How can you sleep peacefully now?

(19) The hymn for the service at the last watch of the night (based on the *Garland Sutra*):

Time has passed in the swiftness of light;
It is already early fifth watch.
Impermanence rushes upon me at every moment;
The King of Death follows me in every step.
Let me urge you, practitioners of the Way,
To strive diligently to attain *Nirvana*. . . .

(20) The hymn for the early morning service (based on the *Mahasamghika-vinaya*):

If you are seeking the pleasure of tranquility,
You should learn to live the frugal life of a mendicant.
Clothes and food are just to sustain your bodies;
Let them be as they are given, whether good or not.

(21) The hymns for the midday service (based on the *Sutra on Worshiping the Six Directions*):

Man's life, if wasted in idleness,
Is like a plant without roots
Or like a cut flower placed in the sun;
How long can it remain fresh?

Man's life is like this. Impermanence will seize you at any moment.
I urge you, all the practitioners of the Way,
To practice diligently to attain Truth.
(Hisao Inagaki, trans., *Shan-tao's Liturgy for Birth* [*Ojoraisan*], http://www12.canvas.ne.jp/horai/raisan.htm)

Shan-tao
-340- Sincere request:
 The Buddhas, the peerless Honored Ones of great compassion,
 Constantly illumine the three worlds with the wisdom of voidness.
 Blind and ignorant, sentient beings are unaware of this,
 Sinking eternally in the great ocean of birth-and-death.
 In order to free sentient beings from various sufferings,
 I beseech the Buddhas to turn the wheel of *Dharma* always.
 Having made this request, I sincerely take refuge in Amida Buddha.

 Sincere rejoicing:
 Jealousy, haughtiness, and indolence which I have had for many *kalpas*
  arise from stupidity;
 With the fire of anger and malevolence I have always
 Burnt the good roots of wisdom and compassion.
 As I contemplate today, I have realized this for the first time;
 Then I have awakened the mind of making great efforts and rejoicing
  (in others' good acts).
 After having thus rejoiced, I take refuge in Amida Buddha with sincerity
  of heart.

 Sincere merit-transference:
 Wandering about in the three worlds,
 I have been conceived in the womb-jail through blind love;
 Having been born, I am destined to old age and death.
 Thus I have been sinking in the ocean of suffering.
 Now I perform these meritorious acts;
 I turn their merit over to the Land of Peace and Bliss to attain birth there.
 After having thus transferred the merit, I take refuge in Amida Buddha
  with sincerity of heart.

 Sincere vow:
 I wish to abandon the body enclosed in the womb
 And attain birth in the Land of Peace and Bliss,
 Where I will quickly behold Amida Buddha's
 Body of boundless merits and virtues

And see many *Tathagatas*
And holy sages as well.
Having acquired the six supernatural powers,
I will continue to save suffering sentient beings
Until all their worlds throughout the universe are exhausted.
Such will be my vow. After having thus made a vow, I take refuge in
    Amida Buddha with sincerity of heart.
    (Hisao Inagaki, trans., *Shan-tao's Liturgy for Birth* [*Ojoraisan*] http://
www12.canvas.ne.jp/horai/raisan.htm)

Genshin
-341- That today I desire Paradise and wish to have all beings obtain the
same and that I am going throughout the ten directions to draw living beings
to myself, is just like Amida Tathagata's great vow of mercy. Is not such grace
joy? Truly the affairs of this life are in the interval of a dream. Why then not
fling away everything and seek after the Paradise of the Pure Land? May all
believers beware of being idle. (A.K. Reischauer, "Genshin's *Ojo Yoshu*: Collected Essays on Birth into Paradise," *The Transactions of the Asiatic Society
of Japan* [December 1930], Second Series Vol. VII, p. 75.)

Honen
-342- There are numerous pure Buddha-lands in the ten directions, but we
desire to be born specifically in the Western Pure Land of Amida Buddha
because even one who commits the ten transgressions or the five grave
offenses can be born there. Among all Buddhas, we rely exclusively upon
Amida Buddha because he will personally welcome into the Pure Land
the *nembutsu* devotees who recite his name a mere three to five times. We
choose the practice of *nembutsu* over all other practices because *nembutsu* is
in accordance with the essential vow of Amida Buddha.

    Now, if we desire birth in the Pure Land through *nembutsu* by relying
upon the essential vow, then birth in the Pure Land is definitely assured.
Reliance on the blessing of the essential vow is a presupposition of our depth
of faith. (Joji Atone, Yoko Hayashi, trans., *The Promise of Amida Buddha:
Honen's Path to Bliss* [Boston: Wisdom Publications, 2011], pp. 240-241)

Ippen
-343- Further he [Ippen] said: The Pure Land has been established to
engender in us a longing for it and to encourage us to aspire for birth there.
And our longing is aroused, in short, so that we say the Name. Thus the
explanation of deep mind states, "Sakyamuni Buddha leads people to aspire
for the Pure Land [by praising Amida's fulfilled body and land]." As we hear
of the wondrousness of the Pure Land, aspiration for birth naturally awakens

in us. When this aspiration has arisen, the Name unfailingly comes to be uttered. Thus our desire for birth is the incipient thought that leads to taking refuge in the Name. Since ours are false minds of the six forms of consciousness and discriminative thinking, it is impossible that they should hold the accomplished cause of attaining the Pure Land. It is the Name that is birth. Hence the expression, "birth through Other- Power." Ordinarily, people think they should be able to attain birth because they ardently desire it and their aspiration is so keen. (Dennis Hirota, trans., *No Abode: The Record of Ippen* [Honolulu: The University of Hawai'i Press, 1997], p. 75)

4. Contemplation/Meditation on the Buddha and Visualization of the Pure Land
Vasubandhu
-344- How does one contemplate? One contemplates with wisdom, that is, contemplates [the Pure Land] with mindfulness, wishing to practice *vipashyana* in accord with the *Dharma*.

The contemplation is of three kinds: (1) contemplation of the glorious manifestations of the merit of the Buddha-land; (2) contemplation of the glorious merit of Amida Buddha; (3) contemplation of the glorious merit of various *Bodhisattvas*.

How does one transfer [the merit of the practice]? One does not forsake suffering beings, but constantly resolves in one's mind to perfect the Great Compassion by putting merit-transference above anything else. (Hisao Inagaki, trans., *Vasubandhu's Discourse on the Pure Land* [*Jodoron*]http:// www12.canvas.ne.jp/horai/jodoron.htm; see also Hisao Inagaki, trans., *T'an-Luan's Commentary on Vasubandhu's Discourse on the Pure Land* [*Ojoronchu*] (Kyoto: Nagata Bunshodo, 1998), pp. 213-216)

Ching-ying Hui-yuan
-345- Before manifesting the Land of *Dharma*-nature, the *Bodhisattvas* relentlessly cultivate the inexhaustible practices of true reality. By means of the power generated by the merits from these pure practices, the *Bodhisattvas* decorate the boundless realm of the pure true reality with an immeasurable variety of adornments. This realm is named the "Land of True Reward." (Kenneth K. Tanaka, trans., *The Dawn of Chinese Pure Land Buddhism: Ching-ying Hui-yuan's Commentary on the Visualization Sutra* [Albany, NY: State University of New York Press, 1990], p. 105)

Ching-ying Hui-yuan
-346- There are two kinds of visualization of the Buddha: first, the True-body visualization and, second, the Response-body visualization. To visualize the Buddha as the body of the impartial *Dharma* gate is the "True-body visual-

ization." In contrast, to visualize the Buddha as the body of the *Tathagata*, who shares [characteristics] with a worldly body, is called the "Response-body visualization.". . . To summarize, visualization requires the practitioner to completely sever all [deluded] forms and to be fully endowed with virtues. The complete severance of all [deluded] forms does not allow even of a form. With the full endowment of virtues, the practitioner does not lack even one moral good. Even though one possesses all moral goods, they are of the same essence and are distinguished only in terms of virtues. (Kenneth K. Tanaka, trans., *The Dawn of Chinese Pure Land Buddhism: Ching-ying Hui-yuan's Commentary on the Visualization Sutra* [Albany, NY: State University of New York Press, 1990], p. 120)

T'an-luan

-347- "Buddhas, *Tathagatas*, have the *Dharma*-realm bodies" means: the *Dharma*-realm is the mind-element of sentient beings. As mind produces all worldly and supra-worldly *dharmas*, it is called the *Dharma*-realm. The *Dharma*-realm produces the *Tathagatas'* body possessing [thirty-two] physical characteristics and [eighty] secondary marks, just as an object and other conditions produce visual consciousness. For this reason, the Buddha's body is called *Dharma*-realm body. This body does not appear as an object of other [perceptive faculties, such as eyes and ears]. Hence, it is said, "[the *Dharma*-realm bodies] enter into the meditating minds of all sentient beings."

"When one visualizes a Buddha, the mind itself produces the thirty-two physical characteristics and eighty secondary marks of a Buddha" has the following meaning: when sentient beings meditate on the Buddha, his body with physical characteristics and secondary marks appears in the minds. It is just as clear water reflects objects; the water and the images are neither different nor identical. For this reason, it is said that the Buddha's body with physical characteristics and secondary marks is [not different from] the meditating mind.

"That mind itself produces Buddhas" means that the [meditating] mind can produce Buddhas. "That mind is itself the Buddha" means that there is no Buddha apart from the [meditating] mind. It is just as fire comes from wood but is not separate from the wood. Because it is not separate from the wood, it burns the wood. The wood becomes fire, which burns the wood and turns it, too, into fire.

"The ocean of correct and universal wisdom of Buddhas is produced from one's meditating mind" means: "perfect, universal knowledge" is the knowledge of truth which is in conformity with the *Dharma*-realm. The *Dharma*-realm has no form, so the Buddhas [which it produces] do not know [by distinguishing objects]. Because of no knowing, there is nothing which they do not know. Not knowing and yet knowing is the correct and universal wisdom. This knowledge is vast and deep, and unfathomable, and so is compared to the ocean. (Hisao Inagaki, trans., *T'an-Luan's Commentary on Vasubandhu's Discourse on the Pure Land [Ojo Ronchu]* [Kyoto: Nagata Bunshodo, 1998], pp. 176-177)

T'an-luan

-348- Having seen them all, we should realize that [the Pure Land] is free of defilements; hence, we contemplate the brilliant light of the Buddha's wisdom. Having realized its purifying power, we should see how far the name [of the Pure Land] extends; hence, we contemplate the far-reaching sound of the sacred name. Then, we should know who possesses the sovereign power [in the Pure Land]; hence, we contemplate the Lord Buddha. Having visualized the Lord Buddha, we should know who his kinsmen are, hence, we contemplate them. After that, we should know how they are sustained; hence, contemplate their nourishment. Next, we should know whether or not it causes afflictions; hence, we contemplate their freedom from afflictions. Next, we should know the cause of the absence of afflictions; hence, we contemplate the gate of the great principle. Having observed it, we should know whether or not hence, we contemplate the fulfillment it fulfills [our aspirations of all aspirations]. (Hisao Inagaki, trans., *T'an-Luan's Commentary on Vasubandhu's Discourse on the Pure Land [Ojo Ronchu]* [Kyoto: Nagata Bunshodo, 1998], pp. 242-243)

Shan-tao

-349- [1. Method of Practicing the Buddha-contemplation *Samadhi*]
Contemplate Amida Buddha whose body is the color of pure gold, with a halo emitting light pervasively and with unparalleled dignity. Aspirants, keep this image, day and night, wherever you are. Keep this image while walking, standing, sitting, or lying down. Always direct your thought to the west and imagine that even the host of sages and all the adornments made of various treasures are manifest before your eyes. This you should remember.

Further, aspirants, when you sit in meditation, you should first sit in the full cross-legged posture. Place your left leg on the right thigh, with the sole in harmony with the contours of the body; then, place your right leg on the left thigh, with the sole in harmony with the contours of the body. Rest your right hand on the palm of the left hand, and touch the soft tip of one thumb with that of the other. Next, keep your body upright and close your mouth. Close your eyes so that they appear open but not exactly open, appear closed but not exactly closed. . . .

. . . If you always practice this meditation, you will be rid of a great amount of hindrances and karmic evils. Besides, you will acquire immeasurable merits and so all the Buddhas will be pleased and rejoice. . . .

. . . The contemplation of the Buddha from the top of the head down to the marks of the thousand-spoked wheel on the soles is called the complete contemplation of the glorious merit of the Buddha's body. This is called the contemplation in the proper order. . . .

. . . If you follow the Buddha's teaching, you will be able to visualize various things in the Pure Land. If you have perceived them, keep them to yourself and do not talk to others about them. For talking about them is a grave offense that will invite the retribution of a bad illness and shortening of life. If you follow the teaching, you will upon death attain the birth of the highest grade in the land of Amida Buddha. (Hisao Inagaki, trans., *Shan-tao's Kannenbomon: The Method of Contemplation on Amida* [Kyoto: Nagata Bunshodo, 2005], pp. 2-4, 6, 8, 10)

Shan-tao

-350- Question: Since the Queen (Vaidehi) had a strong and superior merit-power, she was able to see the Buddha. How can sentient beings of the last *Dharma* age, who have deep and heavy karmic evils, be compared with the queen? As this implication is extremely profound and broad, please show me clear evidence by quoting extensively from the Buddhist sutras.

Answer: The Buddha is a sage of the three transcendental knowledges, possessed of the six supernatural powers which know no obstructions. After observing the people's capacities, he gives them [appropriate] teachings. Whether the teaching [one practices] is shallow or deep, if only one devotes oneself sincerely to it, there is no doubt that one will see [the Buddha]. It is stated in the *Contemplation Sutra*:

> The Buddha praised Vaidehi, saying: "It is good that you have asked me about this matter. Ananda, keep the Buddha's words and expound them widely to the multitudes of beings. I, the *Tathagata*, will teach Vaidehi and all sentient beings in the future how to con-template the Western Land of Utmost Bliss. Through the Buddha's Vow-Power they will be able to see that land as clearly as if they look into a clear mirror and see their own images in it."

This quotation from the sutra is further evidence showing that, due to Amida Buddha's three powers working from outside, one is able to see the Buddha. Hence, we call this the dominant force enabling one to attain the *samadhi* of seeing the Buddha and the Pure Land. (Hisao Inagaki, trans., *Shan-tao's Kannenbomon: The Method of Contemplation on Amida* [Kyoto: Nagata Bunshodo, 2005], p. 44, #24)

Shan-tao

-351- Due to Amida Buddha's three powers working from outside, ordinary beings who meditate on him are made to avail themselves of their own three-mind power and are, therefore, enabled to see the Buddha. [The aspirants'] sincere mind, believing mind, and aspiring mind are the internal cause; and Amida's three kinds of Vow-Power on which they depend are the external condition. Through the coordination of the external condition and the internal cause one can see the Buddha. Hence, this is called the dominant force enabling one to attain the Buddha-visualization *samadhi*. (Hisao Inagaki, trans., *Shan-tao's Kannenbomon: The Method of Contemplation on Amida* [Kyoto: Nagata Bunshodo, 2005], p. 54)

Shan-tao

-352- I take refuge in and prostrate myself with sincerity of heart to Amida
      Buddha in the Western Quarter.
    Amida's mind and body pervade the whole universe,
    And so his images are perceived in the minds of sentient beings.
    Hence, I urge you to contemplate Amida all the time.
    Envisioning him in the mind, expect him to show his true body.
    When you perceive the jeweled image of his true form on the flower-
      seat,
    Your mind's eye opens and you can see glorious adornments of his land.
    The lotus-seats for the three Holy Ones under the jeweled trees fill the
      land;
    The sounds of the bells ringing in the wind and music are just as
      described in the sutra.
    I wish to be born in the Land of Peace and Bliss together with all sentient
      beings.
    (Hisao Inagaki trans., *Shan-tao's Liturgy for Birth* [*Ojoraisan*], http://www12.canvas.ne.jp/horai/raisan.htm)

Shan-tao

-353- All the Buddhas *Tathagathas* are [identified with] *dharmadhatu-kaya*: they universally enter into the minds of all sentient beings. Therefore, when your mind visualizes the Buddha, this [very] mind is [identified with] the thirty-two body marks and the eighty minor marks. This mind "creates" the Buddha; mind is the Buddha. The ocean of true and universal knowledge (omniscience) of the Buddhas arises from the mind. Therefore, you should with single-mindedness and close mindfulness thoroughly inspect that Buddha *Tathagata*, the *Arhat*, the Fully Enlightened One. . . .

[First] I will only explain [the words] "to create the Buddha." This is to visualize mentally without interruption [the body marks], starting from the top of the head down to the feet, and inspect them one by one without a moment's rest. One first visualizes the mark of the top of [the Buddha's] head, next the mark of the white hair-twist between his eyebrows, and so on down to the mark of the thousand-wheel's imprint on his foot soles. While performing this visualization (*hsiang*), all the major and minor marks of the Buddha image will appear perfectly clear with propriety and majesty. . . .

. . . The words "This mind creates the Buddha" signify that when [the meditator], relying on a mind of self-faith, conditions the marks, it is as if he creates them [himself].

The words "This mind is the Buddha" signify that when the mind visualizes the Buddha, then relying on this visualization the body of the Buddha appears: this is a mind-Buddha (or a mental Buddha). Outside this mind [-Buddha], there is no other Buddha.

The words "The [ocean of] true and universal knowledge of the Buddhas" clarify that the Buddhas have obtained perfect and all-pervasive (literally, unhindered) wisdom. Whether consciously or not consciously aware, they possess at all times a universal knowledge of the *dharmadhatu* mind. You have only to perform this imagination, and out of this imagination of the mind he will appear [to you] as if truly alive. . . .

. . . When we say, "to visualize the image [of the Buddha]," [it is] to erect empirically the thirty-two marks. How can the *Tathagata's dharmadhatu-kaya* possess external characters, which can be conditioned, or a body that can be grasped? Indeed, the *dharma-kaya* is immaterial and escapes from being presented to sight; even less can it be analyzed [i.e., classified according to its various components]. Just for that reason the term *sunyata* is chosen in order to symbolize the essence of the *dharma-kaya*. Moreover, the present method of inspection only points to the [western] quarter and establishes [Amida's] marks to concentrate the mind and thus grasp the object. It does certainly not mean formlessness, which is separated from mindfulness.

In his prophetic vision the *Tathagata* knew that the sin-defiled ordinary beings of the decayed age would not be able to fix their minds, even if characters were established. How much less would they succeed if they tried without characters! They would be like unskilled persons who tried to live and build houses in the air. (Julian F. Pas, *Visions of Sukhavati: Shan-Tao's Commentary on the Kuan-wu-Liang-Shou-Fo-Ching* [Albany, NY: State University of New York Press, 1995], pp. 196-198)

Honen

-354- . . . Jogan-shonin (1168-1251) thus stated: "Someone said to Honenshonin, 'The perception of the physical features of Amida Buddha is taught in the *Meditation Sutra*. Should even the *nembutsu* practitioner observe this meditative practice?'

"Honen-shonin replied, 'I, Genku, also performed such a futile practice at the beginning, but I do not practice it now. I recite *nembutsu* with implicit belief in attaining birth in the Pure Land.'" (Joji Atone, Yoko Hayashi, trans., *The Promise of Amida Buddha: Honen's Path to Bliss* [Boston: Wisdom Publications, 2011], pp. 304-305)

## 5. Name-*Nembutsu*

### T'an Luan

-355- "To call the Name of that *Tathagata*" means "to call the Name of the *Tathagata* of Unhindered Light"; ". . . describes his Light, the embodiment of wisdom of that *Tathagata*" shows that the Buddha's light is the embodiment of wisdom. This light is unhindered in illumining all the worlds of the ten directions. Its activity of removing the darkness of ignorance of all sentient beings throughout the universe cannot be compared with the light of the sun and moon or with the brilliance of the [*mani-*] gem, which can only remove the darkness of a hollow or cave. (Hisao Inagaki, trans., *T'an-Luan's Commentary on Vasubandhu's Discourse on the Pure Land* [*Ojoronchu*] [Kyoto: Nagata Bunshodo, 1998], p. 209)

### Tao-ch'o

-356- The reason why the [*Contemplation*] *Sutra* mentions that those who have committed evil throughout life attain birth in the Pure Land by the ten recitations of the *nembutsu* at the time of death but does not question whether they had some appropriate cause for this in the past is that the World-honored One intended to induce evil people in the future to abandon evil and turn to good at the end of their life, thereby enabling them to attain birth in the Pure Land through saying the *nembutsu* recitations. For this reason, the Buddha did not reveal their past karma. This shows that the World-honored One hid the beginning and revealed the end, concealed the cause and spoke about the effect. . . . It is clear that accomplishing of ten recitations of the *nembutsu* has its due cause in the past. . . . The Buddha's intention was to lead sentient beings to accumulate much good cause and then attain birth through the *nembutsu*. (Hisao Inagaki, "Tao-ch'o's *An-le-chi*, Part 2," *The Pure Land*, New Series 22 [December 2006], p. 202 [adapted])

### Tao-ch'o

-357- The ten repetitions of the Name are ten consecutive thoughts of Amida Buddha, not mingled with other thoughts, whether they arise from contemplation of his entire body or part of it, as the case may be. Also, "ten consecutive thoughts" is simply a numerical expression made by the Sage [Shakyamuni]. When we concentrate and focus our thoughts [on the Name] without thinking of other things, the karma [for our birth in the Pure Land] is accomplished. Why the trouble of counting the number of [*nembutsu*] recitations? Those who have been practicing the *nembutsu* for a long time may well follow this [i.e., not count the number]. However, those who practice the *nembutsu* for the first time may count the number. (Hisao Inagaki, "Tao-ch'o's *An-le-chi*, Part 3," *The Pure Land*, New Series 23 [December 2007], p. 73)

Tao-ch'o

-358- Question 4: I wish to follow your recommendation and practice the *nembutsu samadhi*. I still do not know its characteristic features.

Answer: Suppose a man, traveling in a desolate wilderness far removed from human habitation, encounters bandits, who brandish swords and ferociously threaten to kill him. He dashes off and sees a river to cross. Before he reaches the river, he thinks to himself, "When I reach the river bank, shall I take off my clothes to cross the river or shall I keep them on and swim? Should I take the first choice, I fear I would not have time to undress my clothes. Should I try to cross over while keeping my clothes on, I would be drowned." At that time, he is only too concerned about the way of crossing the river to allow other thoughts to arise to intervene. The practitioner should be like this man. When he thinks of Amida Buddha, his mindful thought continues constantly without other thoughts intervening, just as the traveler only thinks of crossing the river. Similarly, the practitioner thinks of the Buddha's *Dharma*-body, or his supernatural power, or the Buddha's wisdom, or the Buddha's white curl of hair, or the Buddha's physical characteristics, or the Buddha's Primal Vow. It is also the same with recitation of the Name. If only he single-mindedly continues to recite it without interruption, he will surely be born in the presence of the Buddha.

I wish to urge Buddhist students of later generations as follows: If they wish to accord with the principle of twofold truth, to realize that each *nembutsu* thought is ungraspable is the wisdom aspect; and to keep directing *nembutsu* thought continuously without interruption is the merit aspect. Hence, a sutra says, "*Bodhisattvas* and *mahasattvas* always cultivate their minds with merit and wisdom." Those who have just set out on the *bodhisattva*-path are still unable to break the attachment to form in their practice. If, however, they single-mindedly perform practices while attached to form, they will never fail to attain birth in the Pure Land. There should not be any doubt about this. (Hisao Inagaki, "Tao-ch'o's *An-le-chi*, Part 3," *The Pure Land*, New Series 23 [December 2007], pp. 73-74)

Tao-ch'o

-359- When the sutra says "ten consecutive thoughts," this does not appear to be a difficult practice. However, minds of ordinary people are like wild horses and their consciousnesses move about more wildly than monkeys. Chasing after the objects of the six sense-organs, they never cease to move. Therefore, each one should awaken faith, concentrate one's mind, cultivate good nature, and strengthen the roots of good. (Hisao Inagaki, "Tao-ch'o's *An-le-chi*, Part 3," *The Pure Land*, New Series 23 [December 2007], pp. 74-75)

Tao-ch'o

-360- Once the sword-wind blows, a hundred tortures gather around one's body. Without habitual trends from the past, how could the *nembutsu* be practiced now? My advice is: You form a group of three or five and vow that, at the time of death, you remind each other to recite Amida's name and attain birth in the Land of Peace and Bliss; then, let the ten times' *nembutsu* recitation continue voice after voice. It is like a wax seal impressed on the clay; as the wax seal is destroyed, the letter is formed. When one's life ends, one is born in the Land of Peace and Bliss. Once the rightly established stage is attained, there is no more worry [about one's spiritual progress]. One should ponder on the great benefit. Why do you not apply serious mindfulness to this matter beforehand? (Hisao Inagaki, "Tao-ch'o's *An-le-chi*, Part 3," *The Pure Land*, New Series 23 [December 2007], p. 75)

Tao-ch'o

-361- Question 11: You say that if someone only calls Amida's Name, be it any of the sentient beings in the ten quarters, the darkness of their ignorance is removed and they will attain birth in the Pure Land. If what you say is true, why are there people who call the Name and remember [Amida] but find ignorance still persisting in their minds and, consequently, do not have their aspirations [for birth in the Pure Land] fulfilled?

Answer: It is because they have not been practicing in accord with True Suchness: that is, in agreement with the significance of the Name. What is the reason? It is due to failure to understand that the *Tathagata* [Amida] is a Body of Reality and, also, a Body for the Sake of Living Beings. It is also due to the three incorrect faiths: 1) one's faith is not sincere; at one time it exists and at another it does not; 2) one's faith is not single-hearted because it is not firm; 3) one's faith is not constant because it is mingled with other thoughts. These three are mutually inclusive. If one's faith continues, it is single-hearted; if it is single-hearted, it is sincere. If you say that one who possesses these three faiths still cannot be born in the Pure Land, then it does not stand to reason. (Hisao Inagaki, "Tao-ch'o's *An-le-chi*, Part 3," *The Pure Land*, New Series 23 [December 2007], pp. 77-78)

Shan-tao

-362- Further I say to the aspirants: If you desire to be born in the Pure Land, you should intently observe the precepts, recite the *nembutsu*, and chant the *Amida Sutra*. Chant the sutra fifteen times a day, and you will arrive at ten thousand in two years. Chant it thirty times a day, and you will arrive at ten thousand in a year. Recite the *nembutsu* ten thousand times a day, and at the proper time worship and praise the glorious manifestations of the Pure Land with great effort. Those who (daily) make thirty thousand, sixty thousand, or a hundred thousand utterances are all aspirants of the highest birth of the highest grade. In addition, turn all the other merits toward birth. This you should remember. (Hisao Inagaki, trans., *Shan-tao's Kannenbomon: The Method of Contemplation on Amida* [Kyoto: Nagata Bunshodo, 2005], p. 12)

Shan-tao

-363- Next, the *Pratyutpanna-samadhi Sutra* states in the chapter on Practice: . . . The Buddha said to Bhadrapala, "If you wish to attain this quickly, you should always have great resolution. Those who practice it as prescribed can attain it. Do not allow the slightest doubt, even as small as a hair, to creep in. This method for the concentration of thought is called '*bodhisattva practice surpassing all practices.*'"

Raise the singleness of mind and believe in this teaching.
According to the teaching you have received, think of the (western quarter).
Be mindful and sever all other thoughts.
Make firm resolution and have no doubt.
Be diligent in practice, and be not indolent.
Raise not a thought of being nor a thought of non-being.
Think not of advancing; think not of regressing.
Think not of things before you; think not of things behind you.
Think not of things to your left; think not of things to your right.
Think not of non-being; think not of being.
Think not of things remote; think not of things nearby.
Think not of painfulness; think not of itchiness.
Think not of hunger; think not of thirst.
Think not of cold; think not of heat.
Think not of suffering; think not of pleasure.
Think not of birth; think not of becoming old.
Think not of sickness; think not of dying.
Think not of living; think not of the span of life.
Think not of poverty; think not of wealth.
Think not of nobleness; think not of baseness.
Think not of lust; think not of greed.
Think not of things small; think not of things large.
Think not of things long; think not of things short.

Think not of beauty; think not of ugliness.
Think not of evil; think not of good.
Think not of anger; think not of joy.
Think not of sitting; think not of rising.
Think not of walking; think not of standing.
Think not of sutras; think not of teachings.
Think not of justice; think not of injustice.
Think not of abandoning; think not of taking.
Think not of ideas; think not of consciousness.
Think not of detachment; think not of attachment.
Think not of voidness; think not of entity.
Think not of lightness; think not of heaviness.
Think not of difficulty; think not of ease.
Think not of deepness; think not of shallowness.
Think not of broadness; think not of narrowness.
Think not of your father; think not of your mother.
Think not of your wife; think not of your child.
Think not of relatedness; think not of estrangement.
Think not of hatefulness; think not of fondness.
Think not of gaining; think not of losing.
Think not of success; think not of defeat.
Think not of purity; think not of turbidity.
Sever all thoughts and be mindful for a fixed period.
Let not your mind be disturbed; be ever diligent.
And count not the years; be not indolent each coming day.
Raise a determined mind; be not lazy mid-way.
Except when asleep, be zealous in your will.
Always live alone and avoid gatherings.
Eschew evil persons, and approach virtuous friends.
Associate with a good teacher and revere him as a Buddha.
Hold fast to your will and ever be supple-minded.
Meditate on equality in everything.
Stay away from your home town and your relatives.
Abandon love and lust and perform pure practices.
Take the way to the Unconditioned and sever all desires.
When learning literary wisdom, be sure it complies with *dhyana*.
Get rid of the three defilements.
Abandon carnal passions and leave all attachments.
Seek not with a greedy mind to accumulate much wealth.
Learn contentment in eating and be not greedy for tasty food.
Restrain yourself and take no life for food.
Dress yourself as prescribed and decorate not your body.

Ridicule not others; be not proud and haughty.

Be not arrogant; hold not yourself aloof.

When expounding a sutra, be in accord with the *Dharma*.

Know that your body is from the beginning like an illusion.

Cling not to the aggregates; stand aloof from the *dhatus*.

The (five) aggregates are bandits; the four (elements) are snakes.

All are ephemeral, and all momentary.

There is no eternal self; the enlightened know it to be void in itself.

As causes and conditions meet and part, things come into existence and
dissolve.

Having realized this well, you will know that all are void from the beginning.

Having pity and mercy for all sentient beings,

Give free gifts to the poor and benefit the needy.

This is the intense concentration; of all *bodhisattva* practices,

This is the way to the ultimate wisdom, the practice surpassing all.

The Buddha said to Bhadrapala: "If you maintain this method of practice, you will attain the *samadhi* in which all the present Buddhas appear
before you. (Hisao Inagaki, trans., *Shan-tao's Kannenbomon: The Method of
Contemplation on Amida* [Kyoto: Nagata Bunshodo, 2005], pp. 12-18)

Shan-tao

-364- "O Bhadrapala, when the four kinds of Buddhists always do this contemplation, . . . it is not that these four kinds of Buddhists see with a divine
eye, hear with a divine ear, or reach the Buddha-land with divine feet. It is
not that they die here and are born there (in order to see the Land). But they
see all this while sitting here."

The Buddha continued, "The four kinds of Buddhists in this land can
see it by single- mindedly contemplating Amida Buddha. Now, let it be asked
what method of practice they should perform in order to be born in the land.
Amida Buddha replies, 'Those who desire to be born should call my Name
unceasingly. Then you will attain birth.'". . .

I [Shan-tao] have clarified above the method of *nembutsu samadhi*.

The proper way of entering the meditation hall and exposition of the
method of the *nembutsu samadhi*:

When you enter the meditation hall, you should exclusively follow the
Buddhist method. First, prepare a hall, place a sacred statue in it, and cleanse
it with perfumed hot water. If you have no family Buddha room, any clean
room will do. Sweep and wash it clean as prescribed, and place a Buddha's
image on the western wall. Aspirants, it would be better if you divide a
month into four periods, that is, from the first to the eighth, from the eighth
to the fifteenth, from the fifteenth to the twenty-third, and from the twenty-

third to the thirtieth. Aspirants, weighing the burden of your occupation, enter the path of the pure act at a (convenient) period. From the first to the seventh day, wear only clean clothes and new sandals. During the seven days eat only one meal a day. Let your soft rice cake, plain rice, and seasonal pickled vegetable be simple and temperate in quantity.

In the hall, restrain yourself, day and night, and focus your thought on Amida Buddha with uninterrupted, exclusive mind. Let your thought stay in accord with your voice. You are only allowed to sit or stand; do not sleep during the seven days. Also, do not worship the Buddha or recite the sutra. Do not use a rosary, either. Only let the consciousness of your recollection of the Buddha with the joined hands be present, and with every thought, think of seeing the Buddha. The Buddha stated: "Imagine that Amida Buddha's golden body, resplendent with light and incomparably august, resides before your eye." When you properly contemplate the Buddha while standing, keep standing while you call his Name—from ten thousand to twenty thousand times. When you properly contemplate the Buddha while sitting, stay seated while you call his Name—from ten thousand to twenty thousand times. In the hall, do not join heads and talk with each other. (Hisao Inagaki, trans., *Shan-tao's Kannenbomon: The Method of Contemplation on Amida* [Kyoto: Nagata Bunshodo, 2005], pp. 20-24)

Shan-tao

-365- It is stated in the *Prajnaparamita Sutra* expounded by Manjushri, "I wish to expound the single-practice *samadhi*. I only encourage you to dwell alone in a quiet place, concentrate on one Buddha without visualizing his countenance, and exclusively recite his name. Then, while in the recitative practice, you will be able to see Amida and all other Buddhas."

. . . Question: Why do you teach me to recite the name exclusively instead of urging me to practice visualization? What is your intention?

Answer: Sentient beings have heavy karmic hindrances, the objects of contemplation are subtle but the contemplating mind is coarse, and their consciousness is agitated and their mind is distracted; therefore, it is difficult to accomplish contemplation.

For this reason, the Great Sage, out of compassion, straightforwardly encourages people to recite the name exclusively. Since the recitative practice is easy to follow, they can attain birth in the Buddha-land through continuous practice of it. (Hisao Inagaki, trans., *Shan-tao's Liturgy for Birth* [*Ojoraisan*], http://www12.canvas.ne.jp/horai/raisan.htm)

Shan-tao

-366- Further as it is stated in the *Contemplation Sutra*, the Buddha encourages sitting contemplation, worshiping, mindfulness, and so forth. In all these acts, to face west comes before anything else, just as a tree topples in the direction it bends. If there is some hindrance which keeps you from facing west, you can just imagine that you are facing west.

Question: I understand that all Buddhas have equally realized the three bodies and their results of compassion and wisdom are perfect and nondual. If one, facing the appropriate direction, worships and concentrates on one Buddha and recites his name, one should attain birth in his land. Why do you only praise the Buddha in the west and encourage an exclusive practice of worshiping, concentrating on him, and so forth?

Answer: Although all Buddhas have attained one and the same enlightenment, when viewed in terms of vows and practices, their causes and conditions are not indiscernible. Now, Amida the World-honored One formerly made deep and weighty vows, and embraces beings of the ten quarters with his Light and Name. They are only expected to establish faith. By reciting the Name until death or reciting it even ten times or once, one can easily attain birth in his land through the Vow-Power of that Buddha. For this reason, Shakyamuni and other Buddhas especially urge people to face west. This does not mean that recitation of other Buddhas' names cannot remove karmic hindrances and extinguish karmic evils. One should realize this. (Hisao Inagaki, trans., *Shan-tao's Liturgy for Birth* [*Ojoraisan*], http://www12.canvas.ne.jp/horai/raisan.htm)

Shan-tao
-367- Shakyamuni and other Buddhas throughout the ten quarters glorify Amida's Light with twelve names and extensively urge beings to recite the Name and worship him continuously without interruption, for such people will gain immeasurable merits in this lifetime and, after death, definitely attain birth. (Hisao Inagaki, trans., *Shan-tao's Liturgy for Birth* [*Ojoraisan*], http://www12.canvas.ne.jp/horai/raisan.htm)

Shan-tao
-368- I take refuge in and prostrate myself with sincerity of heart to Amida
     Buddha in the Western Quarter.
    The color of Amida's body is like the golden mountain;
    The light issuing forth from each of his physical marks shines throughout
        the ten quarters;
    Only those who recite the Name receive the benefit of the light's embrace.
    You should know that the Primal Vow is most powerful;
    The *Tathagatas* in the six quarters, extending their tongues, testify to
        this.
    By solely reciting the Name, one can reach the Land in the West.
    When one reaches there, the flower one is born into opens and one can

hear the wonderful *Dharma*;

Then the vows and practice in the ten *bodhisattva* stages spontaneously become manifest in one's mind.

I wish to be born in the Land of Peace and Bliss together with all sentient beings.

(Hisao Inagaki, trans., *Shan-tao's Liturgy for Birth* [*Ojoraisan*], http://www12.canvas.ne.jp/horai/raisan.htm)

Shan-tao

-**369**- If we ask, "Where is our true home?"

It is the seven-treasure dais in the pond of the land of bliss.

Amida Buddha, in the causal stage, made the universal Vow:

"When beings hear my Name and think on me, I will come to welcome each of them to my land,

Not discriminating at all between the poor and the rich and wellborn,

Not discriminating between the inferior and the highly gifted;

Not choosing the learned and those upholding pure precepts,

Not rejecting those who break precepts and whose evil karma is profound.

When beings just turn about at heart and often say the *nembutsu*,

It is as if bits of rubble were turned into gold."

(*CWS, Kyogyoshinsho*, I, p. 42, II:35)

Shan-tao

-**370**- The land of bliss is the realm of *nirvana*, the uncreated;

I fear it is hard to be born there by doing sundry good acts according to our diverse conditions.

Hence, the *Tathagata* selected the essential *dharma*,

Instructing beings to say Amida's Name with singleness, again singleness.

(*CWS, Kyogyoshinsho*, I, p. 201, V:33)

Chang-lun[1]

-**371**- The military officer Chang-lun declares:

The Name of the Buddha is exceedingly easy to keep and say; the Pure Land is exceedingly easy to reach. Among the eighty-four thousand *dharma*-gates, none compares with this quick path to birth there. By just setting aside moments of the early morning for the *nembutsu*, one can ultimately make

---

[1] From the Southern Sung, an official in charge of military affairs. In his later years, he made a *nembutsu* practice center and learned from Lu-shan Hui-yuan's White Lotus Society, practicing every day with his wife and children.

an aid for attaining the eternal and indestructible. That is, one's exertion of effort is exceedingly slight, and yet one's obtaining of virtue is inexhaustible. What pains do sentient beings suffer, that of themselves they abandon the *nembutsu* and do not take it up? Ah, all is dream and illusion, and void of reality! Life is short and hard to preserve! An instant between breaths is when the next life begins. Once we lose human existence, we will not repeat it for ten thousand *kalpas*. If at this time we do not realize enlightenment, what can even the Buddha do to save us sentient beings? May all people think deeply on impermanence and act so that they do not vainly harbor regrets! Thus I, Chang-lun, known as Layman Ching-yo, urge those with whom I have ties. (*CWS, Kyogyoshinsho*, I, p. 45, II:46)

Yuan-chao[2]

-372- Needless to say, our Buddha Amida grasps beings with the Name. Thus, as we hear it with our ears and say it with our lips, exalted virtues without limit grasp and pervade our hearts and minds. It becomes ever after the seed of our Buddhahood, all at once sweeping away a *koti* of *kalpas* of heavy karmic evil, and we attain the realization of the supreme enlightenment. I know truly that the Name possesses not scant roots of good, but inexhaustible roots of good. (*CWS, Kyogyoshinsho*, I, p. 48, II:51)

Yuan-chao

-373- As this *kalpa* draws to a close, the five defilements flourish;
    Since sentient beings possess wrong views, they find it hard to have faith.
    We are taught to practice wholeheartedly the *nembutsu* alone, taking refuge in the path to the West.
    But because of others our faith is destroyed, and we remain as we originally were.
    Since innumerable *kalpas* in the past we have always been thus;
    It is not that we realize this for the first time in this present life.
    Because we have not encountered the excellent, decisive cause,
    We have been transmigrating, unable to reach the other shore.
    (*CWS, Kyogyoshinsho*, I, p. 233, VI:55)

Beob-wi[3]

-374- All the Buddhas, after passing countless *kalpas* in practice, awaken to the reality of things as they are, and yet they grasp not a single thing; hence when, on making great vows that are formless, they perform their practices

---

[2] A Sung period *vinaya* master (1048-1116 C.E.). Though he studied Tendai teaching, becoming ill, he eventually turned to Pure Land teaching.

[3] A Korean Silla monk.

they do not abide in those excellent acts. When they realize enlightenment, they do not attain it. When they take abode, they do not adorn lands. When they manifest their powers, their supernatural powers are not supernatural powers. Hence, spreading their tongues over the great thousand-fold world, they teach the non-teaching. Thus they urge us to entrust ourselves to this *Amida Sutra*. This is utterly impossible for us to fathom with our minds or discuss with our lips. I believe that these inconceivable virtues of the Buddhas are instantaneously embodied in Amida's two kinds of fulfilled adornments. Moreover, the practice of holding to a Buddha's name, though performed with the other Buddhas, always includes Amida. (*CWS, Kyogyo-shinsho*, I, p. 51, II:60)

Chiko[4]

-375- There are two types of *nembutsu*. The first is the mental *nembutsu*, and the second is the vocal *nembutsu*. The mental *nembutsu* is also of two types. (The first is to) reflect on the Buddha's physical body. This refers to his eighty-four thousand marks, etc. (The second is to) reflect on the Buddha's wisdom body. This refers to the power of his great compassion. As for the vocal *nembutsu*, if you lack the power (to undertake the mental *nembutsu*), use your mouth to reflect on the Buddha (i.e., recite the *nembutsu*) and prevent the mind from becoming distracted. In this way, you can achieve mental concentration.

There are three types of benefits (to be obtained) by constantly remaining mindful of the name of Amida Buddha. First, by constantly remaining mindful of it, various evils and defilements will ultimately be prevented from arising. Moreover, obstructions (arising from) past karma will vanish. Second, by constantly remaining mindful of it, good roots (leading to enlightenment) will increase. Moreover, you will be able to plant the seeds leading to the karmic nexus enabling you to see the Buddha. Third, by constantly remaining mindful of it, its karmic influence will come to maturity, and you will be able to remain mindful (of Amida) at the hour of your death. (Robert F. Rhodes, "The Beginning of Pure Land Buddhism in Japan: From its Introduction through the Nara Period," *Japanese Journal of Religion* [January 2006, Vol. 31, No. 1], p. 15)

Kuya[5]

-376- Seek fame or lead a following, and both body and mind grow weary. Accumulate merit and practice good, and your desires and ambitions

---

[4] A *Sanron*, or "Three Treatise," school monk of the Nara period.

[5] Known as the "monk of the market place," Kuya (903-972 C.E.) traveled about chanting *nembutsu* and doing social work. He was a precursor of the popular Pure Land movement in Japan.

increase. Nothing is comparable to solitariness, with no outside involvement. Nothing surpasses saying the Name and casting off all concerns. The recluse leading a tranquil life rejoices at poverty; the contemplative in his dim cell makes a companion of stillness. Hempen clothes and paper bedding are robes of purity; they are easily acquired and occasion no fear of bandits. (Dennis Hirota, trans., *No Abode: The Record of Ippen* [Honolulu: The University of Hawaii Press, 1997], p. 118)

Genshin

-377- 1. Think on the Buddha's virtue! All who say "*Namu-butsu!*" even once have already fulfilled the Buddha-way; hence, I take refuge in and worship the supreme, great field of virtues.

2. Think on the Buddha's virtue! The Buddha's regard for each sentient being with eyes of compassion is equal, as though each one was the Buddha's only child; hence, I take refuge in and worship the unsurpassed mother of great compassion.

3. Think on the Buddha's virtue! All the *mahasattvas* of the ten quarters bow reverently to Amida, the honored one; hence, I take refuge in and worship the supreme honored one among beings of two legs.

4. Think on the Buddha's virtue! Hearing the Buddha's Name even once is rarer than encountering the udumbara in bloom; hence, I take refuge in and worship the one exceedingly rare to encounter.

5. Think on the Buddha's virtue! Two honored ones do not appear at the same time in the one hundred *kotis* of worlds; hence, I take refuge in and worship the great *Dharma*-king rarely met with.

6. Think on the Buddha's virtue! The ocean of virtues of the Buddha-*dharma* is one and the same throughout past, present, and future; hence, I take refuge in and worship the honored one who has perfectly fulfilled the myriad virtues. (*CWS, Kyogyoshinsho*, I, p. 52, II:64)

Ryonin[6]

-378- One man equals all men,
　　All men equal one man,
　　One practice equals all practices,
　　All practices equal one practice;
　　This is birth in the Pure Land (attainment) by Other-power.
　　The ten worlds are within a single thought,
　　And if the *yuzu nembutsu* is recited countless times,

---

[6] A *Tendai* monk, Ryonin (1072-1134 C.E.) established the *Yuzu nembutsu* sect. Its teaching of mutually interdependent, interpermeating *nembutsu*, with each person's *nembutsu* helping each other's *nembutsu*, is based on the *Kegon Sutra*.

All virtues will be complete.

(Alicia and Daigan Matsunaga, *Foundation of Japanese Buddhism* [Los Angeles/Tokyo: Buddhist Books International, 1976], II, p. 15)

Honen

-379- [The *nembutsu* that I teach] is not the contemplative *nembutsu* expounded by many learned masters of China and Japan, nor is it the recitative *nembutsu* practiced with full understanding of the meaning of "*nen*" [to recite the name Amida] that becomes clear from study. It is nothing but saying "*namu amida butsu*" with a conviction that by saying it one will certainly attain birth in the Pure Land. The three minds and the four practices, which are spoken of [in relation to the *nembutsu*], are contained in the conviction that all attain birth without fail through *namu amida butsu*. If your faith is based on other ground than this, you may not be received by the compassion of the two Buddhas (Amida Buddha and Buddha Sakyamuni) and may be left outside the Primal Vow.

Those who accept the *nembutsu* in faith, however well versed in the lifetime teachings of the Buddha, should consider themselves as illiterate, stupid persons, and without pretensions to wisdom, should single-heartedly recite the *nembutsu* with ordinary devotees of Buddhism of little learning, whether men or women. (Hisao Inagaki, trans., *Honen's One Sheet Profession of Faith* [*Ichimai-kishomon*], http://www12.canvas.ne.jp/horai/ichimai-kishomon.htm)

Honen

-380- "Great benefit" is the opposite of "small benefit." Hence, the manifold practices of the awakening of the *bodhicitta* and the rest are of small benefit. "Even one *nembutsu*" is of great benefit. Further, the words "unsurpassed merit" are the opposite of "merit that can be surpassed." The remaining practices, then, are regarded as surpassable. The *nembutsu* is said to be unsurpassed. It has already been declared that "one *nembutsu*" contains an unsurpassed quantity of merit. Hence, it ought to be understood clearly that ten *nembutsu* contain ten unsurpassed quantities of merit, that a hundred *nembutsu*, contain a hundred, and a thousand contain a thousand unsurpassed quantities of merit. In this manner, merit evolves and expands few to many. If the *nembutsu* becomes as great in number as the sands of the Ganges, then the unsurpassed quantities of merit too will be as numerous as the sands of the Ganges. One should surely understand it in this manner. If this is the case, then why should people who desire birth abandon the *nembutsu* with its unsurpassed benefits and strive to perform the other practices with their small and surpassable benefits? (*Senchakushu* English Translation Project, *Honen's Senchakushu: Passages on the Selection of the Nembutsu in the Original Vow [Senchaku Hongan Nembutsu Shu]* [Honolulu, HI: University of Hawaii Press, 1998], p. 91)

Honen

-381- The highest level of the lower class is composed of sinful people who commit the ten evils. If, at the end of their lives, they recite but one *nembutsu*, their sins will be eradicated, and they will attain birth. The middle level of the lower class is made up of sinful people who break the precepts; if, at the end of their lives, they hear of the merits of the Buddha and his land, their sins will be eradicated, and they will attain birth. The lowest level of the lower class is made up of the people who commit the five heavy sins. If, at the end of their lives, they recite the *nembutsu* ten times, their sins will be eradicated, and they will attain birth.

Even though the people belonging to these last three levels do nothing but evil deeds throughout their lives and do not desire birth, nevertheless, at the end of their lives they may chance to meet a religious teacher for the first time and thereby obtain birth. . . .

. . . Next, the *nembutsu* is the wholehearted reciting of the name of Amida Buddha. The meaning of the *nembutsu* is as it has been used throughout. Now, the passage says "correctly explains that [Sakyamuni] transmitted Amida's name [to Ananda] so that it would remain far into the future ages." Although [Sakyamuni] had in that sutra already expounded at length that various contemplative and non-contemplative practices [sic], nevertheless, he did not transmit these practices to Ananda for transmission to succeeding ages. Only the single practice of the *nembutsu samadhi* was entrusted to Ananda for transmission into the far distant future. . . .

. . . If one ponders carefully the intent of the *Contemplation Sutra*, however, one will see that it is not these various practices that were entrusted [to Ananda] for future transmission. Only the one *nembutsu* practice was so entrusted for the ages that would follow. One ought surely to know that the reason Sakyamuni did not entrust these various practices [to Ananda] was that they were not in accord with Amida's original vow. The reason [Sakyamuni] transmitted the *nembutsu* to him was that it was in accord with Amida's original vow. . . . One should, therefore, realize that the manifold practices do not suit the capacities of people [in the age of the final *Dharma*] and are not in accord with the nature of the present age [of final *Dharma*]. It is birth through the *nembutsu* that corresponds with [people's] capacities and with the times. How could both the [people's] aspirations and the [Buddha's] response come to naught?

One ought to clearly understand that [Sakyamuni] first opened the gateway of the contemplative and non-contemplative practices in response to the wishes of other people. He later closed this gateway in accordance with his original intent. The only gateway, once opened, that will remain unclosed for long eons is that of the *nembutsu*. . . .

Accordingly, one should understand that the way of birth through the *nembutsu* applies to the three ages of the right, the semblance, and the final *Dharma*, as well as to the hundred-year period after its complete extinction. (*Senchakushu* English Translation Project, *Honen's Senchakushu: Passages on the Selection of the Nembutsu in the Original Vow* [*Senchaku Hongan Nembutsu Shu*] [Honolulu, HI: University of Hawaii Press, 1998], pp. 132, 135-136)

Honen

-382- Someone once said to Honen-shonin, "Your every utterance of the name of Amida Buddha is in accord with the intent of his name." Honen-shonin asked, "What do you mean?" He was then told, "Since you are a learned priest, you fully understand the merits of the name of Amida Buddha and have distinctly mastered the profound meaning of the essential vow of Amida Buddha." Honen-shonin replied, "You do not yet believe in the essential vow. The recitation of the name of Amida Buddha taught in the essential vow was designed for all people, including the woodcutter, grass trimmer, farmer, water carrier—regardless of class or knowledge. If one firmly believes that even an illiterate attains birth in the Pure Land through reciting the name of Amida Buddha, sincerely desires birth in the Pure Land, and repeats the name of Amida Buddha unceasingly, he is considered to be the ultimate devotee for birth in the Pure Land. If we can detach ourselves from the delusive worlds of the transmigration of birth-and-death by pursuing wisdom, why would I, Genku (Honen), have abandoned the Holy Gate to follow the teaching of the Pure Land Gate?"

Honen-shonin further stated, "It should be known that the practice of the Holy Gate endeavors to extricate one from the delusive worlds through the pursuit of wisdom, and that the Pure Land Gate teaches one to return to a state of ignorance in order to be born in the Land of Ultimate Bliss (Pure Land)." (Yoko Hayashi, Joji Atone, trans., *Teachings of Honen* [Los Angeles: Bukkyo University-Los Angeles Extension, 2007 rev.], pp. 8-9)

Honen

-383- Although there are many, practices for birth in the Pure Land can be divided into two. The first is the Exclusive Practice (the recitation of *nembutsu*), and the second are the Miscellaneous Practices (all Buddhist practices other than *nembutsu*). The latter practices are defined as the meditative practices with a concentrated mind and with a distracted mind as detailed in the *Meditation Sutra*.

Master Shan-tao stated in his *Hymns in Praise of Birth in the Pure Land* (*Ojoraisan*), "If people recite the name of Buddha Amida continually throughout their entire lives in the manner mentioned previously, ten out of ten and one hundred out of a hundred people will be assured realization of birth in the Pure Land." This statement clarifies the qualities of merit and demerit in comparing the Exclusive Practice and the Miscellaneous Practices.

Here, merit applies to the attainment of birth in the Pure Land. That is, "ten out of ten and one hundred out of a hundred *nembutsu* devotees will be assured realization of birth in the Pure Land" is the merit of the Exclusive Practice. Master Shan-tao also said, "Demerit means losing the merit of birth in the Pure Land. Rarely will one or two out of a hundred practitioners of the Miscellaneous Practices attain birth in that Land. The rest cannot realize it. Rarely will three or five out of a thousand practitioners of the Miscellaneous Practices attain birth. The rest cannot realize birth in the Pure Land."

Someone asked Honen-shonin, "Why is it possible for all *nembutsu* devotees of the Exclusive Practice to be born in the Pure Land?" He replied that this was in accordance with the essential vow of Amida Buddha and that it was also consistent with the teaching of Buddha Sakyamuni. He was further asked, "Why do so few who follow the Miscellaneous Practices attain birth in the Pure Land?" He answered, "The Miscellaneous Practices are not in accordance with the essential vow of Amida Buddha neither are they consistent with the teaching of Buddha Sakyamuni."

The *nembutsu* devotees who aspire to birth in the Pure Land are indeed following the practice in accordance with the compassionate hearts of two venerable Buddhas (Amida Buddha and Buddha Sakyamuni). The followers of the Miscellaneous Practices who aspire to birth in the Pure Land are not in accord with the hearts of these two Buddhas. (Yoko Hayashi, Joji Atone, trans., *Teachings of Honen* [Los Angeles: Bukkyo University-Los Angeles Extension, 2007 rev.], pp. 28-29)

Honen

-384- Knowing that birth in the Pure Land is possible through reciting *nembutsu*, yet indulging in evil karma, neglecting compassionate deeds, and not devoting oneself to *nembutsu* is not in accord with the teachings of Amida Buddha.

It is as if the compassion of parents nurtures all of their children whether they are good or bad; yet the parents rejoice in good children and grieve for the bad children. Amida Buddha extends his compassion equally to all beings and saves the good and bad; but he finds joy in the good and feels sorrow for the bad.

Elation over the good is analogous to the good seed sown in fertile soil resulting in a good crop. Even the good person should recite *nembutsu*. This is, in the true sense, the follower of the teachings of Amida Buddha. (Yoko Hayashi, Joji Atone, trans., *Teachings of Honen* [Los Angeles: Bukkyo University-Los Angeles Extension, 2007 rev.], p. 95)

Honen

-385- Question: Which recitation is more virtuous—to use a string of prayer beads while reciting sixty thousand to a hundred thousand *nembutsu* everyday; or to use the prayer beads with deliberation and accomplish twenty to thirty thousand recitations?

Answer: It is difficult for common people to set the number of *nembutsu* to twenty or thirty thousand as a specific daily goal. It is, however, desirable to recite as many *nembutsu* as possible on a daily basis. Setting a daily goal is to encourage people to continue to recite the name of Amida Buddha. Although a daily quota is not a requisite, one should always be mindful of the goal to recite as many *nembutsu* as possible. Without setting a goal in the number of *nembutsu* recitations, one is prone to laziness. Therefore, a numerical goal serves as an incentive for continual practice. (Yoko Hayashi, Joji Atone, trans., *Teachings of Honen* [Los Angeles: Bukkyo University-Los Angeles Extension, 2007 rev.], p. 86)

Honen

-386- Question: In the recitation of *nembutsu*, should we always use a string of prayer beads?

Answer: You must hold the prayer beads in your hand at all times. In song and dance there must be a beat to guide you in rhythm and timing. In the recitation of *nembutsu* the prayer beads are considered to be the score which guides your tongue and hands. If you do not rid yourself of ignorance, illusory thoughts will arise.

This is like the relationship between a host and guests. When you hold the prayer beads your intention should not be the eradication of illusory thoughts but the counting of the number of recitations of *nembutsu*. Therefore, *nembutsu* is the host, and illusory thoughts are the guests. The guests are free to come and go; however, one should not entertain illusory thoughts while reciting *nembutsu*. You would be terribly misguided should you be holding the prayer beads and uttering slander simultaneously. (Yoko Hayashi, Joji Atone, trans., *Teachings of Honen* [Los Angeles: Bukkyo University-Los Angeles Extension, 2007 rev.], p. 87)

Honen

-387- A Reply to the Priestess Holding the Second Rank in the Court of Kamakura:

I have humbly read your letter in detail.

Buddha Sakyamuni once stated, "The virtue of the recitation of *nembutsu* is so profound that even I cannot expound upon it all." Both Sariputra, the most knowledgeable disciple of Buddha Sakyamuni, and Ananda, the most erudite disciple of the Buddha, also admitted to their lack of complete knowledge regarding the merit of *nembutsu*. *Nembutsu* has an extensive root of virtue; therefore, one such as I could not possibly expound upon its merit.

I, Genku, have studied the voluminous Buddhist scriptures that have found their way to our country; however, I do not think that all Pure Land texts are in existence here. Even the Pure Land Scriptures from China cannot be fully elucidated in one or two years. Nonetheless, since you have asked, however, I will relate some thoughts to you.

The non-believers in *nembutsu* say that because the lay priest of Kumagai and Saburo of Tsunoto are unschooled, I, Honen-bo Genku, encourage them to recite *nembutsu* exclusively rather than to pursue other practices. This is a totally mistaken criticism.

The practice of *nembutsu* does not discriminate between the learned and the unschooled. Long ago the essential vow of Amida Buddha was designed for saving all sentient beings. It does not promote *nembutsu* for the unschooled nor other practices for the scholarly. The essential vow was established for all beings in the ten directions; therefore, *nembutsu* does not discriminate between the learned and the unschooled, the virtuous and the non-virtuous, those who observe the precepts and those who violate them, those of high and low status, nor between male and female.

For those who lived in the time of Buddha Sakyamuni, those who lived after his death, and even those who will live during the extinction of the Three Jewels after the period of the decline of the *Dharma* that lasts ten thousand years, *nembutsu* has and will serve as the sole practice for emancipation for deliverance in this world.

Master Shan-tao was the manifestation of Amida Buddha. In his compassion for all sentient beings, Master Shan-tao pursued the study of the entire Buddhist scriptures and encouraged the exclusive practice of *nembutsu*. *Nembutsu*, as a skillful means for saving all sentient beings, is the teaching suitable for this period of the decline of the *Dharma*.

Have faith in the essential vow that you extensively exercise, comply thoroughly with the heart of Master Shan-tao, and exhort the sole teaching of *nembutsu*. How can birth in the Pure Land through *nembutsu* be limited to the unschooled? How can it be impossible for the learned to attain birth in the Pure Land? If this were so, it would be contrary to the essential vow of Amida Buddha and a betrayal of the intent of Master Shan-tao. I, therefore, encourage all who come asking about the way to birth in the Pure Land to commit themselves to the exclusive practice of *nembutsu* regardless of their intellectual abilities.

Those who attempt to discourage the exclusive practice of *nembutsu* through such falsehoods did not hear the teachings of the *nembutsu samadhi* for attaining birth in the Pure Land in their previous existence, and in their next lives they are most certainly destined to return to the three lower realms. Therefore, they promote lies as if they were true. Such erroneous views are extensively described in the holy texts. To cite an example, Master Shan-tao stated:

> There are people who give rise to the poison of anger who, when they see a serious *nembutsu* practitioner, struggle to incite intrigue and create grudges. Such people seem blind by nature and have no intrinsic goodness. Destroying the teaching designed for the instantaneous realization of enlightenment, they will sink into the three lower realms for a long time. They will never be released from the three lower realms, even though innumerable eons pass, more innumerable than the number of particles released in the explosion of the earth.

This passage refers to someone who generates the worldly passion of anger upon witnessing a practitioner of *nembutsu* who desires to be born in the Pure Land. This person contrives various dastardly schemes and ill-advisedly causes termination of the exclusive *nembutsu*, thus succeeding in his malicious intent. Such a person lacking an understanding of the teachings of Buddha Sakyamuni for birth in the Pure Land, has no inherent goodness; he is in want of the seeds of virtuous roots.

Someone who recites the name of Amida Buddha will extricate himself from the delusive worlds of transmigration where he has stayed for so long, and will live eternally in the Pure Land. A person who criticizes and attempts to destroy the teaching of *nembutsu*, however, will sink interminably in the three lower realms. It will be impossible for such a person to escape from the three lower realms for innumerable eons. Hence, this type of person who promotes falsehoods should be looked upon with pity. It is probably futile to urge *nembutsu* upon one who is swayed by such thought, becomes neglectful in his exclusive practice of *nembutsu*, and harbors doubt about birth in the Pure Land through *nembutsu*.

In general, those who have little karmic relationship with Amida Buddha, and who have not discovered his notion of birth in the Pure Land, will not believe in the teaching of *nembutsu* even if they hear it, will become wrathful when they see the *nembutsu* devotee, and will get angry upon hearing *nembutsu*. They will also speak ill of *nembutsu*, which is not found in any sutra or commentary. This should be understood, and you must not deviate, no matter what you are told. Please do not force reciting *nembutsu* on those who do not believe in *nembutsu*.

If it is unfeasible even for Amida Buddha to sway the nonbelievers, it is well nigh impossible for a common mortal. Rather, look upon the nonbelievers as having been your fathers, mothers, brothers, sisters, and relatives in your previous existence. Summon your compassionate spirit, practice *nembutsu* yourself, speedily achieve the high grade of the high category of birth in the Pure Land, realize enlightenment there, return once again to this delusive world of *samsara*, and hope to welcome into the Pure Land all those who slander and hold *nembutsu* in disbelief. I implore you to thoroughly understand this.

1. When you encounter people who engage in cultivating virtuous merit through performing the miscellaneous practices, think of it as the process by which wealth begets wealth. Firmly believe that you will attain birth in the Pure Land through the single-hearted and exclusive practice of *nembutsu*; think of the other as one who is taking the long way and make an effort to establish a karmic relationship that encourages him to take the short way with you. To the extent that it does not interfere with your exclusive practice of *nembutsu*, it is acceptable to make an attempt at bringing in a *nembutsu* devotee.

2. As you behold the people erecting a temple, creating the image of a Buddha, engaging in the reproduction of sutras, and making offerings to a monk, encourage them to believe that they must awaken unshakable faith in birth in the Pure Land and then keep up their effort to cultivate these sundry virtuous roots.

3. There exist those who are unaware of the true meaning of the recitation of *nembutsu*, who pray to Buddhas and gods for fortune in this world, recite and copy sutras, and erect temples. If you behold these people, you should encourage them as mentioned above. The cultivation of these virtuous acts is acceptable if they are performed for the sake of birth in the Pure Land in their next lives. Please do not say that these acts are unnecessary. Do not consider these acts as a deterrent to the exclusive practice of *nembutsu*.

4. There are many implications in the recitation of *nembutsu*. However, the vocalization of the six characters, *na-mu-a-mi-da-butsu*, encompasses the merit of all religious practices. To believe in the essential vow, to utter the name of Amida Buddha, to hold a string of prayer beads in hand, and to aspire to birth in the Pure Land at all times. These become the ultimate causal practices toward the certain attainment of birth in the Pure Land.

The practice of *nembutsu* does not discriminate among those who are walking, standing, sitting, and lying down; length of time, place, or various karmic conditions; or the purity or impurity of one's mouth and body. The practice of *nembutsu* is, therefore, called the "easy practice for birth in the Pure Land." We must remember, however, maintaining purity of our hearts when *nembutsu* is recited should be foremost.

Putting your total faith in birth in the Pure Land results in the purification of your mind. It is my wish that you encourage others to recite *nembutsu* in this spirit. If you have this spirit all the time, nothing more needs to be said. You, too, should recite *nembutsu* exclusively, believe in certain attainment of birth in the Pure Land, and be stalwart in your belief.

5. Should you encounter a non-believer in the *nembutsu* practice, do not discuss the teaching of *nembutsu*. Neither engage in a debate over doctrine with people who follow teachings and practices other than *nembutsu*. Do not look down on, or slander, people who have views and leanings other than your own. It is lamentable that criticism will result in making the other a grievously defiled person.

Contrarily, should there be a person who has the same heart as us, desiring birth in the Pure Land through reciting *nembutsu*, think of him with no less compassion than that which our fathers, mothers, and masters have shown to us, however low his station is. If such a person is suffering in poverty, come to his aid. At all times, nurture anyone who shows the least bit of interest in the teaching of *nembutsu*. It should be done with the thought that these acts are a service to *Tathagata* Amida.

Some people impudently speak about the teaching of Buddha Sakyamuni as though their own wisdom were comparable, despite knowing that wisdom and practice have gradually waned since the passing of *Tathagata* Sakyamuni. For one who does not peruse the collected works of the Buddhist scriptures and cannot speak of other writings on Buddhism, to assume a stance of wisdom is analogous to the little frog in the well [who is ignorant of the world].

I have collected and studied many Chinese and Japanese holy teachings. Reflecting on these teachings, it is clear that a non-believer of *nembutsu* is someone who committed grave offenses in his previous existence and stayed in hell for a long while and will soon return to hell.

Never believe in the sayings of a thousand false Buddhas, even if they proclaim that *nembutsu* is not the karmic cause for birth in the Pure Land. Firmly believe that *nembutsu* is validated by all Buddhas, as numerous as the sands of the Ganges, not to mention *Tathagata* Sakyamuni as well. Keep your heart as hard and solid as an adamantine stone, and do not change your devotion toward the single-hearted and exclusive practice of *nembutsu*.

Should anyone try to initiate a debate on *nembutsu*, suggest that he come to me to learn the meaning of *nembutsu*. I could recommend voluminous worthy documents concerning *nembutsu* to you, but this explanation suffices.

For people in this delusive world where life is the endurance of pain, desiring a pure Buddha-land other than that of Amida Buddha would be as futile as hunting a bird flying high when one has no bow, or attempting to pluck a flower from a tree-top when one has no legs on which to stand.

The exclusive practice of *nembutsu* becomes the prayer for the present and the future. This is taught in the sutras. Please encourage your kin to practice the recitation of *nembutsu* throughout their entire lives in order to realize the nine grades of birth in the Pure Land in accordance to their abilities.

Respectfully yours.

(Yoko Hayashi, Joji Atone, trans., *Promise of Amida: Honen's Path to Bliss* [Boston: Wisdom Publications, 2011], pp. 178-184; this letter is addressed to Hojo Masako, wife of Minamoto Yoritomo, the first Shogun in Kamakura, 1147-1197)

Honen

-388- No practice other than *nembutsu* is taught in the essential vow of Amida Buddha. Even though other practices are excellent, they are not superior to *nembutsu*. In general, if one desires to be born in a pure land of a Buddha, then follow the vow of that Buddha. It is apparent that one who wishes specifically to be born in the Pure Land of Amida Buddha should abide by his essential vow. Do not compare *nembutsu* taught in the essential vow with Buddhist practices other than *nembutsu* to see which is superior. It is for these reasons that there is no better practice than *nembutsu* for the attainment of birth in the Pure Land. (Yoko Hayashi, Joji Atone, trans., *Teachings of Honen* [Los Angeles: Bukkyo University-Los Angeles Extension, 2007 rev.], p. 227)

Honen

-389- One or Many *Nembutsu*

The second fascicle of the *Two-Fascicle Sutra* (*Larger Sutra*) teaches, "Even a single utterance of *nembutsu* causes joy to well up in one's devout heart. And Master Shan-tao instructed (in *Hymns in Praise of Birth in the Pure Land*), "Believe, without doubting even for a moment, that the upper limit of life—lifelong *nembutsu*—and the lowest limit—ten recitations or a single utterance of *nembutsu*, enable you to attain birth in the Pure Land." Those who misinterpret these statements have proposed the great heretical view that birth in the Pure Land is assured by just a single utterance of *nembutsu*. In truth, the words "even" and "the lowest limit," imply that one should continue to recite *nembutsu* for life.

Recently, however, many ignorant people have become exclusively attached to the ten repetitions, or even a single utterance of *nembutsu*, and have eventually abandoned the life-long practice of *nembutsu*. This is most certainly shameful.

You must believe that *nembutsu* possesses supreme merit and that Amida Buddha with his great compassion of the essential vow, will come to embrace one who recites *nembutsu* even ten times or just once. Thus believing this, practice *nembutsu* for your entire lifetime without negligence. Although there are many writings that attest to this teaching, citing these sources is unnecessary. The advocacy of the attainment of birth in the Pure Land through a single utterance of *nembutsu* is not worth mentioning.

Regarding this perverse view, someone replied upon encountering criticism, "I, too, advocate extreme devotion to a single utterance of *nembutsu*, and although a single utterance guarantees birth in the Pure Land, I do not advocate forsaking *nembutsu* thereafter." These words seem logical, but his heart is attached to an aberrant view. This implies the belief that if one utters *nembutsu* once with steadfast faith, one is free to commit the ten transgressions or the five grave offenses after the single utterance of *nembutsu*, much less other venial offenses.

How can one who espouses such a belief be in compliance with the intent of Buddha Amida even though he recites multiple *nembutsu*? In which sutra and commentary is such a teaching found? Such a belief is indicative of total indolence; it is a lack of aspiration for birth in the Pure Land, and is an attempt of unjust and depraved people to cause iniquity. Further, if one does not continually recite *nembutsu* after a single utterance, one's karmic negativity would be a hindrance toward accomplishing birth in the Pure Land and would ultimately cast one down into the three lower realms.

However, one who has committed a lifetime of evil deeds may still attain birth in the Pure Land through reciting *nembutsu* ten times at the time of his death. This is due to the compassionate power of *nembutsu* in repentance. This person should not be confused with one who has the mistaken notion that evil is nullified by a single utterance of *nembutsu*. The former is one in repentance; the latter is one with a perverse view. There is no need for further explanation. (Yoko Hayashi, Joji Atone, trans., *Teachings of Honen* [Los Angeles: Bukkyo University-Los Angeles Extension, 2007 rev.], pp. 243-245)

Honen

-390- Whenever reciting *nembutsu*, hold your palms together with your eyes always closed and with tranquility in your heart. Recite *nembutsu* with the belief that Amida Buddha, in accordance with the essential vow, will definitely appear before you at the time of death, and that he will impart his compassion to you and make you abide in the rightly settled state of mind. This is the ultimate stance for birth in the Pure Land. Your heart must not falter. (Yoko Hayashi, Joji Atone, trans., *Teachings of Honen* [Los Angeles: Bukkyo University-Los Angeles Extension, 2007 rev.], p. 251)

Honen

-**391**- With [*namu*]-*amida-butsu* this heart of mine
[has been ushered] to the West[ern land],
At last free of this shell,
how coolly the voicing [of *namu-amida-butsu*]
fills the void!

On saying the ten thoughts before retiring at night
It's always best to say ten voicings of
[*namu*]-*amida-butsu* before dropping off at night,
For who knows: this just might be the night
that one falls into that long sleep.
(Wayne Yokoyama and Yukie Dan, trans., *Honen's Waka Verse* #9, #12, based on the text supplied in the entry on *waka* in *Jodoshu jiten*, III.512-13. For a previous English translation, see H. H. Coates and R. Ishizuka, trans., *Honen the Buddhist Saint: His Life and Teaching* [Kyoto: Chion'in, 1925], pp. 542-545, where rhymes are made of seventeen of the *waka*)

Seikaku

-**392**- When persons aspire to free themselves from birth-and-death and attain enlightenment, there are two routes open to them: the gate of the Path of Sages and the gate of the Pure Land. The Path of Sages consists of performing practices and accumulating merit while living in this *saha* world, striving to attain enlightenment in this present life. People who practice the Shingon teaching aspire to rise to the stage of great enlightenment with their present bodies. All followers who endeavor in the Tendai school seek to attain the enlightenment known as "the stage of purifying the six sense organs" in this life. Although such indeed is the final objective of the teaching of the Path of Sages, since the world has reached the age of the corrupt *dharma* and entered the period of defilement, not even a single person among millions can attain enlightenment in this present life. Hence, those who endeavor in the gate of the Path of Sages in the present age become weary and withdraw in their attempt to attain enlightenment of becoming Buddha with this present body. . . .

Second is the gate of the Pure Land, in which, directing the merit of practice in the present life, one aspires to be born in the next life in the Pure Land to fulfill the *bodhisattva* practices and become a Buddha. This gate meets the needs of people of these latter days; it is truly a marvelous path. But this gate is itself divided into two: birth through various practices and birth through the *nembutsu*. . . .

. . . "Birth through various practices" means to aspire to be born in the Pure Land through observing filial piety toward one's parents, serving one's teacher and elders, maintaining the five precepts or eight precepts, and practicing charity and patience, and also through such practices as the three mystic acts (Shingon) or the meditation exercise of the One Vehicle (Tendai). One may attain birth through these practices, for all are, without exception, none other than practices for birth into the Pure Land. But in all of them one aspires for birth by applying oneself relentlessly to practices, so they are called "birth through self-power." If the practices are done inadequately, it is impossible to achieve birth. They do not accord with Amida's Primal Vow; they are not illuminated by the radiance of Amida's grasp.

"Birth through the *nembutsu*" is to aspire for birth through saying the Name of Amida. Because this is in accordance with the Buddha's Primal Vow, it is called the act of true settlement; since one is pulled solely by the power of Amida's Vow, it is called birth through Other-Power. (*CWS, Seikaku's Essentials of Faith Alone*, I, pp. 685-686)

## Seikaku
-393- In this gate of birth through the *nembutsu*, moreover, two practices are distinguished: single practice and sundry practice. Single practice is to perform simply the one practice of the *nembutsu*, awakening the aspiration for the land of bliss and the faith of entrusting to the Primal Vow, never mixing any other practices whatsoever with it. . . . People who enter the gate of the *nembutsu* but combine it with other practices are attached to their former practices and have difficulty abandoning them. Those who hold to the One Vehicle or practice the Three Mystic Acts do not change their aspiration to attain birth in the Pure Land by directing the merits of such practices, wondering what can be wrong with pursuing them together with the *nembutsu*. Without endeavoring in the *nembutsu* of easy practice that accords with the Primal Vow, meaningless is it to follow various practices rejected by the Primal Vow. (*CWS, Seikaku, Essentials of Faith Alone*, I, pp. 688-689)

## Ryukan
-394- Many-calling is nothing but the accumulation of single callings, for human life is such that a person should consider each day that this may be

his last, each minute that this may be the end. From the very moment of our birth, this realm of impermanence is merely a fleeting and temporary dwelling; our lives may be compared to a lantern flame before the wind, or likened to dew upon a blade of grass, and there is no escape anywhere for even a single person, whether wise or foolish, from the extinction of breath and the draining away of life. If our eyes may close forever even in this present instant, then we say *namu-amida-butsu*, aspiring to be saved by Amida's Primal Vow and welcomed into the Pure Land of perfect bliss, based on our trust in the supreme virtues embodied in a single calling and our reliance on the great and vast benefit of that one calling.

As life continues, this single calling becomes two or three callings; they accumulate, so that one moment becomes an hour, then two hours; a day or two; a month, a year, two years, ten or twenty years, eighty years. The immutable nature of our existence is expressed truly in the statement that we should wonder how it is that we are still alive today, and whether this very instant will be our last in this world. (*CWS*, Ryukan, *The Clarification of Once-calling and Many-calling*, p. 701)

Shinran

-395- Attaining Buddhahood through the *nembutsu* is the true essence of
   the Pure Land way;
 The myriad practices and good acts are the temporary gate.
 Unless one distinguishes the accommodated and the real, the temporary
   and the true,
 One cannot possibly know the Pure Land that is naturalness (*jinen*).
 (*CWS*, *Hymns of the Pure Land*, I, p. 344, #71)

Shinran

-396- The saying of the Name arising from true and real *shinjin*
 Is Amida's directing of virtue to beings;
 Therefore, it is called "not directing merit,"
 And saying the *nembutsu* in self-power is rejected.
 (*CWS*, *Hymns of the Dharma-Ages*, I, p. 408, #39)

Shinran

-397- Those who deeply entrust themselves
 To Amida's Vow of great compassion
 Should all say *namu-amida-butsu* constantly,
 Whether they are waking or sleeping.
 (*CWS*, *Hymns of the Dharma-Ages*, I, p. 411, #54)

Shinran

-398- Thus, Shan-tao rephrases the selected Primal Vow, "If, when I attain Buddhahood, the sentient beings of the ten quarters say my Name even ten times but do not attain birth, may I not attain the supreme enlightenment." Here, in Amida's Primal Vow, *even* includes "few" in contrast to "many," teaching us that sentient beings who say the Name as few as ten times will without fail attain birth. Know that "thinking" and "voicing" have the same meaning; no voicing exists separate from thinking, and no thinking separate from voicing. (*CWS, Notes on Essentials of Faith Alone,* I, p. 468)

Shinran

-399- "Saying my Name perhaps even ten times": In encouraging us to say the Name that embodies the vow, the *Tathagata* added "perhaps even" to the words "ten times" to show that there is no set number of times the Name must be said and to teach sentient beings that there is no determined hour or occasion for saying it. Since we have been given this vow by the *Tathagata,* we can take any occasion in daily life for saying the Name and need not wait to recite it at the very end of life; we should simply give ourselves up totally to the entrusting with sincere mind of the *Tathagata.* When persons realize this true and real *shinjin,* they enter completely into the compassionate light that grasps, never to abandon, and hence become established in the stage of the truly settled. Thus it is written. (*CWS, Notes on Inscription on Sacred Scrolls,* I, p. 494)

Shinran

-400- "Even down to ten times" refers to people who say the Name as few as ten times. "Even down to" means that neither those who say the Name more than ten times nor those who only hear the Name are omitted or excluded from birth in the Pure Land. (*CWS, Notes on Inscription on Sacred Scrolls,* I, p. 506)

Shinran

-401- For Amida vowed to take into the land of bliss those who say the Name, and thus to entrust oneself deeply and say the Name is to be in perfect accord with the Primal Vow. Though a person may have *shinjin,* if he or she does not say the Name it is of no avail. And conversely, even though a person fervently say the Name, if that person's *shinjin* is shallow he cannot attain birth. Thus, it is the person who both deeply entrusts himself to birth through the *nembutsu* and undertakes to say the Name who is certain to be born in the true fulfilled land.

In short, although persons say the Name, if they do not entrust themselves to the Primal Vow that is Other-Power, they will surely be born in the borderland.[7] But how can it be that those who deeply entrust themselves to the power of the Primal Vow are also born there? Please say the *nembutsu* fully understanding what I have explained above. (*CWS, Lamp for the Latter Ages*, #12, I, p. 539; see also, *CWS*, p. 555)

Shinran

-402- Now then, what you ask is indeed an excellent question. To begin, you state that with one utterance of the *nembutsu* the cause of birth is fulfilled. It is truly so. Even so, however, it does not mean that a person should not say the *nembutsu* beyond the one utterance. This matter is explained fully in *Essentials of Faith Alone*. Please read this work carefully. That the *nembutsu* said beyond one utterance should be directed to the sentient beings of the ten quarters is also correct. Since one is directing the *nembutsu* to the sentient beings of the ten quarters, it is an error to think that saying it twice or three times is bad for one's attainment of birth. I have been taught that, since it is the Primal Vow of birth through the *nembutsu*, whether one says the *nembutsu* many times or whether one says it only once, one will be born. It must never be taught that one will certainly attain birth with only one utterance but will not attain birth if one says it many times. (*CWS, A Collection of Letters*, #3, I, p. 561)

Shinran

-403- As for me, Shinran, I have never said the *nembutsu* even once for the repose of my departed father and mother. For all sentient beings, without exception, have been our parents and brothers and sisters in the course of countless lives in the many states of existence. On attaining Buddhahood after this present life, we can save every one of them.

Were saying the *nembutsu* indeed a good act in which I strove through my own powers, then I might direct the merit thus gained towards saving my father and mother. But this is not the case.

If, however, simply abandoning self-power, we quickly attain enlightenment in the Pure Land, we will be able to save, by means of transcendent powers, first those with whom we have close karmic relations, whatever karmic suffering they may have sunk to in the six realms through the four modes of birth. (*CWS, A Record in Lament of Divergences*, 5, I, p. 664)

Shinran

-404- The *nembutsu* is the single path free of hindrances. Why is this? To

---

[7] The borderland is a type of limbo mythically located adjacent to the Pure Land where people who engage in self-power practices are born. It is a realm of spiritual immaturity, self-complacency, and indolence.

practicers who have realized *shinjin*, the gods of the heavens and earth bow in homage, and *maras* and non-Buddhists present no obstruction. No evil act can bring about karmic results, nor can any good act equal the *nembutsu*. (*CWS, A Record in Lament of Divergences*, I, p. 665)

Shinran

**-405-** The *nembutsu*, for its practicers, is not a practice or a good act. Since it is not preformed out of one's own designs, it is not a practice. Since it is not good done through one's own calculation, it is not a good act. Because it arises wholly from Other-Power and is free of self-power, for the practicer, it is not a practice or a good act. (*CWS, A Record in Lament of Divergences*, 8, I, p. 665)

Kakunyo

**-406-** The cause and condition relationship maintains between the radiant Light and the Name. In the twelfth of Amida *Tathagata*'s forty-eight vows, it is promised, "My Light shall shine forth without limit." What this means is, [the Light] is for the sake of receiving the sentient beings of the *nembutsu*. As this vow has already been culminated, this Light shines unhindered everywhere in the worlds as fine as dust particles in every direction, and has already been shining for the longest time on the blind passion and evil karma of sentient beings. Therefore, those sentient beings who meet with this condition of the Light, as the darkness of ignorance begins to fade and they begin to notice the seeds of goodness that dwell within them, they hear the Name that is the cause of the eighteenth vow's promise of impending birth by *nembutsu* that [guarantees] they shall truly be born in the reward land.

However, the Name they embrace is not a form of self-power. Rather, it is done solely by relying on the radiant Light that has started to work on them. On this basis, as the condition of the radiant Light becomes more pronounced, the cause of the Name begins to grow faint. For that reason Shan-tao says, "Through the radiant Light and the Name, [Amida] receives and converts [all beings] in every direction; however, [he] does this through imparting them with *shinjin* that makes them turn their thoughts to seeking salvation." The phrase, "however, [he] does this through imparting them with *shinjin* that makes them turn their thoughts to seeking salvation," means the radiant Light and the Name are like the father and mother who strive to raise a child, but without the seed by which the child is produced, there is nothing to be called father and mother. Once there is a child, then the names father and mother apply.

Likewise, though we may say the radiant Light is like the mother and the Name is like the father, the mother of radiant Light and the father of the

Name cannot be said to exist without the seed of *shinjin* by which we are truly born in the reward land.

Thus, when *shinjin* emerges [in us] and we vow to aspire for impending Birth, we find ourselves chanting the *nembutsu*, and also [being enfolded by] the radiant Light that receives all. Thus, unless there is a seeker in whom *shinjin* awakens with regard to the Name, Amida *Tathagata*'s promise to receive all and reject none would never be fulfilled. Without Amida *Tathagata*'s promise to receive all and reject none, on what basis would the seeker's wish for Birth in the Pure Land be fulfilled? Thus it is said, "The vow is the Name, the Name is the vow. The vow is the seeker, the seeker is the vow." (W.S. Yokoyama, *Kakunyo's Embracing the Name*, #4, unpublished translation)

Shoku

-407- People who depend on themselves for their emancipation discolor the *nembutsu* itself. One person gives a different color to it, because of the convictions he has reached regarding the Mahayana teachings. Another does the same by the understanding he has of other Buddhist principles. Another does it by her way of keeping the precepts, while a fourth by his method of meditative absorption (*samadhi*). In the end, those who color their *nembutsu* practice with many meditative and non-meditative practices boast that they will definitely attain birth in the Pure Land.

Meanwhile those who cannot develop these practices and whose *nembutsu* is utterly colorless grow discouraged about their ability to attain birth in the Pure Land. Well, both the boastful and the discouraged are illusions coming from self-dependence. The fact is that the *nembutsu* taught in the *Sutra of Immeasurable Life* for people who live a hundred years after the Dharma has perished, and the *nembutsu* taught in the *Meditation Sutra* for those who belong to the lowest three of the nine ranks of sentient beings is the very *nembutsu* I mean when I use the term "unvarnished wood." In his explanation of the passage in the *Meditation Sutra* which deals with the Original Vow, Shan-tao uses the words "with a sincere and believing mind" and "calling upon my name" in an identical manner—and these correspond to the "unvarnished" *nembutsu*.

Now according to the *Meditation Sutra*, people destined to be born into the lowest of the lowest rank in the Pure Land have no power to discolor anything whatever, because they are just common fools without any goodness either spiritual or secular. In their death-agony, they are so devoid of consciousness that they cannot act, speak, or think. They've been bad their whole lives through, so in the anguish of the last crisis, there is nothing they can fall back upon. They are powerless to do good or refrain from bad, much less grasp the meaning of Mahayana or Theravada teachings. Nor can they see the ultimate goal of all Buddhist aspiration or the ordinary means by which it can be gained. At such a time, there is no use in trying to make merit by building a pagoda or shrine. The coming separation with home and friends and the abandoning of worldly desires tears at their hearts. They are in fact deluded beings of the worst kind, quite beyond all hope of salvation. So a spiritual guide comes and asks, "Can you understand a little about Amida Buddha's power and realize something of the great power of the *nembutsu.*" But the person is so overwhelmed in the death struggle that such thoughts are totally beyond him. Then the person is advised to repeat the words of the *Meditation Sutra*, "If you cannot think upon Amida Buddha's power, then call upon the name of Amida." In spite of all the mental confusion and distress, the person goes on repeating the sacred name ten times. With each repetition the karma, which was bad enough to condemn the person to eight million *kalpas* of transmigration, is completely wiped away. Instead of such an awful fate, the person takes a place of honor upon the "golden lotus which shines in glory like the sun." A person in such an extreme case as this has nothing like what we call the aspiration for enlightenment (*bodhicitta*), nor can their *nembutsu* take any coloring from either meditative or non-meditative practices. By simply following the directions of the guide and without any pretentions to wisdom, the person attains birth in the Pure Land by the mere repetition of the "unvarnished" *nembutsu*. It's just like if you take hold of a child's hand and make it write something. Would such writing be a reason for praising the child? This is the kind of *nembutsu* repeated by those who belong to the lowest classes of the lowest rank. They attain birth in the Pure Land by merely taking Amida's name on their lips as advised by their spiritual guides.

Now if a person just says the *nembutsu*, he or she will attain birth—no matter whether the person leads a pure or impure life, whether their karma is bad or good, whether the person is of high class or low, a scholar or a fool. And yet people committed to the self-power method of emancipation keep on making meditative and non-meditative practices their objective. They insist that it is useless to try to attain birth without the coloring these practices give to their *nembutsu*. But they are all totally out of line. That is why we teach the method of emancipation by dependence upon other power and the complete rejection of the principles of the self-power method. Now this doesn't mean that there's no value in the *nembutsu* of people either deeply or just ordinarily knowledgeable of the Mahayana teachings, or of those who keep the precepts. It's very important to avoid all confusion of thought here. (Jonathan Watts, Yoshiharu Tomatsu, eds., *Traversing the Pure Land Way: A Lifetime of Encounters with Honen Shonin* [Tokyo: Jodo-shu Press, 2005], pp. 116-118)

Ippen

-408- Without deliberating or designing in any way at all, entrust yourself to the Primal Vow and say the *nembutsu*. Whether you say it with mind firmly settled or not firmly settled, the *nembutsu* cannot deviate from the all-surpassing Primal Vow that is Other Power. In Amida's Primal Vow there is nothing lacking, nothing superfluous. Beyond this, what is there to say of a proper attitude? Just return to the mind and heart of a simple, foolish person and say the *nembutsu*. (Dennis Hirota, trans., *No Abode: The Record of Ippen* [Honolulu: The University of Hawai'i Press, 1997], p. 30)

Ippen

-409- Encounters in this world result from close ties in the past borne through many lifetimes; it is indeed joyous, then, to be together in taking refuge in one Buddha. Birth-and-death is the delusional thinking rooted in self-attachment; enlightenment is the One Mind free from such thought. Since birth-and-death is originally nonexistent, though we engage in study, [emancipation] cannot be thus attained. Since enlightenment is originally nonexistent, though we undergo practice, it cannot be thus realized. Nevertheless, those who do not study wander deeper and deeper in illusion, those who do not practice wind further and further in the cycle of birth-and-death. Discarding our bodies, then, we must perform practice; emptying our minds, we must strive. With regard to this truth, the Path of Sages and the Pure Land way are, in the final analysis, one, though their terms differ. The *Lotus Sutra* admonishes us with the words, "We do not hold our lives and bodies dear, but cherish only the unexcelled enlightenment." *The Contemplation Sutra* teaches, "Abandoning the body in other worlds, one is born without fail in that Land." In the Path of Sages, which is the practice of self-power, it is a matter of course that one must give up the body and life of the self in order to realize enlightenment. In the Pure Land way, since it is the practice of Other-Power, we entrust our bodies and lives to the Buddha, and after this life comes to an end, we realize Buddha-nature. Foolish beings like ourselves should seek no path of liberation outside of wholehearted utterance of the Name. . . . Apart from just these six characters—*namu-amida-butsu*—we have no body or mind. Pervading all sentient beings everywhere, the Name is One/All.[8] (Dennis Hirota, trans., *No Abode: The Record of Ippen* [Honolulu: The University of Hawai'i Press, 1997], pp. 30-31)

Ippen

-410- "Birth through the *nembutsu*" means that *nembutsu* itself is birth.

---

[8] Here the name *amida-butsu* in the *nembutsu* is the Buddha nature in all things, the essence of reality.

*Namu* is the mind that entrusts, *Amida-butsu* is the practice entrusted to. The one thought-moment in which mind and practice interfuse is birth.

People who, upon saying *namu-amida-butsu*, cease to weigh the good and evil or right and wrong of their own hearts and minds, and who possess no anticipation of anything coming after, are said to be practicers in whom true entrusting is decisively settled.

There must be no point of facing death outside the utterance of the Name in the immediate present. Simply say *namu-amida-butsu, namu-amida-butsu*, to the very end of life. (Dennis Hirota, trans., *No Abode: The Record of Ippen* [Honolulu: The University of Hawai'i Press, 1997], p. 32)

Ippen

-411- One utterance of [the Name embodying] the universal Vow is the
ultimate among practices;

The three characters of the fulfilled Name [*a-mi-da*] are the wellspring of all virtues;

Without gaining footing in the ground of our minds, we mount the sacred lotus dais;

Without depending on effort in meditation, we open the storehouse of enlightenment.

(Dennis Hirota, trans., *No Abode: The Record of Ippen* [Honolulu: The University of Hawai'i Press, 1997], p. 38)

Ippen

-412- Further he said: Though you take it upon yourself to say the *nembutsu*, that utterance may not be true *namu-amida-butsu*. For to say the Name with thoughts of your own self-being as basis is to take false, discriminative thinking for the *nembutsu*. Further, although you recite the Name with your lips, since you have this basic thought [of self] in your heart, surely that thought is what will emerge at the point of death, and the *nembutsu* will be forfeit. Hence, you must stir up no delusional thinking in your heart. This does not mean, of course, that you must completely rid yourself of all other thoughts. (Dennis Hirota, trans., *No Abode: The Record of Ippen* [Honolulu: The University of Hawai'i Press, 1997], p. 103)

Kakunyo

-413- On the idea that single *nembutsu* is not enough, and that we should strive to do multiple *nembutsu*:

With regard to this idea, both multiple *nembutsu* and single *nembutsu* are in the statement of the true vow, that is, as commented on to mean "up to the very end when your present life form is exhausted, down to a single *nembutsu*" (Shan-tao's *Ojoraisan*); this is the statement. However, "down to a single *nembutsu*" refers to the instant in time when our impending Birth, guaranteed by the true Vow, is decided, while "up to the very end when your present life form is exhausted" refers to our efforts to repay the kindness of the Buddha upon the immediate attainment of our impending birth. . . .

. . . Thus, as we have been taught by our past teachers on more than one occasion, when we experience the faith imparted to us by Other-Power, in the single *nembutsu* [of that moment], the determination of the instant attainment of our impending Birth takes place; at that time if a person's life has yet to come to an end, they should use the life remaining to them to do the *nembutsu*. This, then, is what is meant by "up to the very end when your present life form is exhausted."

. . . If we were to pursue the true vow through multiple *nembutsu*, at what point in time would there be a culmination of multiple *nembutsu*? When it comes time to die, the condition of death for the *bombu* comes in all shapes and sizes. He might be burned to death by fire, drowned to death by water, pierced to death by swords, or die in his sleep. These are all the results of past karma that descend upon us, nor is there any way to avoid them. But supposing that your karma calls it time for you to cash in on your life, just say to yourself, "Well, it looks like I have to call an end to these multiple *nembutsu*," and without flinching, start in on completing the ten *nembutsu* for being taken up by the welcoming Buddha; for the person in question, this event is an instance they would like to take place, and while one of the vows says this welcome is sure to happen, whether it will happen or not is not certain. . . .

. . . In the words of the *Kiten* (*Hakushi monju*, by Haku Cho'i, 772-846 C.E.), "The journey of a thousand *li* starts from beneath your feet, the highest mountain began as particles of dust." The single *nembutsu* is the beginning of the multiple *nembutsu*, the multiple *nembutsu* is built up from the single *nembutsu*. The two form a whole that cannot be divided, but are not people confusing the front with the back? The present understanding was transmitted in the statement that, "The single *nembutsu*, through the superb Buddha-wisdom, leads the *bombu* to the highest reaches of impending birth; the lifetime *nembutsu* in remembrance, through the Name and the Vow, is to return the Buddha's kindness in the course of daily life." (Wayne Yokoyama, *What Shinran Taught* [*Kudensho*], #21, unpublished translation.)

Kakunyo

-414- As for the Founding Master's sentiments, he left us no instruction whatever on how to draw our voice for *nembutsu* or on how to arrange the music sheets [for chanting]. He simply told us that the mystery of Amida's Vow power singly directs its Other-Power toward the ordinary person's Birth [in the Pure Land], and strives to work out the transformation of others by its own natural activity. He had no comment on what to do about tones or scales. However, there was a time when many-*nembutsu* chanting was the vogue in society, and many people experimented with it; even the people who lived together within our temple tried their hand at this, and there were some who even held lessons to practice it. During that time, if there were monastic or lay visitors from the eastern countries who came to the capital (Kyoto), if they stayed at our temple they may perchance have heard it. But in the Shonin's instructions, we never come across any comments on what to do about arranging the music [for *nembutsu* chanting], nor does he urge us to do chanting. In addition to having no comment on musical arrangement [for *nembutsu* chanting], he had no comment as to whether we should say [the *nembutsu*] with a drawl, and that even those who had no drawl should acquire one. However, if one is not born with a twangy voice, to stipulate that you have to train the voice you were born with to drawl in a Bando accent on purpose, twisting your pronunciation, this is much like saying that our receiving birth [in the Pure Land] depends on whether or not we can hold a tune. To sum up, we should simply leave it all up to the voice we were born with; there is no power to the country voice as it says the *nembutsu* with a drawl; you do not have to replace your King's castle voice with a drawl; simply use your own voice to say the *nembutsu*. This is the connection between the voice and the Buddhist service. [However,] the true cause for our birth in the reward land is not to be found in [how well we hold] a tune. It is thus stipulated that, simply through holding with singleness of heart to Other-Power, the time for our birth is settled. (W.S. Yokoyama, *Setting the Claims Straight* [Kakunyo's *Gaijasho*], #14, unpublished translation)

## Zonkaku

-415- The single-minded exclusive practice of *nembutsu* is essential for confirmed birth in the Pure Land. While this is taught among the forty-eight Primal Vows of *Tathagata* Amida, the eighteenth vow recommends the *nembutsu* of true entrusting and does not teach [birth in the Pure Land] through the manifold practices. However, it teaches that the practitioner of "as many as ten thoughts" surely can attain birth. Not only that but the Sutra similarly teaches in the passage on the birth of the three companions (*Larger Sutra*, part 2) that they all single-mindedly and exclusively think on the Buddha of Eternal Life. "Single-minded" means to proceed ahead singly, that is, to proceed with the one practice of *nembutsu*; "to think exclusively" means "to think solely," that is, not to have two [practices] other than thinking earnestly/solely on the one Buddha, Amida. (Alfred Bloom, trans., *Zonkaku's Jodo Shinyosho* [*Jodo Shinshu Seiten*] [Kyoto: Hongwanji Shuppanbu, 1988], I, p. 957)

*Anjinketsujosho*

**-416-** What is sad to see is people chanting the Name believing in the Vow, yet thinking the Buddha's estate is something "out there," and that that energy has to somehow be siphoned into the Name otherwise we cannot achieve Birth. When the informed heart arises in us to urgently call *namu amida butsu* as the condition for our birth, that is where the Buddha's estate and our performance of birth come together in a single voicing that determines our birth once and for all.

Thus, when we hear the Name of Amida Buddha, we should see it as a sign of our birth, a birth identical with the Buddha's enlightenment. Even if we should have lingering doubts as to whether or not Amida Buddha's enlightenment is complete, never should we doubt whether or not our birth is complete. If even a single one of the assembly of the mindful were not to attain birth, never would the Buddha attain enlightenment. To understand this is to gain insight into the eighteenth Vow. (W.S. Yokoyama, *How to Be at Peace with Yourself: In the Spirit of the Anjinketsujosho*, #4, unpublished translation; see also -026-; -071-; -076-; -126-; -128-; -143-; -145-; -146-; -162-; -203-; -250-; -273-; -278-; -286-; -288-; -319-; -483-; -558-)

## 6. Benefits

Honen

**-417-** Question: When does one receive the protection of the light of Amida Buddha? Does one benefit in his daily life or at his time of death?

Answer: The merit of protection by Amida Buddha is received in daily life. This is because one who is genuine in his belief in birth in the Pure Land, holds no doubt, and awaits the coming of Amida Buddha, is the *nembutsu* devotee who embodies the three-fold devotional heart.

The *Meditation Sutra* teaches that one who is of the threefold devotional heart will be born, with certainty, in the Land of Ultimate Bliss. Amida Buddha casts the eighty four thousand rays of His light of compassion upon one who is resolute in the attainment of his goal. He shines this light continually on the *nembutsu* practitioner in daily life and up to the final moment of that person's life. Accordingly, it is called the "vow in which Amida Buddha abandons no one." (Yoko Hayashi, Joji Atone, trans., *Teachings of Honen* [Los Angeles: Bukkyo University-Los Angeles Extension, 2007 rev.] p. 100)

Honen

**-418-** All Buddhas and *bodhisattvas* in the ten quarters, *Bodhisattva* Avalokitesvara, *Bodhisattva* Mahasthamaprapta, and countless other *bodhisattvas* as well as Amida Buddha, surround one who is faithful to the essential vow of Amida Buddha and practices *nembutsu* to attain birth in the Pure Land.

They are in his shadow day and night whether he is walking, standing, sitting, and lying down. They dispel evil spirits and deities which deceive him. They relieve him from any trouble inconsistent with reason and enable him to live in peace. They come to welcome him into the Land of Ultimate Bliss when his end arrives. Therefore, one who believes in *nembutsu* and desires birth in the Pure Land need not pray to other Buddhas or deities or observe abstinence in order to ward off evil spirits.

Those who rely upon the Buddha, the *Dharma*, and the *Sangha* are always protected by the benevolence of the King of Deities and His attendant deities, as numerous as the sands of the Ganges. How could any Buddha or deity torment you or deter you from your goal when the blessings of innumerable benevolent Buddhas and deities surround and protect you? (Yoko Hayashi, Joji Atone, trans., *Teachings of Honen* [Los Angeles: Bukkyo University-Los Angeles Extension, 2007 rev.], p. 102)

Honen

**-419-** The lessening of residual karma has its limits. An illness which one contracts in daily life cannot be overcome by prayers to various Buddhas and deities. If prayer healed and prolonged life there would be no illness or death.

However, the burden of one's karma is lessened by the compassionate power of Amida Buddha for those who are faithful in *nembutsu*. This is called a "burden is lessened." Amida Buddha indeed protects one from an untimely accidental death. Whatever illness befalls the *nembutsu* devotee, that misfortune is the result of residual karma. He should think that although he was supposed to receive a heavy burden, the compassionate power of Amida Buddha lessened the burden.

Amida Buddha eliminates our burden of evil karma and enables us to attain birth in the Land of Ultimate Bliss, the great religious goal. There is no reason not to believe that Amida Buddha can prolong our short life and lessen our illness in daily life.

Consequently, Master Shan-tao said that those whose faith in birth in the Pure Land in the next life and in the essential vow was less than profound would not enjoy the embrace and protection of celestial beings. While reciting *nembutsu* we must arouse in ourselves profound faith, loathe this defiled world of suffering, and long for the Land of Ultimate Bliss. (Yoko Hayashi, Joji Atone, trans., *Teachings of Honen* [Los Angeles: Bukkyo University-Los Angeles Extension, 2007 rev.], p. 104)

Shinran

**-420-** When we say "*namu-amida-butsu*,"
    The benefits we gain in the present are boundless;
    The karmic evil of our transmigration in birth-and-death disappears,

And determinate karma and untimely death are eliminated.
(*CWS, Hymns of the Pure Land*, I, p. 353, #99)

Shinran

-421- The gods of the heavens and earth
　　Are all to be called good,
　　For together they protect
　　The person of the *nembutsu*. . . .

　　*Shinjin* that is the inconceivable working of the power of the Vow
　　Is none other than the mind aspiring for great enlightenment;
　　The evil spirits that abound in heaven and earth
　　All hold in awe the person who has attained it.
　　(*CWS, Hymns of the Pure Land*, I, p. 354, #106-107)

Shinran

-422- Through the benefit of the unhindered light,
　　We realize *shinjin* of vast, majestic virtues,
　　And the ice of our blind passions necessarily melts,
　　Immediately becoming water of enlightenment.

　　Obstructions of karmic evil turn into virtues;
　　It is like the relation of ice and water:
　　The more the ice, the more the water;
　　The more the obstructions, the more the virtues.

　　The ocean of the inconceivable Name does not hold unchanged
　　The corpses of the five grave offenses and slander of the *dharma*;
　　The myriad rivers of evil acts, on entering it,
　　Become one in taste with the ocean water of virtues.

　　Rivers of blind passions, on entering the ocean—
　　The great, compassionate Vow
　　Of unhindered light filling the ten quarters—
　　Become one in taste with that sea of wisdom.
　　(*CWS, Hymns of the Pure Land Masters*, I, [T'an-luan], I, p. 371, #39-42)

Shinran

-423- In entrusting ourselves to the *Tathagata*'s Primal Vow and saying the Name once, necessarily, without seeking it, we are made to receive the supreme virtues, and without knowing it, we acquire the great and vast benefit. This is dharmicness, by which one will immediately realize the various facets of enlightenment naturally. "Dharmicness" means not brought about in any way by the practicer's calculation; from the very beginning one shares in the benefit that surpasses conception. It indicates the nature of *jinen*. "Dharmicness" expresses the natural working (*jinen*) in the life of the person who realizes *shinjin* and says the Name once. (*CWS, Notes on Once-Calling and Many-Calling*, I, p. 481)

Shinran

-424- *It quickly brings to fullness and perfection the great treasure ocean of virtues*: Able to bring quickly means that the great treasure ocean of virtues is effectively brought to perfect fulfillment in the persons who entrust themselves to the power of the Primal Vow. The boundlessness, expansiveness, and all-inclusiveness of the *Tathagata*'s virtues is likened to the unobstructed fullness of the waters of the great ocean. (*CWS, Notes on Inscription on Sacred Scrolls*, I, p. 502)

Shinran

-425- *Constantly illumines me*: Unhindered light constantly illumines the person of *shinjin*. *Constantly illumines* means constantly protects. *Me*: Realize that great love and compassion tirelessly and constantly protects this self. This is the blessing of being grasped, never to be abandoned. Know that this passage sets forth the meaning of the words, "Sentient beings of the *nembutsu* are grasped, never to be abandoned." (*CWS, Notes on Inscription on Sacred Scrolls*, I, p. 510)

7. Repentance
Shan-tao
-426- Sincere repentance: (Brief repentance)
   . . . Ever since my existence came to be in the beginningless past,
   I have continuously done ten evil acts to other beings;
   To my parents I have neglected duties and I have abused the three treasures;
   I have committed the five gravest offenses and other evil acts.
   As the results of various karmic evils like those,
   Delusory thoughts and perverse views have arisen and produced bondages,
   Which will cause me to suffer immeasurable pain of birth-and-death.
   I bow to the Buddha in worship and repent. I beseech you to remove those evils.
   Having thus repented, I sincerely take refuge in Amida Buddha. . . .
     (Hisao Inagaki, trans., *Shan-tao's Liturgy for Birth* [*Ojoraisan*], #30, http://www12.canvas.ne.jp/horai/raisan.htm)

Shan-tao

-427- I have above explained the first two levels of repentance and aspiration. If you wish to follow the most essential mode of repentance, take the first one. If you wish to follow the abridged mode of repentance, take the second one. If you wish to follow the most extensive mode of repentance, take the last one. I will recommend the extensive mode of repentance to those who sincerely aspire for birth. Confess and repent your karmic evils to the four groups of Buddhists, or to Buddhas of the ten quarters, or before the holy relics, images of the sages or assemblies of monks, or to a specific person, or to yourselves, or to the three treasures throughout the space in the ten quarters and to all the sentient beings.

There are three grades of repentance: high, middle, and low. The high grade of repentance is to shed blood from the hair pores of one's body and also shed blood from one's eyes. The middle grade of repentance is to shed hot sweat from the hair pores of one's whole body and also shed blood from one's eyes. The low grade of repentance is to feel feverish all over the body and also shed tears from one's eyes

These three grades of repentance are different from each other, but they can all be carried out by those who have long cultivated the roots of good in the stage leading to emancipation. If people in this life revere the *Dharma*, pay respect to preachers, practice without regard for their lives, and repent even small transgressions, then their repentance will penetrate to their bones and marrow. If repentance is performed in this way, their heavy hindrances, whether accumulated for a long time or short time, will instantly perish. Unless done in this way, any assiduous practice that one may perform throughout the twelve periods of the day and night will not yield any benefit. Those who do not repent in the proper way should know this. Even though one is unable to shed tears and blood, one will get the same result as described above if one thoroughly attains the True Faith.

Reverently I announce: May all the Buddhas in the ten quarters, the twelve-divisioned scriptures, all the great *bodhisattvas*, all the holy sages, all the eight groups of demi-gods, including *devas* and dragons, sentient beings in the entire universe, and the audience in the present assembly become my witnesses. I, so and so, confess my offenses and repent them. From the beginningless past up to now, I have killed or destroyed all the members of the three treasures, masters and monks, parents, relatives down to the sixth blood-relation, good teachers of the Way, and sentient beings in the entire universe, whose numbers are beyond calculation. I have stolen property and belongings of all the members of the three treasures, masters and monks, parents, relatives down to the sixth blood-relation, good teachers of the Way, and sentient beings in the entire universe, whose numbers are beyond calculation. I have approached with lascivious thoughts all the members of the three treasures, masters and monks, parents, relatives down to the sixth blood-relation, good teachers of the Way, and sentient beings in the entire universe, whose numbers are beyond calculation. I have deceived with lies all the members of the three treasures, masters and monks, parents, relatives down to the sixth blood-relation, good teachers of the Way, and sentient beings in the entire universe, whose numbers are beyond calculation. I have ridiculed with insincere words all the members of the three treasures, masters and monks, parents, relatives down to the sixth blood-relation, good teachers of the Way, sentient beings in the entire universe, whose numbers are beyond calculation. I have calumniated, abused, and rebuked with harsh words all the members of the three treasures, masters and monks, parents, relatives down to the sixth blood-relation, good teachers of the Way, and sentient beings in the entire universe, whose numbers are beyond calculation. I have caused enmity and mutual destruction with calumnious words among all the members of the three treasures, masters and monks, parents, relatives down to the sixth blood-relation, good teachers of the Way, sentient beings in the entire universe, whose numbers are beyond calculation. I have broken all the precepts and rules of conduct, including the five precepts, eight precepts of abstinence, ten precepts, ten precepts of good acts, two hundred and fifty precepts, five hundred precepts, threefold precepts for *bodhisattvas*, and tenfold inexhaustible precepts. Not only have I broken these precepts, but also I have incited others to break them, and rejoiced at seeing them do so—this I have repeated uncountable times.

Such transgressions are innumerable, just as the great earth extending in the ten directions is boundless and the number of dust-particles is incalculable. Just as the open space is limitless, my offenses are equally limitless. Just as the means of salvation are boundless, my offenses are boundless. Just as the *Dharma*-nature is boundless, my offenses are boundless. Just as the *Dharma*-realm is boundless, my offenses are boundless. . . .

Since sentient beings are innumerable, my offenses of robbery and manslaughter are innumerable. Since the members of the three treasures are innumerable, my offenses of destruction, theft, and killing are innumerable. Since the precepts provided are innumerable, my breach of them has been repeated innumerable times.

Any one of the sages, from *bodhisattvas* down to *shravakas* and *pratyeka-buddhas*, cannot know the extent of my offenses. Only the Buddha knows it.

Now, before the three treasures and sentient beings of the entire universe, I confess and repent my offenses, without hiding them. I pray that all the members of the three treasures throughout the ten quarters and sentient beings of the entire universe recognize my repentance and wish that I will be purified of the offenses. From today on, together with sentient beings, I wish to abandon wrong views and take right ones, awaken the *bodhi*-mind, see each other with a compassionate heart, look at each other with the eye of the Buddha, become a companion of *bodhi*, become a true teacher of the Way, attain birth in Amida Buddha's land together, discontinue committing those offenses forever and never commit them again.

Having thus repented, I take refuge in Amida Buddha with sincerity of heart.

When you begin a contemplative practice or go to sleep, you should make this vow, whether sitting or standing, with the palms of your hands joined together with singleness of heart, after facing to the west and repeating the holy names ten times, "Amida Buddha, Avalokiteshvara and Mahasthamaprapta *Bodhisattvas*, and the great ocean of the hosts of pure sages": "I, so and so, the Buddha's disciple, am actually an ordinary man of birth-and-death, burdened with heavy karmic hindrances, transmigrating in the six realms and undergoing inexpressible suffering. Today, I have met a good teacher of the Way and have been able to hear from him the Name of Amida's Primal Vow. I single-heartedly recite it, aspiring for birth in his land. May the Buddha, out of compassion, keep the original Primal Vow and embrace me, his disciple. Being ignorant of Amida's bodily light, I pray that the Buddha, out of compassion, may manifest for me his bodily features, Avalokiteshvara, Mahasthamaprapta, other *bodhisattvas*, and the glorious pure light of that land."

Having uttered these words, you should concentrate your thought and begin a contemplative practice or go to sleep. Perhaps you will see these manifestations right at the time when you make the vow, or perhaps you will see them while asleep. If you lack sincerity of heart, you will not see them. I have found that this vow often brings about miraculous signs. (Hisao Inagaki, trans., *Shan-tao's Liturgy for Birth* [*Ojoraisan*], #46, 47, 48, http://www12.canvas.ne.jp/horai/raisan.htm)

Shan-tao

-428- There are three grades of repentance: . . . high, middle, and low. In the high grade of repentance, blood flows from the hair pores of one's body and issues from one's eyes. In the middle grade of repentance, hot beads of sweat appear from the hair pores of one's whole body, and blood issues from one's eyes. In the low grade of repentance, one's whole body is pervaded by heat and tears flow from one's eyes. Although there are differences among these three levels, they are all performed only by those who have long cultivated roots of good for emancipation. But if people in this life revere the teaching, pay homage to monks, do not cherish their lives, and repent even small transgressions, this will penetrate to their hearts' core, and if they repent in this way, their heavy obstructions, whether accumulated over a long or short time, will all swiftly be eradicated. People who do not do so may urgently seek [emancipation] through the twelve periods of the day and night, but in the end it will be of no avail. People who do not repent should know: Although one may not be able to shed tears and blood, if one is simply pervaded by true mind, it will be the same as [the repentance] described above. (*CWS*, *Kyogyoshinsho*, I, pp. 218-219, VI: 25)

Shan-tao
-429- There are three kinds of repentance: principal, short, and extensive, which are explained in detail below. Any of the three can be done as one pleases. Otherwise, one will not be continuously mindful of repaying the Buddha's benevolence, one will give rise to haughty thoughts which allow one's acts to be tainted with desires for reputation and profit, one will be covered with self-attachment which alienates one from fellow-practitioners and good teachers, and one will be drawn to miscellaneous influences, resulting in hindering oneself and others from performing the right practice for birth in the Pure Land. (Hisao Inagaki, trans., *Shan-tao's Liturgy for Birth* [*Ojoraisan*], #6, http://www12.canvas.ne.jp/horai/raisan.htm)

Shan-tao
-430- The Buddha said, "Good men, the purpose of the *Tathagata's* appearance in the world is to destroy your karmic transgressions and offenses. You should now recite the names of the seven past Buddhas and worship them. I will explain to you the karmic transgressions of entertaining wrong views in your previous lives. You should confess and repent them to the multitude of revered monks. In accordance with the Buddha's instruction, you should throw your bodies on the ground before the assembly of the followers of the Buddha-*Dharma*, like a high mountain crumbling, and repent before the Buddha. When you have repented, your spiritual eye will be opened. Then you will see the Buddha's body and attain a great joy. Then you will see the Buddha's body and attain a great joy." (Hisao Inagaki, *Shan-tao's Kannenbomon: The Method of Contemplation on Amida* [Kyoto: Nagata Bunshodo, 2005], p. 90)

8. Gratitude
Shan-tao
-431- Respectfully I urge you, all aspirants: When you have heard those words, you should accordingly shed tears of anguish like rain and resolve to repay your indebtedness to the Buddhas even by grinding your bodies into powder and breaking your bones for many *kalpas* to come. Then you will come into accord with their original intent. Why should there be doubt, even as minute as a hair, which keeps you from accepting these words? I also urge you, all followers of the Way: All ordinary persons of karmic evils can still have their evils destroyed and realize attainment of birth; how much more

so with sages? How could they desire birth and yet fail to reach [the Pure Land]? (Hisao Inagaki, *Shan-tao's Kannenbomon: The Method of Contemplation on Amida* [Kyoto: Nagata Bunshodo, 2005], p. 30)

Honen

-432- With great joy, express sincere appreciation for your encounter with the essential vow of Amida Buddha and be so moved that you look skyward and prostrate yourself with joy. Walking, standing, sitting, or lying down, always recite *nembutsu* and be thankful for the benevolence bestowed by Amida Buddha. (Joji Atone, Yoko Hayashi, trans., *The Promise of Amida Buddha: Honen's Path to Bliss* [Boston: Wisdom Publications, 2011], p. 241)

Shinran

-433- Such is the benevolence of Amida's great compassion,
    That we must strive to return it, even to the breaking of our bodies;
    Such is the benevolence of the masters and true teachers,
    That we must endeavor to repay it, even to our bones becoming dust.
    (*CWS, Hymns of the Dharma-Ages*, I, p. 412, #59)

Shinran

-434- Doubting the inconceivable Buddha-wisdom,
    People devote themselves to saying the *nembutsu* in self-power;
    Hence they remain in the borderland or the realm of indolence and
        pride,
    Without responding in gratitude to the Buddha's benevolence.
    (*CWS, The Hymns of the Dharma-Ages*, I, p. 413, #61)

Rennyo

-435- Rennyo Shonin said, "After you have acquired *shinjin*, the *nembutsu* you say, whether with a feeling of gratitude or casually, is an expression of your indebtedness to the Buddha. In other schools, the *nembutsu* is used for deceased parents or for some specific objectives. In the school of Shinran Shonin, the *nembutsu* is entrusting to Amida. The *nembutsu* you say with this realization, in whatever way you say it, serves as acknowledging your indebtedness to the Buddha." (Hisao Inagaki, trans., *Thus Have I Heard From Rennyo Shonin* [*Rennyo Shonin's Goichidaikikigaki*] [Judet Dolj, Romania: Dharma Lion Publications, 2008], # 179, p. 88; see also -286-; -518-)

9. Merit Transference
Vasubandhu
-436- What is the *Bodhisattvas'* transference of merit by skilful means? The *Bodhisattvas'* transference by skilful means is that they turn over all the

merits and roots of good accumulated by performing the five kinds of practice, such as worship, to all sentient beings to remove their sufferings, for they do not seek to enjoy the pleasures for their own sustenance, but wish to embrace all sentient beings and help them attain birth in the Buddha-land of Peace and Bliss together with themselves. This is called "*Bodhisattvas'* accomplishment of the transference of merit by skilful means." (Hisao Inagaki, trans., *T'an-Luan's Commentary on Vasubandhu's Discourse on the Pure Land* [*Ojoronchu*] [Kyoto: Nagata Bunshodo, 1998], p. 271)

T'an-luan

-437- The merit transference has two aspects: (1) the "going" aspect and (2) the "returning" aspect. The "going" aspect is that one turns one's merit over to all sentient beings with the aspiration that all will be born together into Amida *Tathagata's* Pure Land of Peace and Bliss. The "returning" aspect is that after having been born in his land, one acquires the fruit of the *samatha* and *vipasyana* practices and attains the power of employing expedient means, whereby one enters the dense forest of birth-and-death and leads all sentient beings into the Buddhist Path. Whether "going" or "returning" one seeks to deliver sentient beings from the sea of birth-and-death. (Hisao Inagaki, trans., *T'an-Luan's Commentary on Vasubandhu's Discourse on the Pure Land* [*Ojoronchu*] [Kyoto: Nagata Bunshodo, 1998], p. 216)

Shan-tao

-438- Question: After the Buddha's death, ordinary people, whether good or evil, who will awaken *bodhi*-mind and aspire to be born in the Land of Amida Buddha, may apply their minds, day and night, until the end of their lives, to reciting [his Name], meditating [on him], worshiping and praising him, and offering incense and flowers to Amida, Avalokitesvara and other sages, and also to the glorious adornments of the Pure Land. With continuous contemplation, they may or may not attain the *samadhi*. What sort of merit will accrue to such people? . . .

Answer: It is good that you have asked me this question. It will lead to the termination of causal acts—for cycles of birth and death in the six realms—and forever open the essential gate for the Pure Land of eternal bliss. . . . Now, based on a sutra, I will answer your question in detail.

It is stated in the *Pratyutpanna-samadhi-sutra*:

The Buddha said to Bhadrapala, "Concerning this *nembutsu samadhi*, there are four things to offer up [to Amida]: food, clothes, bed, and medicinal drink. They serve as an aid [to the accomplishment of the *samadhi*] and produce joy. All the Buddhas of the past (present and future) attained enlightenment by keeping in mind this

Amida-recollection *samadhi* and performing the joy-giving act of offering four things as the auxiliary practice." . . .

The Buddha said, "I will further demonstrate to you and other *bodhisattvas*. Suppose a good man or woman acquires rare treasures which fill the space this man has covered and then donates them to charity. The merit of the donation cannot be compared with that of a person who hears of this Amida-recollection *samadhi* and performs the joy-giving act of offering four things as the auxiliary practice. This person's merit is thousands of millions of times as much as that of the donor. It is indeed impossible to compare." . . .

The Buddha said, "Even if there is a distance of a hundred *li*, a thousand or four thousand *li* to travel to hear an exposition of this *nembutsu samadhi*, you should go and seek it. How much more so if there is only a short distance to travel."

(Hisao Inagaki, trans., *Shan-tao's Kannenbomon: The Method of Contemplation on Amida* [Kyoto: Nagata Bunshodo, 2005], pp. 80-84)

Shan-tao

-439- *Bodhisattvas* have already escaped from *samsara*, and are now seeking to attain Buddhahood by transferring their good towards it; this is self-benefiting. Teaching and guiding sentient beings until the end of all future ages is the benefiting of others. Sentient beings today are bound by evil passions and so have not yet escaped from the suffering of birth-and-death in evil realms and other realms of *samsara*. Let us set about practicing in accordance with appropriate conditions and quickly transfer all the good we may do towards the land of Amida Buddha, aspiring to be born there. When we have reached that land, we will have no fear any longer. While performing the above-mentioned four kinds of practice, we will naturally and spontaneously benefit ourselves and others fully. We should be aware of this. (Hisao Inagaki, trans., *Shan-tao's Liturgy for Birth* [*Ojoraisan*], http://www12.canvas.ne.jp/horai/raisan.htm)

Shan-tao

-440- Question: What merit and benefit do we acquire in the present life calling the Name of Amida Buddha and worshiping and contemplating him?

Answer: One utterance of the Name of Amida Buddha can remove the heavy evil karma that will cause one to transmigrate in *samsara* for eight billion *kalpas*. Worshiping and focusing our thoughts upon Amida—along with other acts—have the same effect. *The Sutra on the Ten Ways of Attaining Birth* states:

If there are sentient beings who focus their thoughts upon Amida Buddha and aspire for birth in his land, the Buddha immediately sends twenty-five *bodhisattvas* to protect them, keeping evil spirits and evil gods away from them at all times and in all places, day and night, whether they are walking, standing, sitting or lying down. . . . Since there are such excellent benefits, you should accept this in faith. May all practicers receive Amida's sincere heart and seek to attain birth in the Pure Land.

(Hisao Inagaki, trans., *Shan-tao's Liturgy for Birth* [*Ojoraisan*], http://www12.canvas.ne.jp/horai/raisan.htm)

Honen

-441- The merit of our daily recitation of *nembutsu* should be transferred to those who have preceded us in death. If this happens, Amida Buddha will emit rays of light over the worlds of hell, starving spirits, and beasts. The dead who are suffering in these three evil worlds of hell, starving spirits, and beasts would be absolved of their pain, their lives in those worlds would come to an end, and emancipation will come to pass.

The *Larger Sutra* states: "If those who suffer indescribable pain in the three evil worlds see this light, they shall gain relief, pain will be eliminated, and when their lives in those realms come to an end, they shall attain emancipation." (Yoko Hayashi, Joji Atone, trans., *Teachings of Honen* [Los Angeles: Bukkyo University-Los Angeles Extension, 2007 rev.], p. 110; see also -230-; -248-)

10. Self-Power and Other-Power

T'an-luan

-442- Question: For what reason is it said: "quickly attain *anuttara-samyak-sambodhi*?"

Answer: Because, as it is said in the Discourse [Vasubhandu's *Treatise on the Pure Land* (*Jodoron*)], "by performing the five mindful practices, [*bodhisattvas*] accomplish both self-benefit and benefit for others." When we deeply probe to the roots, we find that Amida *Tathagata* provides the predominant condition. There is a difference between "benefit by the Other" (*tari*) and "benefit for others" (*rita*). Speaking from the Buddha's viewpoint, one should say "benefit for others." Speaking from the viewpoint of sentient beings, one should say "benefit by the Other." Since the Buddha's power is under discussion, one should say, "benefit for others." One should realize this implication.

Generally speaking, attainment of birth in the Pure Land and the various practices performed by the *Bodhisattvas* and human and heavenly beings living there are brought about by the Primal Vow-Power of Amida *Tatha-*

*gata*. The reason for saying so is that if it were not for the Buddha's Power, the forty-eight vows would have been made in vain. Now, I will select three vows to demonstrate the import of this. (Here the eighteenth, eleventh and twenty-second vows are quoted with comment.)

The [eighteenth] vow (comment): . . . Due to the Buddha's Vow-Power, one attains birth by invoking the Name ten times. Since one attains birth [in the Pure Land], one is freed from transmigration in the three worlds. Since one thus attains deliverance from transmigration, this is the first proof for the rapid attainment [of *anuttara-samyak-sambodhi*].

The [eleventh] vow (comment): . . . Due to the Buddha's Vow-Power, one dwells in the Definitely Assured Stage. Because one dwells in the Definitely Assured Stage, one unfailingly reaches *Nirvana*. Once one has reached *Nirvana*, there will be no more suffering of transmigration. Hence, this is the second proof for the rapid attainment [of *anuttara-samyak-sambodhi*].

The [twenty-second] vow (comment): . . . Due to the Buddha's Vow-Power, one transcends the practices of ordinary *Bodhisattva* stages and actually practices the virtues of Samantabhadra. Since one thus transcends the ordinary *Bodhisattva* stages, this is the third proof for the rapid attainment [of *anuttara-samyak-sambodhi*].

. . . When we ponder on the Other-Power, it is the predominant condition [for our rapid attainment of *anuttara-samyak-sambodhi*]. How can it be otherwise? I will present another illustration to show the distinctive features of "self-power" and "other-power." One observes the precepts from fear of the three painful states of existence. Because one observes the precepts, one is able to practice meditation. By practicing meditation, one cultivates transcendent powers. With the transcendent powers one is able to travel freely in the four continents. This is called "self-power." Though a man of little virtue who rides a donkey cannot fly, if he were to follow the procession of a *chakravartin*, he could fly in the air and travel in the four continents without any hindrance called "other-power." How fortunate we are to have met with the Other-Power! Students of the future, having heard that the Other-Power is to be trusted in, should accept it in faith, and should not entertain restricted views. (Hisao Inagaki, trans., *T'an-luan's Commentary on Vasubandhu's Discourse on the Pure Land* [*Ojoronchu*] [Kyoto: Nagata Bunshodo, 1998], pp. 287-291; see also *CWS, Kyogyoshinsho*, I, p. 60, II:82)

Tao-ch'o

-443- Question: There is only one *Bodhi*, and so the causal practice for realizing it should be non-dual. For what reason is there the Path of Difficult Practice whereby one seeks to attain the Buddha's fruition by performing causal practices here in this world and the Path of Easy Practice whereby one seeks to realize the Great *Bodhi* after attaining birth in the Pure Land?

Answer: In the practices presented in various Mahayana sutras, distinctions are made with regard to self-power and other-power: embracing by oneself and embraced by other power. For instance, if one, out of fear of transmigration in birth and death, awakens aspiration for *bodhi*, renounces the world, practices meditation and, with transcendent power, travels freely in the four continents, this is called "self-power." What is other-power? Though a man of little virtue who rides a donkey cannot fly, if he were to follow the procession of a *chakravartin*, he would be able to fly in the air and travel over the four continents. Since this is enabled by the *chakravartin's* majestic power, we call it "other-power." So it is with sentient beings. To make an aspiration for *bodhi* in this world and to perform practices with a desire for birth in the Pure Land is the path of self-power. At the end of an aspirant's life, a glorious lotus seat is sent to him by *Tathagata* Amida; thus he is enabled to attain birth in the Pure Land. This is the path of other-power. (Hisao Inagaki, trans., "Tao-ch'o's *An le chi* (4)," *The Pure Land*, December 2008, #24, p. 240)

## Genshin
-**444**- Although I too am within Amida's grasp, blind passions obstruct my eyes and I cannot see [the light]; nevertheless, great compassion untiringly and constantly illumines me. (*CWS, Kyogyoshinsho*, I, p. 93, III:17)

## Honen
-**445**- One who firmly believes in the teaching of birth in the Pure Land through *nembutsu* and who diligently recites *nembutsu* without doubts is referred to as "one who has faith in the power other than self." There are similar concepts in our society. For instance, it is impossible for an individual whose legs are weak and whose back is bent to go a long distance using his own efforts. Knowing this, he rides a boat or some vehicle to reach his destination—this is much easier. This is not done by using his own power, but by using the power of a boat or vehicle; that is, by the power other than self. Even a vehicle made by ignorant people with perverted hearts in the defiled world possesses such power. However much clearer is it that one can cross the delusive ocean of *samsara* in the boat or raft of the essential vow made by Amida Buddha who practiced virtue for five eons? One must not harbor doubts about this.

Likewise, there exist magical powers in medicinal herbs to cure an illness, in a magnet to attract iron, in musk to emit a fragrance, and in the horn of a rhinoceros to repel water. Although herbs are merely vegetation which do not have hearts and animals never awaken spiritual aspiration, they have magical powers within. The power of the teachings of Buddha Sakyamuni must be even more wondrous. (Joji Atone, Yoko Hayashi, trans., *The Promise of Amida Buddha: Honen's Path to Bliss* [Boston: Wisdom Publications, 2011], p. 392)

Seikaku

-446- In considering this matter over again now, single practice is still superior. The reason is that we are essentially foolish beings of this defiled world who experience obstacles in everything. Amida, observing this, taught the path of easy practice. One who plays and frolics all day is a person of great distraction and confusion. One who sleeps the whole night is a person of great lethargy. All are consequences of blind passions, difficult to sunder and difficult to control. When playing has ended, say the *nembutsu*; when awakening from sleep, recall the Primal Vow. This does not violate the performance of single practice. To recite the *nembutsu* ten thousand times and afterward hold in mind other sutras and other Buddhas seems splendid upon first hearing, but who determined that the *nembutsu* should be limited to ten thousand times? If you are a person of diligence, then recite all day. If you take up the *nenju*-beads, then utter the Name of Amida. If you face an object of worship, then choose the image of Amida. Directly await Amida's corning; why depend on the eight *bodhisattvas* to direct your way? You should rely solely on the guidance of the Primal Vow. Do not struggle to undertake the exercises of the One Vehicle (Tendai). In the capacities of *nembutsu* practicers there are the superior, the ordinary, and the inferior. Those of superior nature constantly say the *nembutsu* both night and day; in what interval, then, can they turn their attention to other Buddhas? You should reflect on this deeply and not become entangled in distracting doubts. (*CWS*, Seikaku, *Essentials of Faith Alone*, I, p. 690)

Shinran

-447- "To abandon the mind of self-power" admonishes the various and diverse kinds of people—masters of Hinayana or Mahayana, ignorant beings good or evil—to abandon the conviction that one is good, to cease relying on the self; to stop reflecting knowingly on one's evil heart, and further to abandon the judging of people as good and bad. When such shackled foolish beings—the lowly who are hunters and peddlers—thus wholly entrust themselves to the Name embodying great wisdom, the inconceivable vow of the Buddha of unhindered light, then while burdened as they are with blind passion, they all attain supreme *nirvana*. "Shackled" describes us, who are bound by all our various blind passions. Blind passions refers to pains which torment the body and afflictions which distress the heart and mind. The hunter is one who slaughters many kinds of living things; this is the huntsman. The peddler is one who buys and sells things; this is the trader. They are called "low." Such peddlers, hunters, and others are none other than we, who are like stones and tiles and pebbles. (*CWS, Notes on Essentials of Faith Alone*, I, pp. 459-460)

Shinran
-448- *I fear it is hard to be born there by doing sundry good acts according to our diverse conditions*:

*According to our diverse conditions* refers to directing the merit of practicing various good acts, which one performs according to one's own particular circumstances and opportunities, toward birth in the land of bliss. There are eighty-four thousand gates of *dharma*. Since they are all good practices done in self-power, they are rejected as not leading to birth in the true fulfilled land. Thus, I fear it is hard to be born. (*CWS, Notes on Essentials of Faith Alone*, I, p. 462)

Shinran
-449- The eighty-four thousand *dharma*-gates are all good practices of the provisional means of the Pure Land teaching; they are known as the "essential" or provisional gate. This gate consists of the good practices, meditative and non-meditative, taught in the *Contemplation Sutra on the Buddha of Immeasurable Life*. Meditative good refers to the thirteen contemplations; non-meditative good refers to the good acts of the three types of meritorious behavior and the nine grades of beings. These all belong to the "essential" gate, which is the provisional means of the Pure Land teaching; it is also called the provisional gate. Encouraging and guiding all sentient beings with various means through this "essential" or provisional gate, the Buddha teaches and encourages them to enter "the great treasure ocean of true and real virtue—the Primal Vow, perfect and unhindered, which is the One Vehicle." Hence, all good acts of self-power are called provisional ways. (*CWS, Notes on Once-Calling and Many-Calling*, I, pp. 485-486)

Shinran
-450- It is not stated at all that any practicers of various other acts are illumined and embraced: Not one of those who perform sundry practices and disciplines is illumined, taken in, and protected. That such practicers are not illumined and protected means that they are not blessed with the benefit of being grasped, never to be abandoned. Know that this is because they are not practicers who have entrusted themselves to the Primal Vow. Hence it is not stated that such people are grasped and protected, never to be abandoned. (*CWS, Notes on Inscription on Sacred Scrolls*, I, p. 508)

Shinran

-451- Birth in accord with the *Larger Sutra* is [brought about by] the *Tathagata*'s Primal Vow, the inconceivable ocean-like vow. This is Other Power. In other words by the cause of the Vow of birth through the *nembutsu*, we gain the fruit of the Vow of necessary attainment of *nirvana*. In this life we dwell in the stage of the truly settled and we necessarily attain the true and real fulfilled land. Thus, because of the true cause—Amida *Tathagata*'s directing of virtue for our going forth—we realize the enlightenment of supreme enlightenment. This is the true intent of the *Larger Sutra*. Hence, it is termed "birth in accord with the *Larger Sutra*," and also "birth that is inconceivable." (*CWS, A Collection of Passages on the Types of Birth in the Three Pure Land Sutras*, I, p. 639)

Shinran

-452- According to Shin Buddhism, there are two kinds of people who seek birth in the Pure Land: those of Other-Power and those of self-power. This has been taught by the Indian masters and Pure Land teachers.

Self-power is the effort to attain birth, whether by invoking the names of Buddhas other than Amida and practicing good acts other than the *nembutsu*, in accordance with your particular circumstances and opportunities; or by endeavoring to make yourself worthy through mending the confusion in your acts, words, and thoughts, confident of your own powers and guided by your own calculation.

Other-Power is the entrusting of yourself to the eighteenth among Amida *Tathagata*'s vows, the Primal Vow of birth through the *nembutsu*, which Amida selected and adopted from among all other practices. Since this is the Vow of *Tathagata*, Honen said: "In Other-Power, no working is true working." "Working" [that is negated] is a term connoting calculation. Since the calculation of the person seeking birth is self-power, it is "working." Other-Power is entrusting ourselves to the Primal Vow and our birth becoming firmly settled; hence it is altogether without one's own working. Thus, on the one hand, you should not be anxious that *Tathagata* will not receive you because you do wrong. A foolish being is by nature possessed of blind passions, so you must recognize yourself as a being of karmic evil. On the other hand, you should not think that you deserve to attain birth because you are good. You cannot be born into the true and real fulfilled land through such self-power calculation. I have been taught that with *shinjin* of self-power a person can attain birth only in the realm of indolence, the borderland, the womb-palace, or the city of doubt. (*CWS, Lamp for the Latter Ages*, #2, I, pp. 525-526)

Shinran

-453- Further, Other-Power means that no working is true working. "Working" [that is negated] is the practicer's calculating and designing. *Tathagata's* Primal Vow surpasses conceptual understanding; it is a design of the wisdom of Buddhas. It is not the design of foolish beings. No one can fathom the wisdom of Buddhas, which surpasses conceptual understanding. This includes Maitreya *Bodhisattva*, who is in [the rank of] succession to Buddhahood. Thus, the great teacher Honen said, "No working is true working." My understanding has been that nothing apart from this realization is necessary for the attainment of birth into the Pure Land; therefore, what others may say is of no concern to me. (*CWS, Lamp for the Latter Ages*, #7, I, p. 533)

Shinran

-454- Of the conceivable and the inconceivable *dharma*, the conceivable comprises the 84,000 kinds of good of the Path of Sages. The Pure Land teaching is the inconceivable *dharma*-teaching. (*CWS, Lamp for the Latter Ages*, #8, I, p. 535)

Shinran

-455- The *Sutra of the Treasure Name* states: "The *nembutsu* of Amida's Primal Vow is not our practice, it is not our good; it is simply keeping the Name of the Buddha." It is the Name that is good, the Name that is the practice. When we speak of practice, we mean doing good. The Primal Vow is clearly the Buddha's promise. When we have understood this, we see that the Vow is not our good, nor is it our practice. Hence we speak of Other-Power.

The Name fulfilled in the Primal Vow is the direct cause of our birth; in other words, it is our father. The radiant light of great compassion is the indirect cause of our birth; it is our mother. (*CWS, Lamp for the Latter Ages*, #22, I, p. 555)

Shinran

-456- It cannot be said that the practicer of self-power is equal to *Tathagata*. With one's own mind of self-power, it is impossible to reach the land of the Buddha of inconceivable light. It is taught that only by *shinjin* that is Other-Power does one reach the land of the Buddha of inconceivable light. The person of *shinjin* aspiring to be born in that land possesses inexpressible, inexplicable, and inconceivable virtues that cannot be thought or described. Hence the expression, "Buddha of inconceivable light" (*CWS, The Virtue of the Name of Amida Tathagata*, I, p. 658)

Shinran

-457- He also said, "If it were only by observing precepts and upholding rules that we should entrust ourselves to the Primal Vow, how could we ever gain freedom from birth-and-death?" Even such wretched beings as ourselves, on encountering the Primal Vow, come indeed to "presume" upon it. But even so, how could we commit evil acts without any karmic cause in ourselves? (*CWS, A Record in Lament of Divergences*, 13, I, p. 671)

Kakunyo

-458- In the present case of Shinshu, the school's highest ideal is achieved through leaving self power behind and exclusively returning to Other-Power; on that basis, from among the three karmas [of words, thoughts, and deeds], when the heart of Other-Power is expressed through the karma of words, the one thought of returning [to the source of] our life, the deep remembrance of the karma of thought, arises. Then in order for the karma of deeds [to play itself out] as obeisance, that is, in order for us [to act out] the feelings of reverence that fill [our heart] to the brim, we [commission artists to do] painted depictions or wooden statues of the main image of worship or have sculptures carved. But that is not all; since we feel the need to worship and revere the benevolent virtue that has instructed us in the buddha *dharma*, it is a widespread practice to [also] enshrine the revered images of our founding teachers and worthy predecessors who have appeared in the transmission of our lineage down through the three countries (India, China, Japan). (W.S. Yokoyama, *Kakunyo's Setting the Claims Straight [Gaijasho]*, #2, unpublished translation)

Kakunyo

-459- For that reason, since the gate of the Pure Land teaching is solely for drawing in the *bombu*, the method of contemplating one's body [as Amida Buddha] and the explanation of the Pure Land as one's own mind have no bearing; this is like counting up the treasures of your neighbor. As a result, since the one gate of the Pure Land was already established (by Amida's special vows), the way of drawing in the *bombu* was also formed; here there can be no error in judgment on the part of Nagarjuna Bodhisattva.

With regard to the Shinshu gate, its leading edge has been defined countless times by the process of dumping one proposition so as to establish the true teaching (*hairyu*). The word *hai* means "to dump." The gate of the Holy path's assertions that "we realize the 'effect' of entering the sacred while living in this [worldly] realm," or that "there is no Amida outside of one's body," or that "there is no Pure Land outside of one's mind," and so on, are all ways of cultivating the Way through self-power, that the *bombu* find too extreme; these are to be dumped. The word "establish" (*ryu*), therefore, means [in effect]: Amida Buddha says, "O *bombu*, take my Other power faith as your faith, take my Other-Power practice as your practice, take my Other power activity as your true activity that makes you to go forth to be born in the reward land; do so and you will abandon this defiled world and go forth to be born in the pure realm"; by so doing, this sets up [the parameters] of what we call Shinshu. (W.S. Yokoyama, *Kakunyo's Setting the Claims Straight* [*Gaijasho*], #18, unpublished translation)

*Anjinketsujosho*
-460- In the other power negotiation of the avowed practices, the energy derived from the Buddha's striving to attain Buddhahood is transferred to us who have no store of good merit, this meritorious power being such that it never fails to work its magic even in the hopeless reprobate of a seeker who has spoken ill of the *Dharma* or one who has lived to the grand old age of one hundred in the age after the *Dharma* has vanished. (W.S. Yokoyama, *How to Be at Peace with Yourself: In the Spirit of the Anjinketsujosho*, #2, unpublished translation; see also -148-; -267-; -295-; -298-; -409-)

11. Learning: The Good Teacher
Rennyo
-461- "Those who are learned in the scriptures have never promoted the Buddha-*Dharma*. Having heard laymen or laywomen expressing their gratitude and joy of receiving the *Dharma*, people obtain *shinjin*," said Rennyo Shonin, so I have heard. Even though they may be ignorant of the scriptures, their expression of joy in the *Dharma* induces others to attain *shinjin* through the Buddha's empowerment. However learned you may be in the scriptures, you will not win people's trust if you are too concerned about your reputation and, hence, lacking dedication to the *Dharma*. (Hisao Inagaki, trans., *Thus Have I Heard From Rennyo Shonin* [Rennyo Shonin's *Goichidaikikigaki*] [Judet Dolj, Romania: Dharma Lion Publications, 2008], #95 p. 63)

Rennyo
-462- Although more than a hundred years have already passed since the master's death, we gratefully revere the image before our eyes. And although his benevolent voice is distant, separated from us by the wind of impermanence, his words of truth have been directly transmitted by his descendants; they resound with clarity deep in our ears. Thus it is that our school's faith, grounded in the truth and reality of Other-Power, has been transmitted until today without interruption. Therefore, given this present occasion, if there are people who have not realized the faith that is the truth and reality of the Primal Vow, we must indeed conclude they have not received the prompting

of good from the past. If there were not people for whom good from the past had unfolded, all would be in vain and the birth that is to come [in the Pure Land] could not be settled. This would be the one thing to be lamented above all else. (Minor L. Rogers and Ann T. Rogers, trans., *Rennyo: The Second Founder of Shin Buddhism* [Berkeley, CA: Asian Humanities Press, 1991], pp. 208-209, fascicle III-9)

Rennyo
-463- "It will do you good if you ask your teacher questions even about something you know well, so it is said. How wonderful is the statement that asking questions even about something you are familiar with is beneficial." So said Rennyo Shonin.

He continued, "How much more wonderful it is to ask questions about something you do not know!" (Hisao Inagaki, trans., *Thus Have I Heard From Rennyo Shonin* [Rennyo Shonin's *Goichidaikikigaki*] [Judet Dolj, Romania: Dharma Lion Publications, 2008], #81, p. 59)

Rennyo
-464- When you read the scriptures, there is no use just passing your eyes over them. Rennyo Shonin advised, "Make a point of reading the scriptures over and over." Also, "There is a saying, 'If you read a passage a hundred times, its meaning becomes clear by itself.' Remember this. The passages of the scriptures should be understood as they are. After that, you can refer to the master's personal instructions and orally transmitted teaching. Arbitrary interpretations should never be applied." (Hisao Inagaki, trans., *Thus Have I Heard From Rennyo Shonin* [Rennyo Shonin's *Goichidaikikigaki*] [Judet Dolj, Romania: Dharma Lion Publications, 2008], #89, p. 61)

Rennyo
-465- Listen to the Buddha-*Dharma* by making time in your secular life. It is wrong to assume that you can listen to the *Dharma* when you have time. [Rennyo says] that there is no tomorrow in the Buddha-*Dharma*. A *Wasan* says:

> If you dare to pass through the fire
> Which fills the great-thousand worlds,
> To hear the Name of the Buddha,
> You will never fail to dwell in the Stage of Non-retrogression.
> (*Jodo Wasan*, 31)
> (Hisao Inagaki, trans., *Thus Have I Heard From Rennyo Shonin* [Rennyo Shonin's *Goichidaikikigaki*] [Judet Dolj, Romania: Dharma Lion Publications, 2008], #155, p. 82)

Rennyo

-466- Rennyo Shonin said, "Treat the Buddha-*Dharma* as your master and secular matters as your guests." After you have established your faith in the Buddha-*Dharma*, you should treat the secular matters as you see fit. (Hisao Inagaki, trans., *Thus Have I Heard From Rennyo Shonin* [Rennyo Shonin's *Goichidaikikigaki*] [Judet Dolj, Romania: Dharma Lion Publications, 2008], #157, p. 82)

Rennyo

-467- Generally speaking, we all have the mind to compete with others. Because of this way of thinking, we learn more and more about the world. Since the Buddha-*Dharma* teaches non-ego, we should acquire *shinjin* by submitting to others. To concede out of respect to reason is in accord with the Buddha's compassion, so the Shonin said. (Hisao Inagaki, trans., *Thus Have I Heard From Rennyo Shonin* [Rennyo Shonin's *Goichidaikikigaki*] [Judet Dolj, Romania: Dharma Lion Publications, 2008], #160, p. 83; see also -489-; -493-; -549-)

12. Sharing *Dharma*
T'an-luan
-468- If there is any world in the universe
    Without the treasure of merit of the Buddha *Dharma*,
    I resolve to be born there
    And to preach the *Dharma* like a Buddha.
    (stanza 23)

Why did the Buddha originally make this vow? He saw that there were *Bodhisattvas* of weak will who only wished to practice in a Buddha-land and lacked strong compassion. For this reason, he made a vow, resolving, "When I have become a Buddha, *Bodhisattvas* in my Land will all have the strong and undaunted spirit of compassion; they will desire to leave the Pure Land and go to other lands where Buddha, *Dharma*, and *Sangha* do not exist. Establishing and glorifying the treasures of Buddha, *Dharma*, and *Sangha*, they will preach like Buddhas, so that the seeds of Buddhahood may not be destroyed in any land." (Hisao Inagaki, trans., *T'an-Luan's Commentary on Vasubandhu's Discourse on the Pure Land* [*Ojoronchu*] [Kyoto: Nagata Bunshodo, 1998], pp. 191-192)

T'an-luan

-469- . . . Amida, the Enlightened One, is inconceivable. The Pure Land of Peace and Bliss is firmly upheld by the merit-power of Amida, the Enlightened One, and so how can we conceive of this?

*Ju* means not to change or perish; *ji* means to keep something from dispersing or being lost. It is like applying antiseptic treatment to seeds. The seeds thus processed will not be destroyed by water or fire. When favorable conditions arise, the seeds will sprout. How is this possible? It is due to the power of the treatment. Once a man is born in the Pure Land of Peace and Bliss, if he afterwards desires to be reborn in the three worlds to teach and convert sentient beings, he is able to terminate his life in the Pure Land and be reborn therein according to his wishes. Although he is reborn in the "water" and "fire" of various states of the three worlds, the seed of supreme *bodhi* is never subject to decay. How is this possible? It is due to the power of Amida, the Enlightened One, which firmly supports and maintains [the Pure Land and the beings born there]. (Hisao Inagaki, trans., *T'an-Luan's Commentary on Vasubandhu's Discourse on the Pure Land* [*Ojoronchu*] [Kyoto: Nagata Bunshodo, 1998], pp. 233-234)

Shan-tao

-470- Sorrowful *dharmas* are like poisons, evil *dharmas* like knives: their spread throughout the three states of existence harms all sentient beings. However, good *dharmas* are like bright mirrors and like sweet dew [or ambrosia]. Now mirrors illumine the right path in order to take refuge in the Truth, while sweet dew is the endless flowing down of the *dharma* rain, which makes all living beings receive moisture and everywhere equally assembles together the flow of the *dharma*. For this reason, it is necessary that [practitioners] mutually exhort each other. (Julian F. Pas, *Visions of Sukhavati: Shan-Tao's Commentary on the Kuan-wu-Liang-Shou-Fo-Ching* [Albany, NY: State University of New York Press, 1995], p. 237)

Rennyo

-471- Nothing is dearer to you than your wife and children. It would be a shame if you could not guide them into the Buddha-*Dharma*. Be that as it may, if they lack stored good from previous lives, there is nothing you can do about them. Should you not save yourself in the first place? (Hisao Inagaki, trans., *Thus Have I Heard From Rennyo Shonin* [Rennyo Shonin's *Goichidai-kikigaki*] [Judet Dolj, Romania: Dharma Lion Publications, 2008], #65, p. 53)

Rennyo

-472- Doing something good may bring about an evil result; it also happens that doing something evil can have a good outcome. Even if one has done something good, if one is proud in thinking "I have done good for the *Dharma*" the interpolation of "I" diminishes the good act. Even if one has done something evil, should one convert one's mind and take refuge in the Primal Vow, the evil act done will yield a good result. So it is said. Thus

Rennyo said, "It is a mistake to think of serving Amida." (Hisao Inagaki, trans., *Thus Have I Heard From Rennyo Shonin* [Rennyo Shonin's *Goichidai-kikigaki*] [Judet Dolj, Romania: Dharma Lion Publications, 2008], #189, p. 91)

Rennyo
-473- Rennyo Shonin said, "In talking about the Buddha-*Dharma*, speak precisely." He said to Hokyo, "Speaking of *shinjin* or *anjin*, ignorant people do not know the meaning of the words. They will think that *shinjin* and *anjin* are different things. Simply tell them that *bombu* can become Buddhas. Tell them to entrust themselves to Amida for salvation in the after-life. However ignorant they may be, they will hear the teaching and attain *shinjin*. It is stated in the *Anjinketsujosho*, 'In the Pure Land teaching, there is nothing more to add.' Hence, the Letters have this to say, 'Amida *Tathagata* unfailingly saves those who entrust themselves to this Buddha wholeheartedly with singleness of mind even if their karmic evils are deep and heavy. This is the import of the eighteenth vow for birth through the *nembutsu.*'" (Hisao Inagaki, trans., *Thus Have I Heard From Rennyo Shonin* [Rennyo Shonin's *Goichidaikikigaki*] [Judet Dolj, Romania: Dharma Lion Publications, 2008], #185, p. 90; see also -091-; -234-)

### a. *Bodhisattva* in Return
Honen
-474- Those who make false claims about the teaching of *nembutsu* are to be pitied. As a result of exposure to blasphemy, no person who begins to harbor doubts and infidelity in his mind about the teaching of *nembutsu* is worth our consideration.

Those who are not firmly entrenched in a relationship with Buddha and who have not established implicit belief in birth in the Pure Land become skeptical about the teaching of *nembutsu* when they hear it, get angry with *nembutsu* practitioners when they see them, and undermine them.

Awareness of such situations is critical, and whatever the blasphemous claim, your unshakable faith should not be tainted. Even the power of Amida Buddha will not be effective toward resistant people. A common man would certainly not succeed in bringing light to such people.

If you truly desire to bring merit to those who disbelieve the teachings of Amida Buddha, you should desire to be born in the Land of Ultimate Bliss, to achieve enlightenment, and to return to this illusory world of birth-and-death to save and facilitate birth in the Pure Land for all beings, including those who slander and disbelieve the teachings of Amida Buddha. (Yoko Hayashi, Joji Atone, trans., *Teachings of Honen* [Los Angeles: Bukkyo University-Los Angeles Extension, 2007 rev.), p. 111)

Seikaku

-475- Some people who read this will surely ridicule it. Nevertheless, both belief and slander will become a cause for each one's birth in the Pure Land. With the pledges of friendship in this life—brief as a dream—to guide us, we tie the bonds for meeting before enlightenment in the coming life. If I am behind, I will be guided by others. If I go first, I will guide others. Becoming true friends through many lives, we bring each other to the practice of the Buddha-way, and as true teachers in each life, we will together sunder all delusion and attachment. (*CWS, Essentials of Faith Alone*, I, p. 697)

Shinran

-476- The countless great *bodhisattvas* of the land of happiness
  Have reached "succession to Buddhahood after one lifetime";
  Entering the compassionate activity of Samantabhadra,
  They unfailingly work to save beings in defiled worlds.
  (*CWS, Hymns of the Pure Land*, # 17, p. 329)

Rennyo

-477- Rennyo Shonin said, "Say something, will you? Those who say nothing are to be feared." Also, "Whether you have *shinjin* or not, just say something." Further, "If you say something, what you have in mind will show. Accordingly, you will be corrected by others. So just say something." (Hisao Inagaki, trans., *Thus Have I Heard From Rennyo Shonin* [Rennyo Shonin's *Goichidaikikigaki*] [Judet Dolj, Romania: Dharma Lion Publications, 2008], #86, p. 60; see also -210-)

*I. The Human Condition*

1. Foolish Being
T'an-luan
-478- "The three worlds" are as follows: (1) the world of desire which includes such states of existence as the six heavens of desire, human existence in the four continents, and the realms of animals, hungry spirits, and beings in hell; (2) the world of form which includes the first, second, third, and fourth meditation heavens; (3) the world of non-form which includes such heavens as the planes of boundless space, boundless consciousness, nothingness, and of neither thought nor non-thought.

These three worlds are indeed a house of samsaric gloom for common, unenlightened beings. Although there are slightly different degrees of pain and pleasure experienced by different individuals and the length of life varies, close observation reveals that they are all, without exception, defiled. Alternately relying on happiness and submitting to calamity, they repeat their existence endlessly, as if going round in a circle. While transmigrating through these various states of existence they forever cling to the four mistaken views (regarding permanence, happiness, selfhood, and purity). Delusion persists in causal acts and in resultant states. (Hisao Inagaki, trans., *T'an-Luan's Commentary on Vasubandhu's Discourse on the Pure Land* [*Ojoronchu*] [Kyoto: Nagata Bunshodo, 1998], p. 139)

T'an-luan

-479- Concerning blossoms from the muddy ponds, the [*Vimalakirti*] *Sutra* states, "The lotus does not grow in the solid ground of lofty plateaus, but in the muddy ponds of the lowland marshes." This is an analogy meaning that foolish beings live in the mud of blind passions, but awakened and guided by *bodhisattvas*, they are able to put forth the blossoms of the Buddha's perfect enlightenment. Truly they make the three treasures flourish and keep them ever from decline. (*CWS, Kyogyoshinsho*, I, p. 163, IV:17)

Tao-ch'o

-480- The first volume of the *An le chi* (*Collection of Passages on the Land of Peace and Bliss*) says:

Question: "If all sentient beings have the Buddha nature, and as each of them from ancient times to the present must have encountered many Buddhas, why then do they continue revolving in the circle of birth and death and fail to escape from this burning house?"

Answer: "According to the holy teaching of the Mahayana, it is actually because they have been unable to cast aside birth and death through [exercising one of] the two excellent teachings that they have not been able to escape from the burning house. What then are these two [teachings]? One is called the Holy Path, and the other is called birth in the Pure Land.

"In these days it is difficult to attain enlightenment through the Holy Path. One reason for this is that the Great Holy One's time has now receded far into the distant past. Another is that the [ultimate] principle is profound, while [human] understanding is shallow. That is why it is stated in the 'Moon Storehouse Section' of the *Great Collection Sutra*: 'In the age of the final *Dharma*, even if the countless sentient beings should begin to practice and cultivate the way, not a single one of them would attain the goal.' We are now in the age of the final *Dharma*, that is, the evil world of the five defilements. The Gateway of the Pure Land is the only one through which we can pass [to enlightenment]. Thus, it is stated in the *Sutra of Immeasurable Life*, 'If there should be a single sentient being who, even if he should have committed evil deeds throughout his life, recites my name ten times in succession as death draws near and yet fails to be born in my land, then may I not attain enlightenment.'

"Further, no one among all sentient beings is able to weigh [his own spiritual abilities]. If we rely on the Mahayana [doctrines of attaining enlightenment], then no one has yet contemplated suchness, the true reality, or ultimate emptiness. From the Hinayana point of view, one must enter into the Path of Insight and the Path of Practice, then one must [toil one's way up] through [the stage of] the *anagamin* to that of the *arhat*, severing the five [bonds of the] lower [world of desire] and leaving behind the five [bonds of the] higher [worlds of form and formlessness]. Until now, however, neither monk nor layperson has ever been able to reach these goals. True, there are those who enjoy the benefit of being born as human and heavenly beings. But this benefit is achieved only by having practiced the five precepts and the ten good acts. Now, however, even those who continue to observe these precepts and virtues are very rare.

"But when we consider people's evil doings and sinful deeds, are they not raging everywhere like the storm's winds and lashing rains? It is because of these things that the many Buddhas, in their immense compassion, urge us to aspire to the Pure Land. For, even though someone has done evil for a lifetime, if only he or she is able to practice the *nembutsu* continually, attentively, and single-mindedly, then all obstacles will spontaneously disappear and he or she will certainly attain birth in the Pure Land. Why, indeed, do we fail to take heed of these things? And why are we not determined to depart [this world for the Pure Land]?" (*Senchakushu* English Translation Project, *Honen's Senchakushu: Passages on the Selection of the Nembutsu in the Original Vow* [*Senchaku Hongan Nembutsu Shu*] [Honolulu: University of Hawai'i Press, 1998], pp. 56-57)

Shan-tao

-481- As this *kalpa* draws to a close, the five defilements flourish;
    Since sentient beings possess wrong views, they find it hard to have faith.
    We are taught to practice wholeheartedly the *nembutsu* alone, taking refuge in the path to the West,
    But because of others our faith is destroyed, and we remain as we originally were.
    Since innumerable *kalpas* in the past we have always been thus;
    It is not that we realize this for the first time in this present life.
    Because we have not encountered the excellent, decisive cause,
    We have been transmigrating, unable to reach the other shore.
    (*CWS, Kyogyoshinsho*, I, p. 232, VI:51)

Shan-tao

-482- Question: Sakyamuni's sermons were meant to enlighten sentient beings. Why are there people who believe in them and those who do not, each abusing the other?

Answer: Moral natures of ordinary persons are of two kinds: good nature and evil nature. Those of good nature are again of five kinds: 1) good persons who, having heard the teaching, abandon evil and do good; 2) good persons who abandon the wrong and perform the right; 3) good persons who abandon the untrue and perform the true; 4) good persons who abandon the unrighteous and perform the righteous; and 5) good persons who abandon the false and perform the true. Those five kinds of persons are able to benefit both themselves and others if they take refuge in the Buddha. At home they perform filial duties; outside, they bring benefit to others. Among the people, they perform sincerity; in the imperial court, they are called "gentlemen," being loyal to the king and bent on fulfilling their duties as loyal subjects. Hence, they are called persons who are good in their own nature.

Persons of evil nature are: 1) evil persons who slander the true and engage in the false; 2) evil persons who slander the right and engage in wrong-doings; 3) evil persons who slander the righteous and engage in unrighteous deeds; 4) evil persons who slander the true and engage in the untrue; and 5) evil persons who slander good and engage in doing evils. Even if those five kinds of persons wish to take refuge in the Buddha, they are not able to attain their own benefit, nor bring benefit to others. At home they do not perform filial duties; among the people, they have no sincerity. At the court, they are called "petty-spirited persons"; when they serve the king, they always entertain flattery and insidious thoughts; hence, they are called "disloyal persons." Furthermore, in their attitudes towards wise, virtuous, and good people, those persons deny righteousness and fabricate unrighteousness; they see only evils in others. Hence, they are called persons who are evil in their own nature. All the good and righteous people among human and heavenly beings as well as Buddhas and sages are slandered and shamed by those evil persons. Wise people should be aware of this. I have above given detailed explanation of the persons of good nature and those of evil nature, thereby clarifying the way things are. I have thus answered your question. (Hisao Inagaki, trans., Shan-tao's Kannenbomon: The Method of Contemplation on Amida [Kyoto: Nagata Bunshodo, 2005], pp. 66-68, #39)

Shan-tao

-483- I am in reality a foolish being of birth-and-death, possessed of deep and heavy karmic evil and transmigrating in the six courses. The suffering is beyond words. Now, encountering a true teacher, I have been able to hear the Name that embodies Amida's Primal Vow. The Buddha instructs me to say the nembutsu single-heartedly and aspire for birth. May the Buddha's compassion, never abandoning the universal Primal Vow, grasp me, a disciple. (CWS, Kyogyoshinsho, I, p. 34, II:27)

Shan-tao

-484- The five defilements and the five forms of suffering are common throughout the six courses; not a single being has ever been free of them. We are constantly assailed and afflicted by them. If there were a person not afflicted by such suffering, he would not belong to the group of ordinary beings. (*CWS, Kyogyoshinsho*, I, p. 84, III:12)

Shan-tao

-485- They will pass *kalpas* countless as the Ganges' sands in the six courses.
   It is truly hard to continue cultivating merits through myriads of *kalpas*;
   In each moment, blind passions intrude a hundred or a thousand times;
   Though some may hope to realize *dharma*-insight in this *saha* world,
   And still the time of realization will not come.

   The various *dharma*-gates are not the same; they are called teachings of
      gradual attainment;
   And one realizes non-origination only through a myriad *kalpas* of
      painful practice.
   Therefore, throughout your life, practice the *nembutsu* alone;
   At the moment your life ends, the Buddha will come to receive you.

   Even in the interval of a single meal, there is time
   For greed and anger to arise; how would they not in a myriad *kalpas*?
   Greed and anger obstruct the path to the human and *deva* realms;
   One will come to settle in the three evil courses or the four evil realms.
   (*CWS, Kyogyoshinsho*, I, pp. 219-220, VI:28)

Shan-tao

-486- Depending on the minds [of beings], excellent practices are performed. There are gateways numbering eighty-four thousand and more. Whether they are gradual or sudden, they are suited to the capacities of beings. Hence, those who practice them according to their circumstances all gain emancipation. (*CWS, Kyogyoshinsho*, I, p. 222, VI:34)

Shan-tao

-487- The *Tathagata* already knows that foolish beings of the latter age possessed of karmic evil and defilements are incapable of visualizing forms and fixing the mind on them. How much harder is it to seek realization without visualizing forms; it is like a person lacking transcendent powers building a house in the air. (*CWS, Kyogyoshinsho*, I, p. 222, VI:34)

Shan-tao

-488- As this *kalpa* draws to a close, the five defilements flourish;
Since sentient beings possess wrong views, they find it hard to have faith.
We are taught to practice wholeheartedly the *nembutsu* alone, taking refuge in the path to the West,
But because of others our faith is destroyed, and we remain as we originally were.
Since innumerable *kalpas* in the past we have always been thus;
It is not that we realize this for the first time in this present life.
Because we have not encountered the excellent, decisive cause,
We have been transmigrating, unable to reach the other shore.
(*CWS, Kyogyoshinsho*, I, p. 232, VI:51)

Shan-tao

-489- It is regrettable indeed that sentient beings doubt what should not be doubted;
The Pure Land is right before us and never out of harmony with us.
Do not ponder whether Amida will take you in or not;
The question is whether or not you wholeheartedly turn about at heart.
It is said that from this moment until the attainment of Buddhahood,
For vast *kalpas*, we will praise the Buddha out of gratitude for his compassion and benevolence.
Had we not received the power of Amida's universal Vow,
When—in what *kalpa*—could we part from this *saha* world?
And how could we now expect to reach that precious land?
It is indeed the power of our Guide, who appeared in the *saha* world.
But for the encouragement of our Guide, our true teacher,
How would we be able to enter Amida's Pure Land?
Attaining birth in the Pure Land, respond in gratitude for the compassion and benevolence!
(*CWS, Kyogyoshinsho*, I, p. 238, VI:63)

*Rakuho monrui*[9]

-490- There are always many who endeavor to be born in the Pure Land, but exceedingly few reach the gateway and immediately attain birth. There are always many who discuss the Pure Land, but few indeed grasp what is essential and directly point it out. I have yet to hear a person explain [*nembutsu*] with reference to self-obstruction and self-obscuration. Having grasped this matter, I explain it here.

---

[9] A five volume anthology from the Southern Sung period, c. 1200.

There is no greater self-obstruction than attachment, no greater self-obscuration than doubt. As that which finally eliminates these hindrances of doubt and attachment, we have only the teaching-gate of the Pure Land. Never has there been any separation: Amida's vast vow always, of itself, grasps and holds beings. This is the necessary way of its working. (*CWS, Kyogyoshinsho,* I, p. 110, III:59)

Genshin

-491- The cloud of the heart which desires Paradise will become the cloud of welcome.

I was seeking the way of Buddha all through the night but it was really to find my own heart.

When I obtain enlightenment and enter the bright sunlight of understanding, immediately the shallow snow of sin melts away.

(A.K. Reischauer, "Genshin's *Ojo Yoshu*: Collected Essays on Birth into Paradise," *The Transactions of the Asiatic Society of Japan* [December 1930], Second Series Vol. VII, p. 25)

Genshin

-492- It is a great joy for us sentient beings to escape from the three evil realms and be born as humans. Even if our status in society is low, could it be worse than the state of animals? Even if we are born in a poor family, we are in a far better condition than hungry spirits. Even if our wishes are not fulfilled, our suffering cannot be compared with tortures of hell. We should not sorrow over unhappiness in this life; we should consider our lower social position as an incentive to seek enlightenment. For this reason, we should rejoice at having been born as humans.

Even though the mind of faith is shallow, anyone who takes refuge in Amida will unfailingly attain birth, because the Original Vow is deep. Even though the *nembutsu* comes from a reluctant heart, anyone who recites it never fails to see Amida welcoming him to his Pure Land; so great is the merit of the *nembutsu*. For this reason, we should rejoice at having encountered the Original Vow.

Delusion is the nature of ordinary beings. Apart from delusion, there is no mind in us. If we recite the *nembutsu* while resigned to the fact that we are to remain ordinary beings full of delusion until death, we shall be received in welcome by Amida; then, as soon as we mount the lotus seat, our mind of delusion will be turned into that of Enlightenment. The *nembutsu* that is uttered with the mind of delusion is like a lotus flower unstained by the muddy water. There should not be any doubt as to our attainment of birth.

We should not be concerned about our delusion, but reflecting on the shallowness of our mind of faith, continually recite the Name in earnest.

(Hisao Inagaki, *Dharma Words at Yokawa* [*Yokawa Hogo*], http://www12. canvas.ne.jp/horai/yokawa-hogo.htm)

Genshin

**-493-** (1) Even an illiterate person can see that the one who holds such a view suffers from illusion. . . . How, then, can such a one understand the real nature of things, namely, that there are fundamentally wonderful laws by which there is an interaction of the negative and positive principles in the four great elements! In the world there are many people, priests and laymen, learned and unlearned, or even those who have superior knowledge—but not enough really to enjoy the nature of things—who are not different from those who hold such errors.

What pitiable objects these are! They may be versed in the three teachings but their learning is only mouth and ear learning, a fancy for flowery words. They pride themselves on their great learning but if one looks into their inner heart and examines what they really say and enjoy then things seem quite different. Nevertheless, it is difficult to discriminate between the true and the false. Such people not only destroy the seeds of Buddhahood and are far from the circle of the saints; they cannot fail to reap in things great and little the fruits of the seeds they have sown. I beseech you, therefore, to reform your self-centered views and go forward in your knowledge of the truth. Constantly embracing sorrow but finally finding constant joy, overcoming and being indifferent to poverty and wealth, to positions of honor and low estate, to sorrow and happiness, because knowing the principle of fundamental truth and not resting in false views but fearing the various hells, seek ye to live on the lotus leaf of non-retrogression. (A.K. Reischauer, "Genshin's *Ojo Yoshu*: Collected Essays on Birth into Paradise," *The Transactions of the Asiatic Society of Japan* [December 1930], Second Series, Vol. VII, p. 38)

Honen

**-494-** It is extremely difficult to be born as a human being, to encounter the essential vow, to awaken the aspiration for birth in the Pure Land, to detach ourselves from the delusive worlds of transmigration, and to be born in the Pure Land; this is our ultimate good fortune.

Believing that even a person who has committed the ten transgressions or the five grave offenses will be born in the Pure Land, you should strive not to commit even the most minor of offenses. As even a wrongdoer can attain birth in the Pure Land, there is no doubt the virtuous can. Further, believing that just a single utterance of *nembutsu*, or ten repetitions, is never futile, you must exercise *nembutsu* continuously for life. If a single utterance assures birth in the Pure Land, think how much more powerful many repetitions would be. (Joji Atone, Yoko Hayashi, trans., *The Promise of Amida Buddha: Honen's Path to Bliss* [Boston: Wisdom Publications, 2011], p. 141)

Honen
-495- Amida Buddha does not discriminate between one who observes the precepts and one who violates them, nor does he discriminate between the poor and the wealthy, and pays no regard to any social class. His power changes the karmic nature of man like a stone or tile turned into gold through *nembutsu*. He also promised that he will come to welcome all *nembutsu* devotees without exception. (Joji Atone, Yoko Hayashi, trans., *The Promise of Amida Buddha: Honen's Path to Bliss* [Boston: Wisdom Publications, 2011], p. 393)

Honen
-496- People naturally know how to commit a karmic wrong without having been taught. This is because they have transmigrated in the six delusive worlds from beginningless time to the present. In each instance, their appearances have changed but their nature remains unchanged. They have performed various non-virtuous actions repeatedly and are now easily accustomed to committing karmic defilements. They have heard of the teaching of birth in the Pure Land through *nembutsu* for the very first time in this life; therefore, it may be natural that they cannot believe in the teaching of *nembutsu* in such a short period of time. (Joji Atone, Yoko Hayashi, trans., *The Promise of Amida Buddha: Honen's Path to Bliss* [Boston: Wisdom Publications, 2011], p. 397)

Shinran
-497- For this reason, in the *Tathagata's* teaching this world is called the defiled world of the corrupt *dharma*. All beings lack a true and sincere heart, mock teachers and elders, disrespect their parents, distrust their companions, and favor only evil; hence, it is taught that everyone, both in the secular and religious worlds, is possessed of "heart and tongue at odds," and "words and thoughts both insincere." The former means that what is in the heart and what is said are at variance, and the latter means that what is spoken and what is thought are not real. Real means "sincere." People of this world have only thoughts that are not real, and those who wish to be born in the Pure Land have only thoughts of deceiving and flattering. Even those who renounce this world have nothing but thoughts of fame and profit. Hence, know that we are not good persons, nor persons of wisdom; that we have no diligence, but only indolence, and within, the heart is ever empty, deceptive, vainglorious, and flattering. We do not have a heart that is true and real. (*CWS, Notes on Essentials of Faith Alone*, I, p. 466)

Shinran

-498- Foolish beings: as expressed in the parable of the two rivers of water and fire, we are full of ignorance and blind passion. Our desires are countless, and anger, wrath, jealousy, and envy are overwhelming, arising without pause; to the very last moment of life they do not cease, or disappear, or exhaust themselves. (*CWS, Notes on Once-Calling and Many-Calling*, I, p. 488)

Shinran

-499- In people who have long heard the Buddha's Name and said the *nembutsu*, surely there are signs of rejecting the evil of this world and signs of their desire to cast off the evil in themselves. When people first begin to hear the Buddha's vow, they wonder, having become thoroughly aware of the karmic evil in their hearts and minds, how they will ever attain birth as they are. To such people we teach that since we are possessed of blind passions, the Buddha receives us without judging whether our hearts are good or bad.

When, upon hearing this, a person's trust in the Buddha has grown deep, he or she comes to abhor such a self and to lament continued existence in birth-and-death; and such a person then joyfully says the Name of Amida Buddha deeply entrusting himself to the Vow. That people seek to stop doing wrong as the heart moves them, although earlier they gave thought to such things and committed them as their minds dictated, is surely a sign of having rejected this world.

Moreover, since *shinjin* that aspires for attainment of birth arises through the encouragement of Sakyamuni and Amida, once the true and real mind is made to arise in us, how can we remain as we were, possessed of blind passions? (*CWS, Lamp for the Latter Ages*, #20, I, pp. 553-554)

Shinran

-500- The sutra states, "The first is sincere (*shijo*) mind." *Shi* means truth, *jo* means reality. This shows that the understanding and practice of all sentient beings, cultivated through their bodily, verbal, and mental acts, unfailingly take as essential what was performed [by Amida] with a true and real mind. We should not outwardly express signs of wisdom, goodness, or diligence, for inwardly we are possessed of falsity. We are filled with all manner of greed, anger, perversity, deceit, wickedness, and cunning, and it is difficult to put an end to our evil nature. In this we are like poisonous snakes or scorpions. Though we perform practices in the three modes of action, they must be called poisoned good acts or false practices. They cannot be called true, real, and sincere action. Firmly setting our minds and undertaking practice in this way—even if we strive to the utmost with body and mind through the twelve periods of the day and night, urgently seeking and urgently acting as though sweeping fire from our heads—must all be called poisoned good acts. To seek birth in the Buddha's Pure Land by directing the merit of such poisoned practice is completely wrong. Why? Because when, in his causal stage, Amida Buddha was performing practices as a *bodhisattva*, in every single moment—every single instant—he performed his practices in the three modes of action with a true and real mind. [True practice] depends on this. (*CWS, Gutoku's Notes*, II.I, p. 601)

Shinran

-501- Even a good person attains birth in the Pure Land, so it goes without saying that an evil person will.

Though it is so, people commonly say, "Even an evil person attains birth, so it goes without saying that a good person will." This statement may seem well founded at first, but it runs counter to the intent of the Primal Vow, which is Other-Power. This is because people who rely on doing good through their self-power fail to entrust themselves wholeheartedly to Other-Power and therefore not in accord with Amida's Primal Vow, but when they overturn the mind of self-power and entrust themselves to Other-Power, they will attain birth in the true and fulfilled land.

It is impossible for us, who are possessed of blind passions, to free ourselves from birth-and-death through any practice whatever. Sorrowing at this, Amida made the vow, the essential intent of which is the evil person's attainment of Buddhahood. Hence, evil persons who entrust themselves to Other-Power are precisely the ones who possess the true cause of birth.

Accordingly he said, "Even the good person is born in the Pure Land, so without question is the person who is evil" (*CWS, A Record in Lament of Divergences*, 3.I, p. 663)

Ippen

-502- *Hymn of Amida's Vow*

Search into your self: but froth on the stream—
Once vanishing, nothing human remains;
Ponder your life, and its shimmer of the moon,
Unstaying through rise and fall of each fleeting breath.
Though we cherish our forms in the good paths—
Human and *deva*—no one can keep them;
The pain in hell, as famished ghosts, as beasts,
We all abhor, yet easily take on again.
Of the various shapes before our eyes,
When we go blind, no form or hue appears;
As for the words that assail our ears,
Once deaf, no voice can be heard.

The smelling of fragrances, tasting of tastes
Are for but a brief span;
When breath's manipulations have come to a halt,
No powers remain to this self.
From far, far in the distant past,
Down to this day, this very instant,
Those things we have longed for most
Have not been attained, and we sorrow.
Some have thoroughly grasped the *Dharma*-gates
Of the Path of Sages and the Pure Land way,
But their false, samsaric thinking unbroken,
It all turns to karma for more transmigration.
With minds that have deviated completely from the truth
Of the non-discrimination of good and evil,
We consider wrong and right to be one:
This insight is darkness; how shameful it is!
While hearing, "Blind passion is itself enlightenment,"
We only go on committing evil;
We say, "Birth-and-death as such is *nirvana*,"
Yet dearly do we treasure this life.
*Dharma*-body, whose original nature is purity,
Is ever-abiding Buddha that is suchness;
Since it transcends both illusion and enlightenment,
It's useless whether we know of it or not.
The fulfilled body, perfectly furnished with a myriad practices,
Is Buddha in whom dharmic reality and wisdom are fused;
Since there's no duality of object and wisdom,
It's useless for our minds to contemplate or lips to utter a name.
The assumed body that has cut off all evil and practices good
Is Buddha who treats the sick according to their condition;
For transgressors who commit the ten evils and five damning acts
And who lack any bonds, there's no help toward their emancipation.
But the fulfilled body arising with the Name as its cause
Is Buddha that liberates the foolish person;
This Buddha's Vow is to save every being in the ten directions,
So there's no lapse of allowing even one to slip away.
The Name of Amida's unique, all-surpassing Vow
Embodies the inconceivable working of Other-Power;
When you just say this Name, leaving everything to your lips,
In that voicing all your evil in birth-and-death vanishes.
Beyond the single thought-moment of *nembutsu* at the start
There are no final ten utterances at death;

Rather, start is made in adding thought-moment on thought-moment
And the thought-moment reaching its limit is the end.
Once our false thinking has completely ceased,
There is neither start nor conclusion, beginning nor end;
In the oneness of Buddha and sentient being
Say *namu-amida-butsu*,
Quickly cast off your myriad entanglements
And, single-heartedly entrusting yourself to Amida,
Let your breath be spent in *namu-amida-butsu*;
This is the finish of all our false thought.
At that moment, from the realm of Perfect Bliss,
Amida, Kannon, and Daiseishi,
With a host of sages, countless as sands of the Ganges,
Manifest themselves before the practicer;
All together they extend their hands
And, welcoming us, they draw us forth.

(Dennis Hirota, trans., *No Abode: The Record of Ippen* [Honolulu: University of Hawai'i Press, 1987, rev.], pp. 3-6)

Ippen

-503- Spring passes and autumn comes, yet it is hard to advance upon the essential path of liberation. We feel the pathos of scattering blossoms and gaze pensively on the moon, yet it is easy for the delusional thoughts of samsaric life to arise. The karmic evil that obstructs us has grown into a mountain, and before we realize, clouds of passion have gathered so thick about it that light of the Buddha-sun does not fill our eyes. Permanently over the ocean of birth-and-death the winds of impermanence rush, so that never can the moon of suchness abide.

As we receive birth, suffering is laden upon suffering, and each time we return to death, we make our way from darkness into further darkness. At the crossroads of the six paths there is nowhere we do not stray; at the doorways of the four modes of arising there is no niche in which we do not take shelter. Should we call this cycle of transformations in birth-and-death dream or reality? When we think to say it exists, it rises in clouds and vanishes like [the pyre's] smoke; there is no one who keeps his shadowy form in the vacant sky. When we think to say it does not really exist, we still find, lodged within our hearts, grief at separation from one we loved that never fails to cut to the bowels and leave the soul distraught.

(Dennis Hirota, trans., *No Abode: The Record of Ippen* [Honolulu: University of Hawai'i Press, 1987, rev.], pp. 32-33)

Kakunyo[10]

-504- At that point the Shonin could not easily slip out of answering, and facing the young child he said, "Rare is it to be born into human form, yet we take the lives of other living things to satisfy our craving for the taste of flesh, this being something that we should never do, and even the *Tathagata* thus sets forth strict precepts against it. However, the sentient beings of the present age of the defiled world of the latter *dharma* (*mappo*) live in a precept-less time, such that there are neither those who hold them nor those who violate them. As a result, although my head is shaved and I wear the dyed robes of a priest, because my heart is identical to those of the ordinary worldly masses, I eat things like this. Ah, if only this massive urge to eat were instead translated into the work of liberating these living things. Although I bear the title of *Shaku-shi* (an ordained disciple of Shakyamuni) it is of little consequence; with a heart steeped in the dust of the worldly life, my wisdom naught, and my merits none, what can I possibly do to save these sentient beings? In this regard there is this *kasaya* (stole) I wear, the holy vestment symbolic of the liberation of all Buddhas in the triple world. When I don this vestment while eating, the meritorious use of the *kasaya* exerts its influence of the vow's thought to save living beings, and thus I wear this while I eat them. When you believe that invisible forces watch over us, there is no need to be concerned over how we appear in the eyes of others, however utterly shameless and unconscionable we may appear to them. And so this is the reason I am so." (W.S. Yokoyama, trans., *Kakunyo's What Shinran Taught* [*Kudensho*], #8, unpublished translation)

Kakunyo

-505- [This is what Shinran taught:] That, as *bombu*, to put on a show of being brave or manly in the face of circumstances, is all for nothing.

We experience the pain of leaving behind our loved ones, when we are bereaved by having to part with a father or mother or wife or child. To those of you who have cleaved to the belief that "The people who hold to the *nembutsu* as their Buddha-*dharma* should never be so sad as to weep or cry inconsolably," and therefore held back, keeping yourselves in control all the time due to the admonishment of your elder brethren, I want to say: it was all for nothing. Such episodes are typical of those who believe themselves to be treading the Way in accord with the various schools of the Path of Sages;

---

[10] This passage is taken from Kakunyo's account of an incident when Shinran was invited to participate in a project to copy the entire canon of sutras. Eating with his *kesa* (Sanskrit: *kasaya*) or stole on was considered a violation of etiquette. He was questioned by a young man concerning his failure to remove the *kesa*. Shinran gave the following reply after giving a nonchalant reply that he had forgotten, when the youth persisted in questioning.

it is not the understanding of the person who identifies himself as a person of the true school of the Pure Land (*Jodo Shinshu*).

First of all, the *bombu*, in the face of such events, simply comes off as foolish. For those of us who put on an act of being wise and good to cover up the fact of our cunning and deceitful nature, it is all untrue and all for nothing. For instance, we may well understand that Amida's reward land is the site of our future birth and have no doubt that we will be reunited with our loved ones in the Pure Land. However, as the first wave of sadness sweeps over us when we send off someone dear, who has departed ahead of us, we, as *bombu* caught up in the confusion, start to wonder why things have to turn out this way. Herein we realize that, after having spent long *kalpas* wandering from life after life and world after world with the noose of transmigration slipped around our neck, we want to bring this tale of transmigration to a close with the present round of life. While in this temporary abode to which we are so inured and attached, this burning house of the human world, we want to leave behind this old home of delusions, with its two kinds of reward, either consolatory or true. Yet what are we going to do about those memories that linger on? Unless this question occurs to us, we can never count ourselves among those who are received as *bombu* [by Amida]. The more we think to put on a brave face at this time, the more we should doubt ourselves, for this feeds the mistaken notion of ourselves as persons pursuing the Path of Sages by self-power; it is not compatible with the person now headed to the Pure Land by Other-Power. To cry and weep away like blubbering fools on this occasion, rather, is exactly what is to be expected of the person who is on course for impending birth by Other-Power. There is no reason for the *bombu* to exhibit any change of behavior other than to carry on in the way they have always carried on.

We leave the one great matter of our impending Birth to the Buddha (Amida *Tathagata*). However, the actions of our body, the drifts of our minds, the words of our mouths as the roots of the three poisons of greed, hate, and stupidity, and the ten evils of taking life and so on, all make our defiled existence so difficult to rise above and make this realm so difficult to leave behind. For the foolish and spiritually-inept *bombu* who has only succeeded in filling his life with blind passion, it is truly wonderful that, in our true school of the Pure Land (*Jodo Shinshu*), the very person for whom Amida made his true vow is simply those who are their unassuming selves, who do not pretend to be other than what they are.

Now, in the way of the world, when a person dying is someone who is deeply attached to wife and children and family and friends, as the final hour approaches, it is customary to keep him separate from them and not allow them to see him. The reason they do this is to keep the dying person who is so attached to them from being distracted and thus falling into evil paths after he dies. This case reflects how ingrained the Path of Sages' self-power view is in the ways of the world. But the true school of Other-Power is not to be found in such a depiction of things. The reason is, no matter how much people may declare their intention to sever themselves from this [worldly] realm, without the Buddha-*dharma* of Other-Power to back up their aspiration, there is nothing they can latch onto to make good their departure from this realm of births-and-deaths. On the other hand, even though a person might be seriously confused by deluded love, from the outset [Amida] has it in his heart to work out the salvation of this person, and through the agency of his true vow to effect just that. Since he has to deal with the grave karmic causes which lead to bottomless hell such as the exceedingly great evils of the five transgressions, slandering of *dharma* and so on, how much less would he be deterred by the heart-rending cries of those who cannot bear the pain of parting from loved ones.

Even if we were to add the condition that they must perfect our *shinjin* for our impending birth in Pure Land, bringing to a close this round of our transmigration in *samsara*, their sadness and grief will be at its deepest point. Though the mourners line themselves up at the foot of the bed and pillow-side and give out stifled cries of grief, with the room cluttered with people left and right who long for the departed and cannot stop crying, the deceased is not distracted in the least. As *bombu* just as we are, with our unassuming self, it is unbecoming for us to wonder whether this is somehow incompatible or not with being persons who will be born through Other-Power. Thus, there is no need to hesitate for fear of disturbing that realm where our loved ones have gone; it is alright to cry and weep away inconsolably. (W.S. Yokoyama, trans., *Kakunyo's What Shinran Taught* [*Kudensho*], #17, unpublished translation)

Kakunyo
-506- (19) On the *Tathagata's* true Vow originally being for the sake of the *bombu*, and not for the saintly:

The Hongwanji Shonin (Shinran), told Nyoshin Shonin something that his late teacher of Kurodani (Genku) once told him, that people ordinarily think, "If the evil-ridden person attains impending birth, how much more so the good person." This view, on the far end, turns it back on Amida's true Vow, and on the near end, contradicts the golden words of Shakyamuni's appearance in this world. For that reason, the five *kalpas* of laboring in contemplation and the myriad practices that he endured on the six paths, were all necessary for the sake of obtaining the release of the *bombu*, and none of it was for the sake of the saintly. Thus, the *bombu* is the main person who is supposed to ride on the true Vow and arrive at birth in the reward land. If the *bombu* was incidental to impending birth, it was all for nothing [that the

Buddha] made the vows and the effort he made to realize them simply dissipated. However, by matching up and loading on the power of the Vow, he was able to achieve great and far-reaching benefit for sentient beings in every direction. As a result, ten *kalpas* have now passed since his attainment of true enlightenment was praised [by all Buddhas]. This testimony of all Buddhas as many as the sands of the Ganges—how can such testimony be empty and false? Moreover, even in the commentary (Shan-tao's *Gengibun*) there are statements such as, "All *bombu* good and evil attain birth." This too regards the evil-ridden *bombu* as main and the good *bombu* as incidental. For that reason, if the good *bombu* who is cast in the incidental role can attain birth, how can the evil-ridden *bombu* who is cast in the main role not be able to attain birth? Thus, I was told, "If the good person can attain birth, how much more so does this apply to the evil-ridden person." (W.S. Yokoyama, trans., *Kakunyo's What Shinran Taught* [*Kudensho*], #19, unpublished translation)

Kakunyo

-507- "The spirit of the Pure Land school is that it is basically for the *bombu* and not for the saints." However, unless what the Buddha taught was false, we must conclude that impending birth [in the Pure Land] most decidedly awaits the *bombu*, whose greed is profound, whose anger is fierce, and whose ignorance smolders, [in] this round [of transmigration]. If by some mistake the three poisons were not to pile up in our hearts and only a good heart was to make itself felt, we would also think that our impending birth is uncertain. That is because the Buddha clearly explains the vow was made for the sake of the *bombu*. But even if we have no feeling of being *bombu* in our hearts, we would think that: "Since we are not *bombu*, are we excluded from this vow?" But all of us are the same in already having the full complement of the three poisons of greed, anger, and ignorance in our hearts, and it is for this reason that if there is a vow that has been raised [for the *bombu*], it is surely decided that such persons [as these] have been slated for impending birth. From these facts we are to understand that, even though our hearts are full of evil, even though we are lowly candidates, we can rest assured that our impending birth will not fail to be brought about in principle and reality, and no one will be left out of, or disappointed by, [the vow of] the *bombu's* impending birth. That is why I have said, "The five *kalpas* of contemplation and the millions of years of practice that the Buddha underwent were all for the sake of this one person Shinran." (W.S. Yokoyama, trans., *Kakunyo's What Shinran Taught* [*Kudensho*], #7, unpublished translation)

Zonkaku

-508- Body impurity means that with regard to the physical form made up of the 360 bones and the 36,000 blood vessels through which blood courses to sustain the life spirit, the five organs and six viscera—all of these are impure; whether we are speaking of tears or sputum or excrement, of these bodily things none of them is pure. Even if you bathe yourself in an oceanful of salt water, there is no cleansing yourself of bodily impurity. Even if you perfume yourself by burning a stick of sandalwood, it will do nothing to change the basic foul smell of the body itself. Though the pretty women may have lovely eyebrows that rival the willowy leaves, if you contemplate the reality, it is something you had better not be too attached to. Even though some faces have features as delicate as flowers, they are like pictures painted on excrement pots. Among wise men who combined wisdom with practice, there are many in the Three Lands (the Buddhist lands of India, China, and Japan) who, becoming fascinated with the temporal beauty of women, utterly destroyed all their efforts at practice. Although they were not unaware of bodily impurity and were not unimpressed by the insights of the sacred teachings, they under the sway of delusions and unable to control the urgings of their own hearts, and when they stood at the nexus of the torments of the world of desire, they were powerless against them. Always trying to feed the hunger of their five senses, they realized what Shan-tao meant when he said: "Even if we can generate a beautiful mind, it is like a beautiful picture painted on water." What it comes down to is, common hearts of the defiled world, of both the clever and the fools alike, cannot be said to be very different. (W.S. Yokoyama, Suzuki Hiroshi, eds., *Zonkaku's Sermons*, #2b2, unpublished translation)

Zonkaku
## —The Wheel of Suffering
-509- . . . as to the Wheel of Suffering, suffering is usually portrayed as the triple world and the six paths, but it is the four sufferings and eight sufferings that pertain particularly to humans. There are the noble and the lowly, but suffering is something that afflicts both in ample quantity. The poor and the wealthy cannot be said to be the same, but they are identical as far as not being free from distress. The four sufferings are (i) birth, (ii) aging, (iii) infirmity, and (iv) death. The eight sufferings are (v) the suffering of parting from loved ones, (vi) the suffering of not getting what you want, (vii) the suffering of being in the company of people you hate, and (viii) the suffering of being attached to the five composite *skandhas*. Should it happen that you are struck down in the prime of life and thus pass from our midst, it may be that you will not undergo the suffering of aging, or should it happen that you are born into good circumstances, it could be that you will escape the suffering of poverty. But for the rest of us, these are sufferings that cannot be avoided. It is in this regard that the Master Shan-tao of Komyo-ji temple (in his *Jobungi*) says:

The five defilements, the five sufferings, the eight sufferings, and so on, are things that are experienced by everyone on the six paths. There has never been anyone who has not. It is a constant for those torments to be universally present. If there is someone who does not experience suffering, then that person is not one of the sentient beings who do.

In the *Abhidharma Kosa* (chapter 22) it explains why the foolish are not aware of suffering while receiving it, saying:

If you have an eyelash and put it on the palm of your hand, you cannot feel it. If that eyelash were put on the eye, though, it would cause it pain and you cannot be at rest. It is said that the foolish, like the palm, do not know what suffering is, while the wise, like the eye, having been touched by the eyelash of suffering, have a great loathing and fear of it.

However, for those who walk the paths of humans and gods it is not the case that they have no enjoyment at all. While the retributions of those who live on earth and in the heavens vary, the pleasures of the heaven of the thirty-three gods sound especially great. However, to merely set out in the pursuit of pleasures makes it impossible to cultivate the Buddhist way. During our long journey of transmigration on the Six Paths over vast *kalpas* it is without doubt that we too have been born in the heavens. But when we enjoyed those sublime states we never once thought to offer up the pure waters of those splendid ponds to the Buddha, we never thought to offer up to the Buddha world the wreaths of flowers from those happy gardens. As a result, we again tumbled down into the lesser worlds where we were unable to avoid entering the cycle of transmigration again. This is truly something to be ashamed about. Among the retributions earned in the human world, though the highest ranks of a Golden Wheel Turning King or Silver Wheel Turning King or Emperor who roams the sky, or the ruler of a foreign land or of this land are out of the question, some people are born to a high ranking lineage to live a leisurely life in fabulous mansions, some live in wealthy homes with stores full of treasures. And the happy cause for all this good fortune in the present life lies in their previous life. You might envy their present good fortune, but this abundant joy they glory in is limited just to this life, and unless they make some investment in the next life, then, like the thousand year pine there will come a time when they reach that final age, and suddenly the fiery vehicle sent from the eight fiery hells will come calling for them—what can they do then to fend for themselves! Though they wish to stop and enjoy, there is no time, for in the next instant they are forced to abandon all, those pleasures mere delusions, their wealth only bringing them suffering.

The triple world of desire, form, and idea is no place to sit back and relax, it is precisely a burning house, filled with suffering, and those who live within its walls should hold it in the greatest of fear.

So said the Buddha, for there is no turn where we are not confronted by this burning house of the torments. Whomever it may be, they experience the sentient beings' suffering of birth and death. Although it is typical of the foolish to imagine the suffering they are experiencing to be pleasure, and not to realize what it is and not to loathe it, if they have an inkling as to the principle of cause and effect and desire to be born in the Pure Land, they need to realize the difficulty of getting the Cause of suffering under control, they need to realize the impossibility of avoiding the Effect of suffering. Once they realize the impossibility of their cutting off the source of birth and death through self-power, they need to turn completely to Other-Power, the power of the Original Vow, to plead, Oh, save me!, reverently opening their hearts to the caring power of the *Tathagata* which is working to save them through Other-Power. (W.S. Yokoyama, Suzuki Hiroshi, eds., *Zonkaku's Sermons*, #2c, unpublished translation; see also -028-; -029-; -064-; -076-; -155-; -245-)

## a. Impermanence
Zonkaku

-510- First, the Wheel of Impermanence means, the world and everything in it exists in a state of change and transience. The *Larger Sutra* extols this truth saying: We cannot hold on forever to those whom we love, to things we want, to the fame and fortune we have; in the end we must part from all these things.

. . . How empty the years seem as our life dwindles to an end. Think it through for yourself: even the world-conquering kings cannot hold on to their high status and many treasures forever; even for the rulers of the heaven of the thirty-three gods, there will surely come a time when they must leave behind the pleasure of riding their jeweled elephants and four gardens (of chariots, battle, desires, delights). As we cast our gaze upward to the six gods in the world of desire and the gods belonging to the fourth stage of meditation [in the world of form], there may be none [in the triple world] whom we envy. As we cast our gaze down upon the three or four evil paths, indeed, there is none on the six paths who can find haven from the sorrows that lie ahead. In the brief time we take human form on this earth born on this forsaken strand (the scattered islands known as Japan) as is our karma, what is there of lasting value we can affix ourselves. Seeking this elixir of immortality, both the First Emperor of the Ch'in (d. 210 B.C.E), and Emperor Wu of the Han dynasty (d. 87 B.C.E.) died miserable deaths, and now only mournful winds howl around their tombs at the foot of Mount Li and the Tu-lung mound. Fan-pei and Chang-kang were men of action who drew up brave plans, but all that is left of them is their names. Never do we hear of a mighty weapon that can protect us from the enemy called Change that lurks around every corner of our existence. All the thousands of court ladies draped in finest silk grew old in vain. The elegant figures of Li of the Han and Yang of the T'ang may have prospered in their day, but in the end they only amounted to small mounds of dust. All of the wise and saintly to whom the Buddha entrusted the *Dharma* store passed away, and however wise and practiced, not one could beat the demon Impermanence. Whether young or old, even in the prime of life, they went down. The Truth be, all who are born must die, and how much truer is it for the elderly who know they cannot tarry here much longer. The smoke rises from the funeral pyres at the top of Mount Toribe just as it rises from those at its base. When will we have to join their numbers? The dewy drops on the fields of Adashino will vanish with the morning's first light, just as they will vanish in the evening— this chilling thought being one which cannot but concern us. The Buddhist Emperor, [former Emperor] Gotoba, contemplating the transiency of the world from his place of exile on a distant island, composed verses orally that he called *Eulogy to Impermanence* (*Mujo ko no shiki*). The truths they point out are familiar to us, resounding as they do with the transiency of the world in which we live. In that regal work we find the following words:

Was it yesterday you were kneeling by the burial mound, wiping away the tears you shed. Or is it tonight you are to send off another, as you break down and weep by the coffin side. So it is that for transients like us, an entire lifetime comes to pass, beginning middle end, as it were a phantasm. The triple world of desire, form, and idea is Impermanence itself. From ancient times to the present, never have we heard of anybody living to be an immortal's age. An entire lifetime slips away quickly, and of the faces we see among us today there is none who will remain a hundred years from now. I might be first to go, you might be first to go; it can happen today, it can happen tomorrow—who can tell. Whether you are left behind or first to go, sooner or later we all pass on like the incessantly vanishing dew.

Also, in recent times are the words written by Gedatsu Shonin (Jokei) of Kasagi, famous for his wisdom and practice, whose subtle message slips into my heart. The words are,

It is hard to keep together this body like a scarecrow of leaves swept up by the wind; how quickly this life vanishes like dew on the grass. Mourning in the southern quarter, mourning in the north village, there is no stopping the stream of tears as we send off our loved ones. In the hills there are funerals, on the plains there are funerals, the soil being turned over so often to receive their bones that it has no chance to dry. How painful it is to think that, once they breathe their last, we must mourn for our dearest friends. Even the unbreakable, solid gold bonds of intimate relationships are such that when a soul must go its way, we have no choice but to mourn our loss alone.

Although we confront this kind of truth, we only pretend to understand it. Inured to a life hemmed in by desires, the ordinary person is not the least astonished by the law of impermanence. Ah, how empty we ordinary persons are! In the *Zazen samadhi sutra* (vol. 1), it says:

All who are born into this world must return to Death. Even if life is as boundless as they say, the end will surely come. Even for one brimming with life there will surely come a time when their energies will flag; all those whom we have met shall surely be parted from us.

Living to do the things we plan for the day and for the morrow, attached to life's pleasures, and refusing to look suffering in the eye, we never even notice the demon Death encroaching. Busied with everything else, we never even notice the days and nights passing by in a blur.

In the *Mahaparinirvana Sutra* (northern edition, vol. 2; southern edition, vol. 2) it says,

The sorrow of impermanence that descends upon us is impossible to avoid outside the Pure Land. Yet it is impossible to transcend our bodies that depend on material things to exist, unless we leave behind the cycle of birth and death. The cultivation of the three vehicles all address this problem of how to avoid the wages of impermanence and how to dwell forever at the highest rank of the Permanent, but it is because we cannot distill the cause that we come up short as far as results go. On the other hand, if we set ourselves in good stead with Amida's Vow Power, when we realize that our birth in the Land of Peace and Sustenance is secure, as this Land is itself the realm of eternal *Nirvana*, it is a world wherein we do not grow weary, a world wherein we do not revert to our former state. Because of this, without having to resort to our own clever actions, we can pin ourselves onto the sleeves of Buddha power to forever avoid the Wheel of Impermanence of birth and death, and reach the vaunted plane of true Permanence.

(W.S. Yokoyama, Suzuki Hiroshi, eds., *Zonkaku's Sermons*, 2a, unpublished translation)

Rennyo

-511- On deep contemplation, we realize that the pleasures of human life last only as long as a flash of lightning or the morning dew, a dream or an illusion. Even if we enjoy a life of pomp and glory and can do as we wish, this is only a matter of some fifty to a hundred years. If the wind of impermanence were to come even now and summon us, would we not suffer illness of one kind or another and die? And indeed, at the time of death, no part of either the family or wealth on which we have depended for so long can accompany us. Thus, all alone, we must cross the great river of three currents, at the end of the mountain path that we take after death. Let us realize, then, that what we should earnestly aspire to is birth [in the Pure Land in] the afterlife, that the one we should rely upon is Amida *Tathagata*, and that the place we should go, faith having been decisively settled, is the Pure Land of serene sustenance. (Minor L. Rogers and Ann T. Rogers, trans., *Rennyo: The Second Founder of Shin Buddhism* [Berkeley, CA: Asian Humanities Press, 1991], pp. 161-162, fascicle I-11)

Rennyo

-512- In particular, as I observe the present state of affairs, [it is clear that] because this is a time of instability, human sorrow exceeds all imagination. If this is a world where we can surely die at once if we want to die, why have I lived on until now? Quite simply, the place where I am eager to be born is the Pure Land of utmost bliss, and what I aspire to and long to attain is the undefiled Buddha body. But then, for a person who has, through the wisdom of the Buddha, realized the settled mind that is Other Power [with the awakening] of the one thought-moment of taking refuge, what could be lacking that he would hasten the time of death established in a previous life (having reached the point of devoting himself until life's end to the saying of the Name in grateful return for the Buddha's benevolence)? To the contrary, he might be foolishly deluded. Such is the reflection of this foolish old man. Others, too, should be of this mind. The way of the world is, above all, that we continue on as if unaware of the uncertainty of life for young and old alike. Existence is as ephemeral as a flash of lightning or the morning dew, and the wind of impermanence may come even now. Yet we think only of prolonging this life for as long as possible, without ever aspiring to [birth in the Pure Land in] the afterlife. This is inexpressibly deplorable. (Minor L.

Rogers and Ann T. Rogers, trans., *Rennyo: The Second Founder of Shin Buddhism* [Berkeley, CA: Asian Humanities Press, 1991], p. 220, fascicle IV-2)

Rennyo
-513- On White Bones
When we deeply consider the transiency of this world, [we realize that] what is altogether fleeting is our own span of life: it is like an illusion from beginning to end. And so we have not yet heard of anyone living ten thousand years. A lifetime passes quickly. Can anyone now live to be a hundred? Will I die first, or will my neighbor? Will it be today or tomorrow? We do not know. Those we leave behind and those who go before us are more numerous than the dewdrops that rest briefly beneath the trees and on their leaf tips. Hence we may have radiant faces in the morning, but in the evening be no more than white bones. With the coming of the wind of impermanence, both eyes are instantly closed, and when a single breath is forever stilled, the radiant face is drained of life, and its vibrant glow is lost. Although family and relatives may gather and grieve broken-heartedly, this is to no avail. As there is nothing else to be done, [the once-familiar form] is taken to an outlying field, and when it has vanished with the midnight smoke nothing is left but white bones. This is indeed indescribably sad. And so, because the impermanence of this world creates a condition of uncertainty for young and old alike, we should all immediately take to heart the most important matter, the afterlife, and, deeply entrusting ourselves to Amida Buddha, say the *nembutsu*. (Minor L. Rogers and Ann T. Rogers, trans., *Rennyo: The Second Founder of Shin Buddhism* [Berkeley, CA: Asian Humanities Press, 1991], p. 255, fascicle V-16; see also -538-)

**b. Equality: Non-discrimination**
Shinran
-514- *Not discriminating at all between the poor and the rich and wellborn*: Not discriminating means not choosing, not rejecting. . . . *Poor* means "impoverished" and "in need." *At all* is for emphasis, meaning "not at all"; it also means "with" and "to lead." *Rich and wellborn* indicates the wealthy and the people of rank. Thus, without in the least differentiating among such people, Amida leads each and every person to the Pure Land.

*Not discriminating between the inferior and the highly gifted*: *Inferior* refers to those whose knowledge is shallow, limited, and slight. *Highly gifted* indicates those with great ability for learning. Amida does not choose between the two.

*Not choosing the learned and those who uphold pure precepts*: *Learned* means to hear and believe in numerous and diverse sacred teachings. (*CWS, Notes on Essentials of Faith Alone*, I, pp. 457-458)

Shinran

-515- That people of the countryside, who do not know the meanings of written characters and who are painfully and hopelessly ignorant, may easily understand, I have repeated the same things over and over. The educated will probably find this writing peculiar and may ridicule it. But paying no heed to such criticisms, I write only that ignorant people may easily grasp the meaning. (*CWS*, *Notes on Essentials of Faith Alone*, I, p. 469; see also *Notes on Once-Calling and Many-Calling*, I, p. 490)

Rennyo

-516- The Shonin said, "To get together, sit around, and talk to each other regardless of different ranks and social status is consistent with (Shinran) Shonin's remark that the people of the world who share the same Faith are all brothers. My sole wish is that if we are sitting together, those who have questions may ask us about the teaching and acquire Faith. (Hisao Inagaki, trans., *Thus Have I Heard From Rennyo Shonin* [Rennyo Shonin's *Goichidai-kikigaki*] [Judet Dolj, Romania: Dharma Lion Publications, 2008], #40, p. 45)

Rennyo

-517- When some members came to Kyoto on cold days, Rennyo Shonin had saké served warm and told them to forget the cold on the way. On hot days, he had saké served cold and consoled them with kind words. He scolded his men when members' visits to Kyoto were announced to him late. He said that it was outrageous to keep visiting members waiting a long time to meet the Shonin. So it is said. (Hisao Inagaki, trans., *Thus Have I Heard From Rennyo Shonin* [Rennyo Shonin's *Goichidaikikigaki*] [Judet Dolj, Romania: Dharma Lion Publications, 2008], #295, p. 126; see also -369-)

## c. Daily Life

Rennyo

-518- First, [realizing] the settled mind in our tradition does not mean that we put a stop to our mind's evil or to rising of delusions and attachment. Simply carry on your trade or position of service, hunt, and fish. For when we realize deeply that Amida *Tathagata*'s Primal Vow promises to save such worthless beings as ourselves, confused morning and evening by evil karma, when we single-heartedly (without any double-mindedness) rely on the compassionate vow of the one Buddha Amida, and when sincere faith is awakened in us with the realization that Amida saves us—then, without fail, we partake of the *Tathagata*'s saving work.

Beyond this, when there is a question as to with what understanding we should say the *nembutsu*, [the answer is that] we are to say the *nembutsu* as long as we live, realizing that it is in gratitude, in return for the gracious benevolence that saves us by giving us the power of entrusting, through which our birth is assured. [Those who do] this are to be called practicers of faith, in whom the settled mind of our tradition is established. (Minor L. Rogers and Ann T. Rogers, trans., *Rennyo: The Second Founder of Shin Buddhism* [Berkeley, CA: Asian Humanities Press, 1991], p. 149, fascicle I-3)

Rennyo

-519- For a long time, people have said uniformly that ours is a ridiculous, degenerate sect. This does indeed point to a certain truth: among those in our tradition, [there are] some who unhesitatingly proclaim our teaching in the presence of those of other schools and other sects. This is a great mistake. Observing our tradition's rules of conduct means keeping firmly to ourselves the teaching transmitted in our tradition and not giving any outward sign of it; those who do this are said to be people of discretion. These days, however, some talk carelessly and without reserve about matters concerning our sect in the presence of those of other schools and other sects; as a result, our tradition is considered shallow. Because there are some with mistaken views, others see our sect as degraded and detestable. We should bear in mind that this is not at all the fault of others, but that it is the fault of our own people.

Next, as for the matter of avoiding things that are impure and inauspicious, it is established that in our tradition, within the Buddha-*dharma*, we do not regard any particular thing as taboo. But are there not things that we should avoid in regard to other sects and the civil authorities? Of course, in the presence of those of other sects and other schools, there are certainly things to be avoided. Further, we should not criticize what others avoid. (Minor L. Rogers and Ann T. Rogers, trans., *Rennyo: The Second Founder of Shin Buddhism* [Berkeley, CA: Asian Humanities Press, 1991], pp. 158-159, fascicle I-9)

## d. Licensed Evil

Shinran

-520- If a person, justifying himself by saying he is a foolish being, can do anything he wants, then is he also to steal or to murder? Even that person who has been inclined to steal will naturally undergo a change of heart if he comes to say the *nembutsu* aspiring for the land of bliss. Yet people who show no such sign are being told that it is permissible to do wrong; this should never occur under any circumstances.

Maddened beyond control by blind passions, we do things we should not and say things we should not and think things we should not. But if a person is deceitful in his relations with others, doing what he should not and saying what he should not because he thinks it will not hinder his birth, then it is not an instance of being maddened by passion. Since he purposely does these things, they are simply misdeeds that should never have been done. (*CWS*, *Lamp for the Latter Ages*, #16, p. 547; see also *CWS*, I, p. 564)

Shinran

-521- You must not do what should not be done, think what should not be thought, or say what should not be said, thinking that you can be born in the Pure Land regardless of it. Human beings are such that, maddened by the passions of greed, we desire to possess; maddened by the passions of anger, we hate that which should not be hated, seeking to go against the law of cause and effect; led astray by the passions of ignorance, we do what should not even be thought. But the person who purposely thinks and does what he or she should not, saying that it is permissible because of the Buddha's wondrous vow to save the foolish being, does not truly desire to reject the world, nor does such a one consciously feel himself a being of karmic evil. Hence such people have no aspiration for the *nembutsu* nor for the Buddha's vow; thus, however they engage in *nembutsu* with such an attitude, it is difficult for them to attain birth in the next life. Please transmit this point fully to the people. There is no need for me to say these things to you, but I write them frankly because you have always shown care and concern for me. (*CWS*, *Lamp for the Latter Ages*, #19, I, pp. 550-551)

Shinran

-522- There was, in those days, a person who had fallen into wrong views. He asserted that since the Vow was made to serve the person who had committed evil, one should purposely do evil as an act for attaining birth. As rumors of misdeeds gradually spread, Shinran wrote in a letter, "Do not take a liking to poison just because there is an antidote." This was in order to put an end to that wrong understanding. It by no means implies that evil can obstruct one's attainment of birth.

He also said, "If it were only by observing precepts and upholding rules that we should entrust ourselves to the Primal Vow, how could we ever gain freedom from birth-and-death?" Even such wretched beings as ourselves, on encountering the Primal Vow, come indeed to "presume" upon it. But even so, how could we commit evil acts without any karmic cause in ourselves? (*CWS*, *A Record in Lament of Divergences*, #13, p. 671)

### e. Practice of Compassion

Shinran

-523- Concerning compassion, there is a difference between the Path of Sages and the Pure Land Path.

Compassion in the Path of Sages is to pity, commiserate with, and care for beings. It is extremely difficult, however, to accomplish the saving of others just as one wishes.

Compassion in the Pure Land Path should be understood as first attaining Buddhahood quickly through saying the *nembutsu* and, with the mind of great love and compassion, freely benefiting sentient beings as one wishes.

However much love and pity we may feel in our present lives, it is hard to save others as we wish; hence, such compassion remains unfulfilled. Only the saying of the *nembutsu*, then, is the mind of great compassion that is thoroughgoing. (*CWS, A Record in Lament of Divergences*, #3, p. 663)

### f. On the Death of Loved Ones
Kakunyo
-524- [On those in mourning]
[This is what Shinran taught:] When you meet someone distraught over the loss of someone dear, recommend to them the medicine of Buddha *dharma*, instruct and guide them in what Buddhism has to tell us at this impasse in our life: Of the eight sufferings of the human realm, there is nothing more painful than that of having to leave our loved ones behind. First, tell them the plain truth: that in this world of birth and death there is no one who lives forever; next, explain to them the condition of the world of peace and sustenance: that though we are caught in misery and suffering, if we do not wish for the Pure Land where there is no misery and suffering, in the future we shall again meet with grief and sorrow. On the other hand, when we leave behind the six paths where "only the screams of suffering are heard" and turn to Amida's Pure Land where "we enter his Nirvana palace" (Shan-tao's *Jozengi* chapter), in this new orientation to our life, the grief and sorrow of the darkness enshrouding us is cleared away, and without knowing it we find ourselves being taken up and brought to benefit from the Light. Next, when you meet someone who is in mourning, the last thing that you want to do is to add more sadness to their existing sadness. When you do this, not only are they mourning, now you are forcing them to become ever lonelier by the minute. Another name for wine is *bo-yu*, meaning "to forget your troubles." Comfort the mourners by having them partake of some wine, leaving them once their smiles have returned. This, then, is how we should treat those in mourning. Keep these points well in mind. (W.S. Yokoyama, *Kakunyo's What Shinran Taught* [*Kudensho*], #18, unpublished translation)

### 2. Personal Confessions
T'an-luan
-525- I have been wandering in the three realms since the beginningless past,
   Turning on the wheel of falsity.
   The karma I commit every moment, every instant,

Is a step bound to the six courses, so that I stay in the three paths.
May the compassionate light protect me
And keep me from losing the mind aspiring for enlightenment.
I praise the voice of the Buddha's wisdom and virtue.
May all beings of the ten quarters having ties with the teaching be
    brought to hear it.
(*CWS*, *Kyogyoshinsho*, I, V:29, p. 196)

Shan-tao

**-526-** (38) I take refuge in the Buddha and repent before him so that my teacher, parents, good friends of the Way, and sentient beings of the universe may destroy the three karmic hindrances and together attain birth in the land of Amida Buddha. . . .

(47) . . . Reverently I announce: May all the Buddhas in the ten quarters, the twelve-divisioned scriptures, all the great *bodhisattvas*, all the holy sages, all the eight groups of demi-gods, including *devas* and dragons, sentient beings in the entire universe, and the audience in the present assembly become my witnesses. I, so and so, confess my offenses and repent them. From the beginningless past up to now, I have killed or destroyed all the members of the three treasures, masters and monks, parents, relatives down to the sixth blood-relation, good teachers of the Way, and sentient beings in the entire universe, whose numbers are beyond calculation. I have stolen property and belongings of all the members of the three treasures, masters and monks, parents, relatives down to the sixth blood-relation, good teachers of the Way, and sentient beings in the entire universe, whose numbers are beyond calculation. I have approached with lascivious thoughts all the members of the three treasures, masters and monks, parents, relatives down to the sixth blood-relation, good teachers of the Way, and sentient beings in the entire universe, whose numbers are beyond calculation. I have deceived with lies all the members of the three treasures, masters and monks, parents, relatives down to the sixth blood-relation, good teachers of the Way, and sentient beings in the entire universe, whose numbers are beyond calculation. I have ridiculed with insincere words all the members of the three treasures, masters and monks, parents, relatives down to the sixth blood-relation, good teachers of the Way, sentient beings in the entire universe, whose numbers are beyond calculation. I have calumniated, abused, and rebuked with harsh words all the members of the three treasures, masters and monks, parents, relatives down to the sixth blood-relation, good teachers of the Way, and sentient beings in the entire universe, whose numbers are beyond calculation. I have caused enmity and mutual destruction with calumnious words among all the members of the three treasures, masters and monks, parents, relatives down to the sixth blood-relation, good teachers of the Way, sentient

beings in the entire universe, whose numbers are beyond calculation. I have broken all the precepts and rules of conduct, including the five precepts, eight precepts of abstinence, ten precepts of good acts, two hundred and fifty precepts, five hundred precepts, threefold precepts for *bodhisattvas*, and tenfold inexhaustible precepts; not only have I broken these precepts, but also I have incited others to break them, and rejoiced at seeing them do so—this I have repeated uncountable times.

Such transgressions are innumerable, just as the great earth extending in the ten directions is boundless and the number of dust-particles is incalculable. Just as the open space is limitless, my offenses are equally limitless. Just as the means of salvation are boundless, my offenses are boundless. Just as the *Dharma*-nature is boundless, my offenses are boundless. Just as the *Dharma*-realm is boundless, my offenses are boundless.

Since sentient beings are innumerable, my offenses of robbery and manslaughter are innumerable. Since the members of the three treasures are innumerable, my offenses of destruction, theft, and killing are innumerable. Since the precepts provided are innumerable, my breach of them has been repeated innumerable times.

Any one of the sages, from *bodhisattvas* down to *shravakas* and *pratyeka-buddhas*, cannot know the extent of my offenses. Only the Buddha knows it.

Now, before the three treasures and sentient beings of the entire universe, I confess and repent my offenses, without hiding them. I pray that all the members of the three treasures throughout the ten quarters and sentient beings of the entire universe recognize my repentance and wish that I will be purified of the offenses. From today on, together with sentient beings, I wish to abandon wrong views and take right ones, awaken the *bodhi*-mind, see each other with a compassionate heart, look at each other with the eye of the Buddha, become a companion of *bodhi*, become a true teacher of the Way, attain birth in Amida Buddha's land together, discontinue committing those offenses forever, and never commit them again.

Having thus repented, I take refuge in Amida Buddha with sincerity of heart. (Hisao Inagaki, trans., *Shan-tao's Liturgy for Birth* [*Ojoraisan*], http://www12.canvas.ne.jp/horai/raisan.htm)

Genshin

-527- The teaching which shows how to obtain birth into Paradise and the easy way of training for becoming a Buddha, is for the sinners of this dark world just as easy as seeing with one's eyes or walking with one's feet. As it is such a blessed teaching, shall not all who seek with an earnest heart enter this way priests and laymen, men and women, the noble and the ignoble, the wise and the foolish? Only the revealed and the hidden teachings are comprehensive, and the causes and circumstances and the religious disciplines are numerous, but these are not difficult for the clever and wise who can easily understand things. But what about myself, one who is only a foolish man? I cannot comprehend these difficult things and walk in this hard way. That is why I have turned to the one gate of nembutsu. I have now peace of heart and so have decided to set forth briefly in outline the teaching of the scriptures in regard to this matter. This should prove a help for easily understanding and for putting the teachings in practice. (A.K. Reischauer, "Genshin's *Ojo Yoshu*: Collected Essays on Birth into Paradise," *The Transactions of the Asiatic Society of Japan* [December 1930], Second Series, Vol. VII, p. 25)

Shinran

-528- Although I take refuge in the true Pure Land way,
    It is hard to have a true and sincere mind.
    This self is false and insincere;
    I completely lack a pure mind.
    Each of us, in outward bearing,
    Makes a show of being wise, good, and dedicated;
    But so great are our greed, anger, perversity, and deceit,
    That we are filled with all forms of malice and cunning.
    Extremely difficult is it to put an end to our evil nature;
    The mind is like a venomous snake or scorpion.
    Our performance of good acts is also poisoned;
    Hence, it is called false and empty practice.
    Although I am without shame and self-reproach
    And lack a mind of truth and sincerity,
    Because the Name is directed by Amida,
    Its virtues fill the ten quarters.
    Lacking even small love and small compassion,
    I cannot hope to benefit sentient beings.
    Were it not for the ship of Amida's Vow,
    How could I cross the ocean of painful existence?
    With minds full of malice and cunning, like snakes and scorpions,
    We cannot accomplish good acts through self-power;
    And unless we entrust ourselves to Amida's directing of virtue,
    We will end without knowing shame or self-reproach.
    As a mark of increase in the five defilements,
    All monks and laypeople of this age
    Behave outwardly like followers of the Buddhist teaching,
    But in their inner thoughts, believe in non-Buddhist paths.
    (*CWS, Hymns of the Dharma-Ages,* I, pp. 421-422, #94-100)

Shinran

-529- While persons ignorant of even the characters for "good" and "evil"
   All possess a sincere mind,
   I make a display of knowing the words "good" and "evil";
   This is an expression of complete falsity.

   I am such that I do not know right and wrong
   And cannot distinguish false and true;
   I lack even small love and small compassion,
   And yet, for fame and profit, enjoy teaching others.
   (*CWS, Hymns of the Dharma-Ages*, I, p. 429, #115-116)

Shinran

-530- I know nothing at all of good or evil. For if I could know thoroughly, as Amida *Tathagata* knows, that an act was good, then I would know good. If I could know thoroughly, as the *Tathagata* knows, that an act was evil, then I would know evil. But with a foolish being full of blind passions, in this fleeting world—this burning house—all matters without exception are empty and false, totally without truth and sincerity. The *nembutsu* alone is true and real. (*CWS, A Record in Lament of Divergences*, postscript, I, p. 679)

Shinran

-531- I know truly how grievous it is that I, Gutoku Shinran, am sinking in an immense ocean of desires and attachments and am lost in vast mountains of fame and advantage; so that I rejoice not at all at entering the stage of the truly settled and feel no happiness at coming nearer the realization of true enlightenment. How ugly it is! How wretched! (*CWS, Teaching, Practice, and Realization*, I, p. 125)

Kakunyo

-532- For the sake of our impending birth in the Pure Land, true entrusting (*shinjin*) comes first and foremost; pay no heed to the rest. When it comes to that one great matter of our impending Birth, [however,] there is nothing that the *bombu* has to especially figure out; simply leave everything to the *Tathagata*. This stipulation is not limited to the *bombu* alone; there is nothing even for Maitreya *Bodhisattva*, who is first as far as the mystery of Buddha wisdom goes, to figure out—how much more so for the wisdom-deficient *bombu*. To my mind we should leave all to the promise of the *Tathagata*. This is the seeker who, subscribing to Other-Power, has actively received true entrusting. As a result, whether I am to make my way to the Pure Land, or whether I am bound for hell, is not within my power to determine. In the words of the late Shonin (Genku [Honen] Shonin of Kurodani),

"Tell yourself that wherever Genku goes, I go," is something I distinctly recall him telling me; that even if he were to go to hell, wherever that place may be I am inclined to follow. On this round of life, should we not meet with a spiritual guide, we *bombu* would surely fall into hell. But having received the guidance of the Shonin (Genku), having heard of Amida's true vow, the principle of receiving all and rejecting none has become lodged in my heart, and leaving behind the (realm of) birth-and-death so difficult to leave behind, I can look forward to being born in the Pure Land so difficult to attain with certainty, even though I have not the least power to bring it about on my own. But suppose that my taking refuge in Amida's Buddha-wisdom and saying the *nembutsu* was the very act for landing me in hell; what if I were tricked by Honen who told me that this was the activating cause for my impending birth in the Pure Land? Even if I were to fall into hell, even then I would not regret it in the least. My reasoning is this: if my life had come to an end before meeting this wonderful teacher, I was a person who was destined to evil paths. But if I were deceived by my spiritual guide and were to end up on evil paths, I would not be traversing them alone; I would have my teacher to accompany me. Thus, even if I were told that this is the path leading to hell, I am obliged to follow it if I know that is where the late Shonin has gone, for whether I am born in a place that is good or bad is something that is not in my power to decide. (W.S. Yokoyama, *Kakunyo's Embracing the Name*, #2, unpublished translation; see also -426-; -427-)

## 3. Karma

### T'an-luan

-533- Regarding the phrase "the manifestation of true merit," there are two kinds of merit:

(1) The merit which accrues from the activity of a defiled mind and is not in accord with the *Dharma*-nature: Such merit arises from the various good acts of ordinary men and heavenly beings. It also refers to the reward of human and heavenly states of existence. Both the cause and effect of such good acts are inverted and false; hence they are called false merit.

(2) The merit which is produced from the wisdom and pure karma of *Bodhisattvas* and which serves to glorify Buddhist action: It conforms to the *Dharma*-nature and has the characteristic of purity. This *Dharma* is not inverted and false; hence it is called "true merit." Why is it not inverted? Because it conforms to the *Dharma*-nature and agrees with the twofold reality. Why is it not false? Because it leads sentient beings to Ultimate Purity. (Hisao Inagaki, trans., *T'an-Luan's Commentary on Vasubandhu's Discourse on the Pure Land [Ojoronchu]* [Kyoto: Nagata Bunshodo, 1998], p. 135; see also *CWS, Kyogyoshinsho*, I, p. 29, II:19)

T'an-luan

-534- He (the Buddha) saw that, in a certain land, there were persons of great fame and high rank who could not live in seclusion [even if they wished to] and also there were ordinary men of humble birth who had no means of rising in the world. Length of life being determined by one's karma, it cannot be controlled as one wishes. . . . People such as these are thus at the mercy of the wind of karma and do not have control [over their destiny]. For this reason, the Buddha made a Vow, resolving, "in my Land people will have their wishes granted and their aspirations fulfilled." (Hisao Inagaki, trans., *T'an-Luan's Commentary on Vasubandhu's Discourse on the Pure Land* [*Ojoronchu*] [Kyoto: Nagata Bunshodo, 1998], pp. 168-169)

Tao-ch'o

-535- Karmas that bind one to the three worlds and acquisition of the fruit of birth in the Pure Land:

Question 1: Since eternally-long *kalpas* ago, all sentient beings have produced innumerable kinds of defiled karma, thereby being bound to the three worlds. If, as you say, without severing the karma which ties you to the three worlds, you attain birth in the Pure Land by applying yourself to mindfulness of Amida Buddha and escape from the three worlds, what will happen to the karma which would bind you there?

Answer: There are two explanations: one is a theoretical clarification and the other is an explanation by parables. The former is that Buddhas, *Tathagatas*, have inconceivable wisdom, boundless Mahayana wisdom, and incomparable, unequaled, unsurpassed supreme wisdom.

(Hisao Inagaki, trans., "Tao-ch'o's *An-le-chi*," 3:22-1, pp. 1-2, unpublished translation)

Tao-ch'o

-536- Question 2: A Mahayana sutra states, "The law of karma is like a balance; a heavier object pulls it down." Sentient beings in their lives, a hundred years (at the longest) or ten years (at the shortest), until this day, commit all kinds of evil. How can they, after meeting a good teacher on their deathbeds, repeat the *nembutsu* for ten times and, thereby, attain birth in the Pure Land? If this actually happens, how could we place our faith in the teaching that a heavier karma pulls one down?

Answer: You consider the bondage of karma as heavy and the good acts of ten repetitions of *nembutsu* by a man of the lowest grade as light. Now, let us study this matter in the light of Buddhist principles.

Whether an act creates dominant karmic force or not is dependent on: 1) the state of mind, 2) the object, and 3) the degree of concentration, and not by the length of time.

1) The state of mind: The evil-doer in question has committed offences in a false and perverted state of mind, whereas the ten repetitions of the *nembutsu* arise when he hears the teaching of Truth from a good teacher who consoles him by various skillful means. One is truthful and the other false. How can they be compared to each other? Suppose there is a room which has been dark for a thousand years. If a light is cast into the room even for a short while, the room will instantly become bright. How could the darkness refuse to leave because it has been there for a thousand years? (Hisao Inagaki, trans., "Tao-ch'o's *An-le-chi*," 3:22-1, p. 3, unpublished translation)

Genshin

-537- Among all winds the wind of karma is the strongest, and it is in this way that the wind of karma of men's evil deeds drags them to their doom. After they reach this place Emma-O tortures them in various ways. Then binding them with the rope of evil karma he drags them toward this hell. From afar the victims catch sight of the raging flames of this hell of the great scorching heat as they belch forth. When they hear the cries of the victims who are already in this hell they are filled with sorrow and fear, and as they come gradually nearer they behold their immeasurable torments. And when they learn that this torture continues for immeasurable hundred thousand times ten thousand hundred millions of years the terror that enters their hearts becomes ten times greater than it was when they had merely heard the wailings of the victims. Then the hell warden, taking each sinner separately, torments him saying: "Are you frightened as you hear the cries and see with your eyes? How much more then will you be terror-stricken when your body is burning like dry grass and tinder! However, the burning by fire here is not that of a literal fire but rather the hot passion of your evil karma. The burning of fire may be extinguished, but the burning of evil karma cannot be put out." (A.K. Reischauer, "Genshin's *Ojo Yoshu*: Collected Essays on Birth into Paradise," *The Transactions of the Asiatic Society of Japan* [December 1930], Second Series, Vol. VII, p. 39)

Genshin

-538- We may take, for example, the life of a man who, let us say, has accumulated good karma throughout a long life, a man cared for by many children and grandchildren who one day enjoy the flower festival and on another day gather to view the moon. They dearly love him with deep filial piety so that others envy him and say: "What a happy man he must be!" But even though he may be happy in this way, still in accordance with the law of the impermanence of things this happiness cannot last. If one or two of his children die he is saddened because they precede him in death and his long life becomes a burden to him. Henceforth he sheds the tears of old age. His body gradually declines in strength and at last becomes a vehicle of impermanency, and he is made a lonely man. He continues to feel sad. Wealth may fill his coffers and he may have a magnificent house with a roof facing east and west and with a far view toward the north and south. The pleasant song of a beautiful woman and the sunshine of spring may charm him. He may be entertained by the dancing of beautiful women whose long sleeves are spread out by the breezes, or he may be fascinated with the autumn scenery; yet all these things pass away with time, the man changes and all becomes but as a dream of yesterday. (A.K. Reischauer, "Genshin's *Ojo Yoshu*: Collected Essays on Birth into Paradise," *The Transactions of the Asiatic Society of Japan* [December 1930], Second Series, Vol. VII, pp. 55-56)

Honen

-539- Regarding "deep faith in [karmic] causality," there are two kinds: one is [faith] in the law of worldly cause and effect, and the other is [faith] in cause and effect that transcends this world. Worldly cause and effect is that of the six paths, as is explained in the *Sutra of Correct Dharma Thought*. Cause and effect that transcends the world is [karmic] cause and effect relevant to the four kinds of holy people, as explained in the sutras of both the Mahayana and the Hinayana. . . .

In this manner, the phrase "deep faith in cause and effect" pervades all the teachings of the Buddha throughout his whole life. For all those who seek birth in the Pure Land, even though they fail to perform the other practices, deep faith in cause and effect can become a karmic action for birth. (*Senchakushu* English Translation Project, *Honen's Senchakushu: Passages on the Selection of the Nembutsu in the Original Vow* [*Senchaku Hongan Nembutsu Shu*] [Honolulu, HI: University of Hawaii Press, p. 129)

Honen

-540- Amida Buddha will transform one's unsettled karma for attaining birth in the Pure Land into the definitely settled karma for birth in the Pure Land and welcome one to the Pure Land if one exclusively relies on Him with a singleness of heart. This is more meritorious for attaining birth in the Pure Land than thoughtlessly invoking Buddhas or gods without knowing that the length of one's life and the depth of one's penalty for previous acts are due to one's residual karma.

To pray for a good fortune in this ephemeral world and forgetting crucial deliverance in the next life are not the true meaning for *nembutsu* devotees. Amida Buddha designed *nembutsu* as the "rightly established practice" for birth in the Pure Land in the life to come; therefore, one should not ignore *nembutsu* and observe other practices. For this reason, I encourage you to recite *nembutsu*. (Joji Atone, Yoko Hayashi, trans., *The Promise of Amida Buddha: Honen's Path to Bliss* [Boston: Wisdom Publications, 2011], p. 365)

Honen

-541- . . . This passage means: There are some people who become enraged upon seeing the *nembutsu* practitioner who aspires to birth in the Pure Land. They also become overwhelmed with malicious thoughts, formulate a plan, utilize misguided schemes in order to undermine the practice of *nembutsu*, and fight to outdo each other in their impious deeds to cause a suspension of the practice of *nembutsu*. These people are referred to as "people with no intrinsic goodness" (Skt. *icchantika*) who since birth lack the ability to understand the teachings of Buddha Sakyamuni and the seed for the attainment of Buddhahood.

If they would vilify and destroy this *nembutsu* teaching of instantaneous enlightenment [that is, to detach immediately from the perpetual transmigration of the delusive realms and to live eternally in the Pure Land through the recitation of the name of Amida Buddha], they will fall into the three lower realms for an extremely long time and will not extricate themselves from the three lower realms due to the gravity of their karmic transgressions. The sutras state that these people will not escape the three lower realms for innumerable eons. In one view, such people who would scheme to spread untruths should be rather pitied. To preach to a person like this who doubts *nembutsu* and becomes distrustful of the teaching would nonetheless be in vain.

As a rule, one whose karmic relationship with Amida Buddha is shallow and who has not thought as far as birth in the Pure Land, will not believe what he hears about the teaching of *nembutsu*, will fume on witnessing its practice, and in anger would try to impede the practice of *nembutsu*. Bear this in your mind, and despite what people say, maintain a stalwart heart.

The power of Amida Buddha is ineffective on those who do not believe in birth in the Pure Land through *nembutsu* at all; the word of a common mortal is even more ineffective. If you are compassionate toward nonbelievers and desire to help them attain birth in the Pure Land, you yourself must first attain birth in the Pure Land immediately. After achieving enlightenment there, return to this delusive world of transmigration and lead those who criticize and do not believe in the teaching of *nembutsu* to achieve birth in the Pure Land, thus saving all sentient beings. Remember this well. (Joji Atone, Yoko Hayashi, trans., *The Promise of Amida Buddha: Honen's Path to Bliss* [Boston: Wisdom Publications, 2011], pp. 236-237)

Seikaku

-542- Next, people often say: "Even if I entrust myself to the power of Amida's vow and aspire to be born in the land of bliss, it is difficult to know my defiled karma from past lives. . . . Thus, although we have received birth into human life now, we may possess the karma for the evil paths without our knowing. If the power of such karma is strong and brings about birth into the evil courses, will it not be difficult to attain birth in the Pure Land?"

Although the sense of this is quite sound, such people are unable to sever the net of doubt and create deluded views by themselves. Karma, more or less, may be compared to a scale. It tips towards the heavier weight. If the power of my karma for birth in the evil courses were strong, then I would not have been born into human life but would have fallen first into the evil paths. This much is clear from having already received birth into human life: though we may possess karma for evil courses, that karma is weaker than the observance of the five precepts which brought about our birth into human life. If this is so, such karma cannot obstruct even the five precepts; how could it obstruct the virtue of ten utterances? . . . The virtue of the *nembutsu*, moreover, is superior to even the ten precepts and surpasses all the good of the three worlds. . . . Evil karma does not obstruct even the five precepts, it can never be an obstacle to birth. (*CWS, Essentials of Faith Alone* [Seikaku], I, pp. 695-696)

Seikaku
-543- We lack a pure heart, however, so we know that our past good is minimal. But though our karmic evil is heavy, we do not commit the five grave offenses, and though our good acts are few, we deeply entrust ourselves to the Primal Vow. Even the ten utterances of someone guilty of the five grave offenses comes about through that person's past good. How could it be, then, that the saying of the Name throughout one's life is not also due to one's past good? (*CWS, Essentials of Faith Alone* [Seikaku], I, p. 696)

Shinran
-544- Karmic evil is from the beginning without real form;
    It is the result of delusional thought and invertedness.
    Mind-nature is from the beginning pure,
    But as for this world, there is no person of truth.
    (*CWS, Hymns of the Dharma-Ages*, I, p. 423, #107)

Shinran
-545- Evil karma is profound: evil people who have committed the ten transgressions or the five grave offenses, people of evil karma who have reviled the teaching or who lack seeds for Buddhahood, those of scant roots of good, those of massive karmic evil, those of shallow inclination to good, those of profound attachment to evil—such wretched men as these, profound in various kinds of evil karma, are described by the word profound. Profound

means bottomless. Good people, bad people, noble and low, are not differentiated in the vow of the Buddha of unhindered light, in which the guiding of each person is primary and fundamental. Know that the true essence of the Pure Land teaching (*Jodo Shinshu*) is that when we realize true and real *shinjin*, we are born in the true fulfilled land. (*CWS, Notes on Essentials of Faith Alone*, I, p. 458)

Shinran
-546- In the Reverend of Komyoji [Shan-tao] commentary on the meaning of the *Larger Sutra of Infinite Life*'s Eighteenth Vow of *nembutsu*-birth, it says, "When ordinary beings, both good and bad (or evil), attain birth, it never takes place without their riding on the activating power of Amida Buddha's great Vow as the leading condition." What this means is that, although you might regard yourself as a good person, it does not mean you will be granted your wish to be born in Amida Buddha's reward land on the basis of the good you have to your name.

[Such good karma] also does not have any consequence to speak of for the bad person. Though you may wish to deflect the power of your bad karma from drawing you into rebirth in the three evil destinies or four realms, [your good karma] is not sufficient to effect your birth in the reward land. Thus, you are caught in the position where your good karma is not sufficient to put you in good stead, nor is it sufficient to undo the effects of your bad karma. For the good person's impending birth, it is virtually impossible for [their wish] to come true without Amida *Tathagata*'s special vow whose great affection (*ji*) and great feeling (*hi*) transcend this world. As for the evil person's impending birth, while those who wish [for impending birth] assume they have no hope of ever being considered by the reward Buddha for the reward land, in order to bring forth the marvelous power of the mystery of Buddha-wisdom [Amida Buddha] spent five *kalpas* meditating on it and long *kalpas* putting it into practice, and with regard to the shallow (wretched) beings, who have no other choice than to be immersed in the six destinies and four forms of birth and have no chance to ever float to the surface, he took special consideration of them, so as to impress upon them the message that your having bad karma is no reason for you to disparage yourself. Thus, if you cannot put yourself aside and truly submit yourself to reverencing the Buddha-wisdom, you find that having bad karma is where you come up short as far as [cinching] the cause of birth in the Pure Land. Clearly if [our having bad karma] is not for the sole purpose of preventing our sinking into the three miserable paths and four realms where we are [forever] being drawn into by the evil causes of the ten evils, five transgressions, four grave wrongs, and slander of the *dharma*, then of what use is it? But, if good is not a seed [cause] for our being born in the land of ultimate bliss, then neither is it of any use for our impending birth, and if what I have stated for evil also holds true, then these are merely the good and bad [karma] that accompany people when they are born [into this world]. If we are ever to hope for that Land, we must come to accept the fact that it cannot be done without our submitting ourselves to Other-Power. On this basis Shan-tao comments, "When ordinary beings, both good and evil, attain birth, it is due [solely] to the activating power of the great vow." When he says that "there is nothing that surpasses this leading condition" he means that there is nothing that surpasses Amida's promise next to which all other things pale by comparison. (W.S. Yokoyama, *Kakunyo's Embracing the Name*, #3, unpublished translation)

Shoku

-547- When a person possesses the three minds (*sanjin*) which the Original Vow calls for, his or her *nembutsu* repetitions guarantee all the benefits of someone who is embraced by Amida. To explain more fully what I mean by Amida's embrace, this relation can be spoken of as intimate, close, and superior. By intimate karmic relation (*shin-en*), I mean that Amida takes us into his embrace no matter how dull or ignorant we may be. This was the very purpose he had for accomplishing enlightenment for himself. The light which streams from his being finds nothing it cannot penetrate. None of the virtues which flow from Amida Buddha's thoughts, words, and actions can fail to affect us, no matter how immersed we may be in affliction and bad karma. This is the reason that when we call, he hears; when we pray, he sees; and when we meditate, he knows, and unfailingly leads us to birth in the Pure Land, regardless of the good or bad in our hearts, as long as we continue to put our trust in him. This is why Shan-tao says that the three acts of Amida Buddha exactly agree with the three acts of the wayfarer. They are inextricably interrelated.

By close karmic relation (*kin-en*), I mean that when this intimacy between us and Amida has reached its height, not only does he know all about our actions, words, and thoughts, but we come to know the significance of his actions, words, and thoughts on our behalf. So if we long to see him, he actually appears at our side in a dream or at life's last hour.

By superior karmic relation (*zojo-en*), I mean the results which flow from the actions set in motion by the preceding two. As Shan-tao says, "All sentient beings who call upon his name will shed all the karma for which they should suffer throughout countless *kalpas* time. When they draw near to life's end, Amida Buddha and his retinue will come to welcome them, and all their inherited hindering karmic relations are dispelled. This is what we call superior karmic relation. (Jonathan Watts, Yoshiharu Tomatsu, eds.,

*Traversing the Pure Land Way: A Lifetime of Encounters with Honen Shonin*
[Tokyo: Jodo-shu Press, 2005], pp. 116-118)

Kakunyo

-548- On good karma and bad karma:

The Shonin (Shinran) once told us, "As for me I have neither a desire for good nor a fear of evil. The reason I have no desire for good is, there is no good that can surpass that of having received the faith, 'to receive the message' of Amida's true vow. The reason I fear no evil is, there is no evil that can prevent [the working of] Amida's true vow. All the same, people in this world think, 'I've got to stock up on my supply of good karma, for unless I have enough *nembutsu* there is no impending birth.' Or, they think, 'Even though I do the *nembutsu*, my evil karma is so deep and grave there is no impending birth in store for me.' We should never let ourselves fall into either one of these extreme views.

"If it were possible for us to dispense with our bad karma at will and to load ourselves with a stock of good karma to our heart's desire, and thus leave behind the cycle of birth and death and embark on the journey to birth in the Pure Land, then we do not have to know the slightest thing about the true vow, for there is nothing we are particularly in need of. As we are unable to leave either one to our hearts to take care of, as to evil karma we keep on producing more even as we live in fear of it, and as to good karma we can't get enough to be sure we've gotten all we need—such is the plight of the *bombu*. In order to take such shallow, evil-ridden beings like us, who are stocked full of the three poisons, who have ample [bad karma] and not enough [good karma] to make good our escape [from *samsara*], [the Buddha] contemplated his true Vow for five *kalpas*, so that all that is needed is for us to turn to [this Buddha vow] to receive the message, "to receive the faith" of Buddha wisdom. But, people have the idea that if the good person does the *nembutsu* their impending birth is a sure thing, but when it is an evil-ridden person who says the *nembutsu*, people have doubts, and think the impending birth of such a person is uncertain. These people have here lost sight of the design of the vow, and seem to have no idea of their own amply evil-ridden self. That is, it is through unconditional compassion that takes up and welcomes the *bombu*, equally allowing those aboard the five vehicles to enter the reward land, awarded to this Buddha who has made a special vow for which the cultivating of the cause and the receiving of the effect are already done. This amounts to a vow of transcendental mystery that none of the other Buddhas have yet to make. For instance, although someone might say he is a good person who has read all the Mahayana scriptures and grasped their ultimate point, no matter how much good he might have made while alive, that alone is not enough to grant his wish to be born in that Land. Moreover, if bad karma is the point where all the Buddhist methods [presuming such a person is hopeless and] simply give up, the evil-ridden person whose bad karma is burgeoning would hardly be the kind that aspires to this Land.

"But, as to the good and bad karma that a person is born with, this of course does not mean that this disqualifies a person from ever attaining birth in the reward land. Thus, other than as a person laden with good and bad karma who is blown away by Amida's Buddha wisdom, how else is the *bombu* to come to attaining birth? Thus it is said, "Our bad karma is not to be feared, nor should we desire to have good karma." Adhering to this [view] the great Master of Komyoji (Shan-tao) says, (in the *Gengi-bun*): 'The all-embracing vow is as explained in the *Larger Sutra*. Every *bombu*, with their good and bad karma, who attains birth, does so through the superior condition of riding on the karmic power of Amida Buddha's great vow.' Thus, 'Those who are born with a thick layer of good karma will prefer to do good in this life and will abhor evil, while those who are born with a thick layer of bad karma will prefer to do evil in this life and will ignore good. Simply leave these two—the good karma and the bad karma—to past causes, and leave the great benefit of impending birth to the Buddha's Other-Power, for it is not up to our judgment who is good or bad so that we can determine who will attain birth or not.'"

In this regard, [Shinran] once said, "You [menfolk, listen to me], there is a way to attain birth that is even easier than doing the *nembutsu* that I want to confer on you." And he said, "If you go out and kill a thousand people you will easily be born—this is the teaching that all of you must follow. What do you say?" At that time there was one person who protested, saying, "As for me it boggles the mind to think of a thousand when I can't find it in me to kill even a single person." The Shonin (Shinran) continued, "Although you do not turn your back on our teachings in the course of the day, you have decided to doubt the instruction that I have just set forth. However, your statement that 'I can't find it in me to kill even a single person' is because there is no past [karmic] cause. If there was such a cause in your past, even if someone were to admonish you saying, 'It is wrong to take life, and if you commit that crime, you will be barred from impending birth,' if the seed cause is part of your [karmic] makeup then you will most certainly commit the crime of taking life. Here the two, our good karma and bad karma, as the determination of the causes we are born with, are making themselves felt. However, it is absolutely the case that, as to our impending birth, the stockpiling of good does not save us, nor does our evil interfere [with our being saved]; take note of this." (W.S. Yokoyama, *Kakunyo's What Shinran Taught* [*Kudensho*], #4, unpublished translation)

Kakunyo

-549- When our Founding Master (Shinran) Shonin was alive, he constantly commented on this situation which persisted among his direct disciples. At that time he instructed us, saying, "The warm family relations maintained between mother and child and those closest to us are of the sort that we should nurture, but they exist only because the past karma we bear inside of us allows them to exist; when the time comes for us to leave our loved ones behind, we have no choice but to cast off those ties and depart. When the time has run out for those karmic ties, although we may wish to stay close to our loved ones and want to be taken along, our wishes are not granted. How much more so does this apply to our fellow travelers and companions, who have only their *bombu* (mortal) powers to call upon that can neither determine whether they stay close to their companions and spiritual teachers or part from them. Though you meet someone with whom you want to live your whole life, when the karmic ties run out you grow estranged and distant; though you meet someone whom you are not especially fond of, unless those karmic ties run out, you may end up living your whole life in their company. All of this is due to our past karmic causes and conditions, and is not just a matter of our life in this one world. Again, on the one hand, the reason that a person who has good past karma comes round to being on intimate terms with a *zenchishiki* (spiritual guide) who can explain the true *dharma* is, that, even without being invited to do so, such a person gravitates toward the light of *dharma* which never leads a person astray. If we were to posit a reason why a person who does not have good past karma, even without being invited to do so, will on his own account naturally gravitate toward wicked friends and will be distant from the *zenchishiki* (the good friend), it might well have to do in part with the surfacing of the inadequacy of the *zenchishiki*. As to whether an initiate's fortune turns out well or not, in addition to whether or not they have good past karma, there is also the much more basic matter of whether teacher and disciple are suited for one another. However, since this principle is often kept in the dark, the first thing that becomes operative is our self-attachment, and as we tend to forget the existence of past karmic connections, we start to engage in arguments over whether this person belongs among our fellow travelers or someone else's; this reaches such foolish and inane heights that everything the Buddhas and founders have done for us become a stumbling block; know well that such nonsense will not be tolerated." (W.S. Yokoyama, *Kakunyo's Setting the Claims Straight* [*Gaijasho*], #8, unpublished translation)

Kakunyo

-550- That, those people who call themselves the members of the school of the same Founder (Shinran) are fond of saying, "We deny there is such a thing as [karmic] cause and effect; this is groundless." Now, in the three sutras, when we seek out this famous phrase, there is the passage in the *Contemplation Sutra*, "to deeply believe in cause and effect." How are we to regard this passage? Generally it is said that there is a single unified principle in the transmission from our Founder, the Shonin (Shinran), that does not discriminate between the three sutras; however, the *Contemplation Sutra* introduces the true model of the person and patently expresses the *Dharma* that applies to it as the good derived from meditation and good deeds. In this transmission, however, the so-called true model of the person is patterned after the woman of the five impediments and the wicked person, the prime example of which is Vaidehi. The *Larger Sutra of Infinite Life* introduces the "manifested Person," and its *Dharma* applies to the same audience of listeners. It speaks of the mystery of [the Vow] necessarily coming to the rescue of the foolish being. The transmission of the great master [Shinran] Shonin lies exclusively in the *Larger Sutra*. The fact that [Shinran] does not adopt the *Contemplation Sutra*'s set explanation of "deep belief in cause and effect" indicates that he was not entirely satisfied with it. For instance, even if we were to accept this Sutra at face value, the disparity between its principle [and our reality] would be so great as to render it meaningless. For that reason this Sutra's "deep belief in cause and effect" is classified under the three happy acts (leading a moral life, upholding precepts, doing good deeds). The three happy acts are in turn the imperfect [unenlightened karmic] acts that lead to our birth among humans and *devas*. Thus by what reach of the imagination can the *bombu* rely on the principle of "deep belief in cause and effect" and expect to realize birth [in the Pure Land]? Firstly, with regard to the ten evils, it is said, "Those on the highest level who commit evils fall into the way of hell; those who offend on the middle rank fall into the way of hungry ghosts; those who offend on the lower rank fall into the way of beasts."

This is a set feature of Mahayana [Buddhism]. If those who are presently *bombu* were to dwell on the "cause" giving rise to their patent offenses, they would sense in them the effect up to now, and would realize they stand on the brink of falling into the paths leading to the three evil realms. Though someone has now won for themselves the effective reward of a place among the humans or *devas* in the heavens above, unless they master the five precepts or the ten goods perfectly, how can they possibly pin their hopes [on a good result in the next life]. How can they possibly imagine that what they are doing captures the principle of birth in the reward land of the kingdom of reward where one enjoys the immaculate [enlightened] state of birthlessness transcending the triple world? (W.S. Yokoyama, *Kakunyo's Setting the Claims Straight* [*Gaijasho*], #17, unpublished translation)

Rennyo

-551- Junsei said to the Shonin, "It is stated in the Letters that at the time of awakening the single thought of *shinjin*, one's karmic evils are all destroyed and one attains the Rightly Established State, or the State of Non-retrogression. However, you have just said that as long as one lives, one is bound to commit evils. Your remark sounds different from what is stated in the Letters."

The Shonin replied, "When it is stated that one's karmic evils are all canceled at the moment of awakening a single thought of *shinjin*, it means that one's birth is settled by the power of the single thought of *shinjin* and that one's transgressions do not create hindrance to birth; therefore, they are as good as non-existent. As long as we live in the *saha* world, our karmic evils are not exhausted. Are you, Junsei, already enlightened and so are you free of transgressions? It is stated in the scriptures that one's karmic evils are canceled at the moment of awakening a single thought of *shinjin*. You should ask yourself over and over again whether you have attained *shinjin* or not, instead of questioning whether you still have karmic evils or not. It is up to Amida to save you after he has destroyed your karmic evils or to save you while leaving them as they stand. You should not inquire into this problem. Remember that *shinjin* is of paramount importance." Thus the Shonin emphatically stated. (Hisao Inagaki, trans., *Thus Have I Heard From Rennyo Shonin* [*Rennyo Shonin's Goichidaikikikigaki*] [Judet Dolj, Romania: Dharma Lion Publications, 2008], #35, p. 43)

Rennyo

-552- "There are bright and dark moods in the world. The flowers favored by the bright mood bloom earlier and those in shade bloom late. Similarly, there are time differences in the maturation of stored good. This explains why there are people who attained birth in the past, those who attain birth at the present, and those who will attain birth in the future. When encountering Amida's light, some people's stored good blooms earlier and some others blooms late. At any rate, whether *shinjin* is firmly established or not, you should endeavor to hear the Buddha-*Dharma*." So it is said. Concerning the time differences—past, present, and future—Rennyo Shonin said, "For some, stored good matured yesterday, and for others, it matures today." (Hisao Inagaki, trans., *Thus Have I Heard From Rennyo Shonin* [*Rennyo Shonin's Goichidaikikikigaki*] [Judet Dolj, Romania: Dharma Lion Publications, 2008], #307, p. 130; see also -029-; -298-; -356-)

4. Violation of *Dharma* and Retribution

T'an-luan

-553- 2. Harmonizing the different descriptions in the two sutras about the salvation of evildoers:

Question: The *Larger Sutra* says, "Aspirants to birth [in the Pure Land] will all attain birth, excepting those who have committed the five gravest offences and abused the right *Dharma*." The *Contemplation Sutra* says, "Those who have committed the five gravest offences and the ten evil acts as well as various other evils will also attain birth." How do you harmonize those descriptions in the two sutras?

Answer: The [*Larger*] *Sutra* mentions the committing of the two gravest evils, namely, the five gravest offences and the abusing of the right *Dharma*. Since one has committed those two kinds of evils, one is not able to attain birth. The other sutra mentions only the committing of the ten evils and the five gravest offences; it does not mention abuse of the right *Dharma*. Since one has not abused the right *Dharma*, one is able to attain birth.

3. Those who have abused the *Dharma* will not be born in the Pure Land:

Question: If there is a man who has committed the five gravest offences but has not abused the right *Dharma*, he will, according to the [*Contemplation*] *Sutra*, be able to obtain birth. Suppose there is a man who has abused the right *Dharma* but has not committed the five gravest offences. If he desires birth in the Pure Land, will he be able to attain it?

Answer: He who has committed the transgression of abusing the right *Dharma* will not be able to attain birth, even though he has not committed any other evils. For what reason? The [*Mahaprajnaparamita*] *Sutra* says:

> Those who have committed the five gravest offences will fall into the Great *Avici* hell, where they will receive retributions of the grave evils in various ways for one *kalpa*. Those who have abused the right *Dharma* will also fall into the Great *Avici* hell. When the period of one *kalpa* comes to an end, they will be sent to the Great *Avici* hell of another world. In this way, such evildoers will consecutively pass through a hundred thousand Great *Avici* hells.

The Buddha thus did not mention the time of their release [from the *Avici* hells]. This is because the transgression of abusing the right *Dharma* is extremely grave.

Further, the right *Dharma* refers to the Buddha *Dharma*. Such ignorant persons have abused it; therefore, it does not stand to reason that they should seek birth in a Buddha-land, does it? If they seek birth merely from desire to enjoy pleasures, it is as if they sought to attain ice which is not made from water, or fire which does not produce smoke. Is it not contrary to reason that they would be able to attain birth?

4. The act of abusing the right *Dharma*:

Question: What is the act of abusing the right *Dharma*?

Answer: If one says, "there is no Buddha," "there is no Buddha *Dharma*," "there is no *Bodhisattva*," or "there is no *Dharma* for *Bodhisattvas*," such views, held firmly in the mind by one's own reasoning or by listening to other's teaching, are called "abusing the right *Dharma*."

5. Graveness of the transgression of abusing the *Dharma*:

Question: The fault of holding such views belongs only to those who hold them. What suffering does it cause to other beings which makes it more serious than the five gravest offences?

Answer: If there were no Buddhas or *Bodhisattvas* who edify living beings by teaching them ways of both worldly and supra-mundane good, how could they know about [the Confucian moral virtues, namely,] humanity, righteousness, propriety, wisdom, and sincerity? The result would be that all worldly good, such as those virtues, would perish and there would be no wise men and holy sages [who practice the way of supra-mundane good]. You only know of the graveness of the five gravest offences. You are not aware that they arise from the absence of the right *Dharma*. For this reason, abusing the right *Dharma* is the gravest of all evils. (Hisao Inagaki, trans., *T'an-Luan's Commentary on Vasubandhu's Discourse on the Pure Land* [*Ojoronchu*] [Kyoto: Nagata Bunshodo, 1998], pp. 195-199)

Shan-tao

-554- Question: Sakyamuni appeared in the world and, in order to save ordinary people in the age of five defilements, compassionately explained the painful aspects of the three evil realms which people undergo as a result of the ten evil acts. Also, with the wisdom of equality, he led human beings and *devas* to turn their thoughts and attain birth in the Land of Amida Buddha. In various sutras there are clear references to this teaching of quick enlightenment. Now there are people who openly express their disbelief of it and compete with each other in abusing it. I do not know what retribution such people will receive in the present life and after death. . . .

Answer: . . . such evil persons are those that I described above. . . . I will now reveal a quotation directly from a sutra as clear evidence. It is stated in the *Sutra on the Ten Ways of Attaining Birth*:

> The Buddha said to Girisagarajna *Bodhisattva*, "You should hold this teaching for the purpose of saving all sentient beings.". . .
> For those sentient beings who have not yet had good karmic relations with the *nembutsu samadhi*, this sutra opens the great *samadhi*-gate. This sutra closes the gate of hell for the sake of sentient beings. Also, for the sake of sentient beings, this sutra keeps away those who inflict harm on them and destroys evil spirits, thereby giving peace to all beings in the four directions.". . .

Girisagarajna said to the Buddha, "Many sentient beings of the future may abuse [this teaching]. What will be the outcome?"

The Buddha said: "In future there will be in Jambudvipa monks and nuns, men and women, who, having seen someone chanting this sutra, will get angry with this person and entertain enmity in their minds. By the cause of abusing the right *Dharma*, they will in the present life suffer from bad and serious illnesses or have impaired limbs; or they will be deaf, blind, or dumb; or they will suffer from harassment by evil spirits, insanity, colds, fever, piles, dropsy, or loss of consciousness. These bad and serious illnesses will beset their bodies life after life. Suffering thus from pains, they will not find rest, whether sitting or lying; they will be unable to ease nature. However strongly they may seek death or life, they will get neither. All such pains result from abusing this sutra. It happens that, after death, they will fall into hell, where they will undergo extreme pains for eighty thousand *kalpas*, and will not be able to hear even the words 'water' or 'food' for thousands of millions of lives to come. These are the karmic retributions they will get by their acts of abusing this sutra. It so happens that when they can come out of hell to be born in the human world, they will be born as oxen, horses, boars, or sheep and end their lives in great pain by being slaughtered by men. This is due to abusing this sutra. Later, when they are born again as human beings, they will always be born in low-class families, unable to enjoy freedom for thousands of millions of lives, or unable to see even the words denoting the Three Treasures for thousands of millions of lives. Such is the painful result one receives by the act of abusing this sutra. For this reason, you should not expound it to ignorant people. Only to those people who possess right contemplation and right mindfulness should you expound this sutra. If one does not revere this sutra, one will fall into hell. If one reveres it, one will attain right emancipation and be born in the Land of Amida Buddha."

(Hisao Inagaki, trans., *Shan-tao's Kannenbomon: The Method of Contemplation on Amida* [Kyoto: Nagata Bunshodo, 2005], pp. 74-78)

Genshin

-555- *Abijigoku* is the Hell of No-Interval. It is situated below the Hell of the Great Scorching Heat and is at the bottom limit of the Realm of Passions. As the sinners approach this hell from the sky above, they wail with a great lamentation, quoting from the Scriptures these words: "Everything is nothing but flames. In the sky there is not a space without flames and the whole land in every direction is covered with them. The whole land is filled with evil doers and there is no room for me. I am alone and like an orphan without a friend. I am in a dark and evil place. I am enveloped in a great raging flame. I can see neither moon nor sun in the sky." Thus they wail. Thereupon the hell wardens reply with wrathful severity, saying: "You fools, we shall burn some of you for a period of an increasing *kalpa* and others of you for a period of a decreasing *kalpa*. You have already created your evil karma and do you now repent? You are not *asuras*, *gandharas*, or dragon demons of the heavenly realm. You are caught in the meshes of your own deeds. You fools, how can others save you since this is not the result of the deeds of others? If you compare the suffering as you see it from the sky with the suffering which you will have to undergo in this hell, it is like comparing a drop of water with the waters of the great ocean. Your present suffering is like a drop of water, your later suffering like the waters of the great ocean." Tormenting the victims with these words, they drag them toward this hell for 25,000 *yojanas*, and as the sinners hear the wailings of the victims in hell, their terror, as the hell wardens had said, is increased tenfold until their souls are consumed with fear as in a nightmare. For two thousand years they are flung headlong down toward this infernal abyss. (A.K. Reischauer, "Genshin's *Ojo Yoshu*: Collected Essays on Birth into Paradise," *The Transactions of the Asiatic Society of Japan* [December 1930], Second Series, Vol. VII, pp. 40-41)

Shinran

-556- Excluded are those who commit the five grave offenses and those who slander the right dharma: *Excluded* means that those who commit the five grave offenses are rejected and reveals how grave the evil of slandering the *dharma* is. By showing the gravity of these two kinds of wrongdoing, these words make us realize that all the sentient beings throughout the ten quarters, without a single exception, will be born in the Pure Land. (*CWS, Notes on Inscription on Sacred Scrolls*, I, p. 494; see also -163-)

## 5. Doubt

Shan-tao

-557- It is indeed that sentient beings doubt what should not be doubted;
  The Pure Land is right before us and never out of harmony with us.
  Do not ponder whether Amida will take you in or not;
  The question is whether or not you wholeheartedly turn about at heart.
    . . .
  It is said from this moment until the attainment of Buddhahood,
  For vast *kalpas*, we will praise the Buddha out of gratitude for his compassion and benevolence.
  Had we not received the power of Amida's universal Vow,
  When—in what *kalpa*—could we part from this saha world? . . .

And how could we now expect to reach that precious land?
It is indeed the power of our Guide, who appeared in the *saha* world.
But for the encouragement of our Guide, our true teacher,
How would we be able to enter Amida's Pure Land?
(*CWS, Kyogyoshinho*, I, pp. 119-120, III:93)

Honen

-558- People entertain various doubts about birth in the Pure Land: some feel that even though they recite *nembutsu*, birth in the Pure Land is impossible due to their own accumulated non-virtuous karma; others think that birth in the Pure Land is impossible through *nembutsu* because they are too busy with everyday life; and some suppose that birth in the Pure Land through *nembutsu* is impossible because their hearts of *nembutsu* are not strong enough to attain this birth. Those who entertain these doubts about birth in the Pure Land do not know the efficacy of *nembutsu*.

In reality, a mortal's karmic burden is so grave that *nembutsu* is encouraged in order to eradicate it. Do not harbor doubts about birth in the Pure Land by saying that such birth is unattainable through *nembutsu* because your karmic burden is too heavy. *Nembutsu* is just like medicine: one who gets seriously ill must take medicine. If one has a serious condition but does not take medicine, the disease will never be cured.

. . . Moreover, that mundane affairs keep us so busy means we should recite *nembutsu* even more. The reason is: that *nembutsu* is designed for all people without distinction as to whether one is male or female, high or low, walking, standing, sitting, or lying down, and without regard for length of time, place, or various karmic relationships. *Nembutsu* can be practiced easily. Only *nembutsu* can be uttered even in one's final moment. Contrarily, practices other than *nembutsu* are difficult to perform in this hectic world. The practice of *nembutsu* does not discriminate between a lay person and a monk, or between the learned and the unschooled. Everyone who recites *nembutsu* will receive the merit of birth in the Pure Land equally. The attainment of birth in the Pure Land must be realized without being hindered by various worldly affairs. (Joji Atone, Yoko Hayashi, trans., *The Promise of Amida Buddha: Honen's Path to Bliss* [Boston: Wisdom Publications, 2011], pp. 361-363)

Shinran

-559- As a mark of not apprehending Buddha-wisdom,
    People doubt the *Tathagata*'s various kinds of wisdom,
    Believe in the recompense of good and evil, rely on their practice
    Of the root of good, and hence remain in the borderland.

No less than people of *shinjin*,
Practicers of doubt who cling to self-power should
Awaken to the benevolence of Amida's great compassion
And endeavor in saying the *nembutsu*.

People who, doubting the inconceivable Buddha-wisdom,
Rely on their practice of the root of good and root of virtue
Are born in the borderland or realm of indolence and pride;
Hence, they fail to realize great love and compassion.
(*CWS, Hymns of the Dharma-Ages*, I, pp. 413-414, #60, 66, 68)

Shinran
**-560-** It further states, "Know that because of doubt one remains in the house of birth-and-death: When one doubts the inconceivable karmic power of the great vow, one remains in the six courses, the four manners of arising, the twenty-five forms of existence, and the twelve kinds of arising. We are to realize that up to now we have been wandering for aeons in such a realm of illusion." (*CWS, Passages on the Nembutsu Selected in the Primal Vow*, I, pp. 512-513; see also alternative reading: "One ought surely to know that it is through doubt that one is held fast within the house of birth and death, while it is through faith that one can enter into the castle of *nirvana*." [*Senchakushu* English Translation Project, *Honen's Senchakushu: Passages on the Selection of the Nembutsu in the Original Vow (Senchaku Hongan-nembutsu-shu)* (Honolulu: University of Hawaii Press, 1998), p. 112])

Shinran
**-561-** Doubting Amida's various kinds of wisdom,
They do not entrust themselves to the Buddha,
And yet they deeply believe in the recompense of good and evil,
And they diligently practice the root of good. . . .

Those who practice the root of good
While believing deeply in the recompense of good and evil
Are good people whose minds are possessed of doubt;
Hence, they remain in the provisional, transformed lands. . . .

The fault of doubting Buddha-wisdom is grave.
Becoming fully aware of this,
You should, with deep repentance,
Entrust yourself to inconceivable Buddha-wisdom.
(*CWS, Hymns of the Dharma-Ages*, I, pp. 415-417, #70, 74, 82)

Rennyo

-562- Rennyo Shonin said, "Doubt and complete ignorance are two different things. It is groundless to call complete ignorance doubt. Doubt is being unclear about 'what is this and what is that?' It is wrong to use the word 'doubt' for asking about something of which you are completely ignorant." (Hisao Inagaki, trans., *Thus Have I Heard From Rennyo Shonin* [*Rennyo Shonin's Goichidaikikigaki*] [Judet Dolj, Romania: Dharma Lion Publications, 2008], #219, p. 102; see also -056-; -214-; -226-; -229-; -253-; -262-; -268-; -269-; -276-; -434-; -489-; -490-)

## 6. Doctrinal Disputes/Deviations and Regulations

Kakunyo

-563- At that time the Founding Master instructed them, saying, "The *honzon* (the main object of worship) and the sacred teachings are *upaya* for the benefit of sentient beings; they should not be made out to be something that I have made out of my foolish and arbitrary will. How is it that we simply assume them to be some kind of worldly treasure that we should try to get them back? If it irks him that [the book] bears the name Shaku Shinran, or if he hates me personally as a *dharma* master even to [wearing] my *kesa*, he should simply abandon the sacred teaching in a field in a mountain somewhere. If someone were to tell me that indeed this is what he has done, it does not perturb me in the least; we should see this, rather, as an occasion to rejoice. The reason that I say this is, by his act of throwing away the sacred teaching on that spot, he has in effect saved the living beings there down to the tiniest crawling insects, for it will help them to avoid drowning in the sea of suffering. Take this point well to heart. Further as his latter day heirs why would we adopt a new principle? Please cease [from it]. . . ." (W.S. Yokoyama, *Kakunyo's Setting the Claims Straight* [*Gaijasho*], #6, unpublished translation)

Kakunyo

-564- I reckon that among the disciples of the Shonin (Shinran) of the Hongwanji, there are some twenty or so learned disciples who formed their own streams; they should follow a system that restricts them [from teaching things that are not based on] what the founding master personally taught them, and they should cease and desist [from spreading] deluded ideas that they arrived at independently. (W.S. Yokoyama, *Kakunyo's Setting the Claims Straight* [*Gaijasho*], #1, unpublished translation)

Kakunyo

-565- Next, when it came to the rule of whether to take back the *honzon* and sacred writings [of a member who had defected], [Shinran told us] not to cherish those objects [as if they were some kind of worldly treasure]. (W.S. Yokoyama, *Kakunyo's Setting the Claims Straight* [*Gaijasho*], #9, unpublished translation)

Kakunyo
-566- Next, when it came time to build a hall, there was a rule that [the members of the fellowship] should not raise any objection [on the grounds of heresy]. Generally speaking, to make statues or erect towers and so on are not activities indicated in Amida's Vow, and so there is no reason that the practicing members of the single direction exclusive cultivation (practice) movement should engage in any such projects. (W.S. Yokoyama, *Kakunyo's Setting the Claims Straight* [*Gaijasho*], #9, unpublished translation)

Kakunyo
-567- While Buddha body and Buddha wisdom do not assume a basic form, to say that a spiritual guide in his mortal frame has direct control over them, and to promote him by saying to others, "Here is the *Tathagata* in physical form for you to see," such a claim is divorced from the provisions of the sacred teachings and turns its back on the words spoken by our Founder [Shinran] that have been handed down in our tradition. [But someone may protest:] Apart from the object of worship, then, in what quarter is the spiritual guide to appear? This is wild and woolly thinking, for there is a fine line of distinction between the two. As far as speaking words of truth to hand down to others, giving expression to Buddha wisdom, and earning the gratitude of those who have settled [the question in their hearts], the *Tathagata* of the living body is always the same. Since the wooden statue [of the object of worship] says nothing and never has any sutra on its lips, it is from their spiritual guide that the seekers can stock up gratefully on the things that are transmitted to them, and with hearts filled with thanks, they should revere and pray to the spiritual guide as the deputy of the *Tathagata*; [but to say] that there is no Buddha other than the spiritual guide, is an assertion that would make the wise laugh and make the foolish go astray. Ah, woe is me, woe is me! (W.S. Yokoyama, *Kakunyo's Setting the Claims Straight* [*Gaijasho*], #18, unpublished translation)

Rennyo
-568- Rennyo Shonin made this remark, "There are some who are learned in the scriptures but are ignorant of them, while there are others who are ignorant of the scriptures but understand them. Even if you do not know a single character of the scriptures, if you get someone to read the scriptures to others and lead them to acquire *shinjin*, you are one of those who are ignorant of the scriptures but understand them. Even if you are learned in the

scriptures but if you do not read them in depth and sincerity, without appreciating the *Dharma*, you are one of those who are learned in the scriptures but are ignorant of them." (Hisao Inagaki, trans., *Thus Have I Heard From Rennyo Shonin [Rennyo Shonin's Goichidaikikigaki]* [Judet Dolj, Romania: Dharma Lion Publications, 2008], #94, p. 63)

Rennyo

-569- Junsei is said to have made the following remark: "Ordinarily, people get angry when they know that someone is speaking ill of them behind their back instead of telling them directly. I have a different opinion. If it is awkward to speak frankly to me, you may criticize me behind my back. Hearing that, I will mend my ways." (Hisao Inagaki, trans., *Thus Have I Heard From Rennyo Shonin [Rennyo Shonin's Goichidaikikigaki]* [Judet Dolj, Romania: Dharma Lion Publications, 2008], #126, p. 73; see also -387-)

## J. Philosophical Aspects

*Contemplation Sutra*

-570- The Buddha said to Ananda and Vaidehi, "After you have seen this, next visualize the Buddha. Why the Buddha? Because Buddhas, *Tathagatas* have cosmic bodies, and so enter into the meditating mind of each sentient being. For this reason, when you contemplate a Buddha, your mind itself takes the form of his thirty-two physical characteristics and eighty secondary marks. Your mind produces the Buddha's image and is itself the Buddha. The ocean of perfectly and universally enlightened Buddhas thus arises in the meditating mind. For this reason, you should single-mindedly concentrate and deeply contemplate the Buddha, *Tathagata, Arhat*, and Perfectly Enlightened One. (Hisao Inagaki, trans., *The Three Pure Land Sutras* [Kyoto: Nagata Bunshodo, 1994], #16, p. 330)

Nagarjuna

-571- [An opponent claims:]

1. If everything is empty, there is no origination nor destruction.

Then you must incorrectly conclude that there is non-existence of holy truths.

2. If there is non-existence of the four holy truths, the saving knowledge, elimination [of illusion],

The "becoming" [enlightened] and the "realization" [of the goal] are impossible.

3 .If there is non-existence, then also the four holy "fruits" do not exist.

In the non-existence of fruit there is no "residing in fruit" nor obtaining.

4. When the community [of Buddhists] does not exist, then those eight

"kinds of persons" [i.e., four abiding in the fruit and four who are obtaining] do not exist.

Because there is non-existence of the four holy truths, the real *dharma* does not exist.

5. And if there are no *dharma* and community, how will the Buddha exist?

By speaking thus, [that everything is empty] certainly you deny the three jewels [i.e., the Buddha, the *dharma*, and the community].

6. You deny the real existence of a product, of right and wrong,

And all the practical behavior of the world as being empty.

[Nagarjuna replies.]

7. We reply that you do not comprehend the point of emptiness;

You eliminate both "emptiness" itself and its purpose from it.

8. The teaching by the Buddhas of the *dharma* has recourse to two truths:

The world-ensconced truth and the truth which is the highest sense.

9. Those who do not know the distribution (*vibhagam*) of the two kinds of truth

Do not know the profound "point" (*tattva*) in the teaching of the Buddha.

10. The highest sense [of the truth] is not taught apart from practical behavior,

And without having understood the highest sense one cannot understand *nirvana*.

11. Emptiness, having been dimly perceived, utterly destroys the slow-witted.

It is like a snake wrongly grasped or [magical] knowledge incorrectly applied.

12. Therefore the mind of the ascetic [Gautama] was diverted from teaching the *dharma*,

Having thought about the incomprehensibility of the *dharma* by the stupid.

13. Time and again you have made a condemnation of emptiness,

But that refutation does not apply to our emptiness.

14. When emptiness "works," then everything in existence "works."

If emptiness does not "work," then all existence does not "work."

15. You, while projecting: your own faults on us,

Are like a person who, having mounted his horse, forgot the horse!

16. If you recognize real existence on account of the self-existence of things,

You perceive that there are uncaused and unconditioned things.

17. You deny "what is to be produced," cause, the producer, the instru-

ment of production, and the producing action,

And the origination, destruction, and "fruit."

18. The "originating dependently" we call "emptiness";

This apprehension, i.e., taking into account [all other things], is the understanding of the middle way.

19. Since there is no *dharma* whatever originating independently,

No *dharma* whatever exists which is not empty,

20. If all existence is not empty, there is neither origination nor destruction.

You must wrongly conclude then that the four holy truths do not exist.

21. Having originated without being conditioned, how will sorrow come into existence?

It is said that sorrow is not eternal; therefore, certainly it does not exist by own nature (*svabhava*).

22. How can that which is existing by its own nature originate again?

For him who denies emptiness there is no production.

23. There is no destruction of sorrow if it exists by its own nature.

By trying to establish "self-existence" you deny destruction.

24. If the path [of release] is self-existent, then there is no way of bringing it into existence (*bhavana*);

If that path is brought into existence, then "self-existence," which you claim does not exist.

25. When sorrow, origination, and destruction do not exist,

What kind of path will obtain the destruction of sorrow?

26. If there is no complete knowledge as to self-existence, how [can there be] any knowledge of it?

Indeed, is it not true that self-existence is that which endures?

27. As in the case of complete knowledge, neither destruction, realization, "bringing into existence,"

Nor are the four holy fruits possible for you.

28. If you accept "self-existence," and a "fruit" is not known by its self-existence,

How can it be known at all?

29. In the non-existence of "fruit," there is no "residing in fruit" nor obtaining [the "fruit"];

When the community [of Buddhists] does not exist, then those eight "kinds of persons" do not exist.

30. Because there is non-existence of the four holy truths, the real *dharma* does not exist.

And if there is no *dharma* and community, how will the Buddha exist?

31. For you, either the one who is enlightened (*buddha*) comes into being independent of enlightenment,

Or enlightenment comes into being independent of the one who is enlightened.

32. For you, someone who is a non-Buddha by his own nature (*svabhava*) but strives for enlightenment,

Will not attain the enlightenment through the "way of life of becoming fully enlightened."

33. Neither the *dharma* nor non-*dharma* will be done anywhere.

What is produced which is non-empty? Certainly self-existence is not produced.

34. Certainly, for you, there is a product without [the distinction] of *dharma* or non-*dharma*.

Since, for you, the product caused by *dharma* or non-*dharma* does not exist.

35. If, for you, the product is caused by *dharma* or non-*dharma*,

How can that product, being originated by *dharma* or non-*dharma*, be non-empty?

36. You deny all mundane and customary activities

When you deny emptiness [in the sense of] dependent co-origination (*pratitya-samutpada*).

37. If you deny emptiness, there would be action which is inactivated.

There would be nothing whatever acted upon, and a producing action would be something not begun.

38. According to [the doctrine of] "self-existence" the world is free from different conditions;

Then it will exist as unproduced, undestroyed, and immutable.

39. If non-emptiness does not exist, then something is attained which is not attained;

There is cessation of sorrow and actions, and all evil is destroyed.

40. He who perceives dependent co-origination (*pratitya-samutpada*)

Also understands sorrow, origination, and destruction as well as the path [of release].

(Frederick J. Streng, *Emptiness: A Study in Religious Meaning* [Nashville/New York: Abingdon Press, 1967], pp. 213-214)


Nagarjuna
-572- On the four reliances:

When Sakyamuni was about to enter *nirvana*, he said to the *bhiksus*, "From this day on, rely on *dharma*, not on people who teach it. Rely on the meaning, not on the words. Rely on wisdom, not on the working of the mind. Rely on the sutras that fully express the meaning, not on those that do not.

"As to relying on *dharma*, *dharma* refers to the twelve divisions of scripture. Follow this *dharma*, not people who teach it.

"With regard to relying on the meaning, meaning itself is beyond debate of such matters as, like against dislike, evil against virtue, falsity against truth. Hence, words may indeed have meaning, but the meaning is not the words. Consider, for example, a person instructing us by pointing to the moon with his finger. [To take words to be the meaning] is like looking at the finger and not at the moon. The person would say, 'I am pointing to the moon with my finger in order to show it to you. Why do you look at my finger and not the moon?' Similarly, words are the finger pointing to the meaning; they are not the meaning itself. Hence, do not rely upon words.

"As to relying on wisdom, wisdom is able to distinguish and measure good and evil. The working of mind always seeks pleasure, and does not reach the essential. Hence it is said, 'Do not rely on mind.'

"As to relying on the sutras that fully express the meaning, among all the sages, the Buddha is foremost. Among all the various scriptures, the Buddha-*dharma* is foremost. Among all human beings, the assemblage of *bhiksus* is foremost."

The Buddha regarded the sentient beings of an age in which there is no Buddha as possessed of deep karmic evil. They are people who have not cultivated the roots of good that would enable them to see a Buddha. (*CWS, Kyogyoshinsho, The Commentary on the Mahaprajnaparamita Sutra*, I, #71, pp. 241-242)

T'an-luan
-573- It is to be noted that all things are transformations of mind; for nothing exists outside of mind. The inhabitants and the land are neither different nor the same. Since they are not the same, they are distinguishable according to their different characteristics. Also, since they are not different, they are both pure. (Hisao Inagaki, trans., *T'an-luan's Commentary on Vasubandhu's Discourse on the Pure Land [Ojoronchu]* [Kyoto: Nagata Bunshodo, 1998], p. 268, adapted)

T'an-luan
-574- *This mind attains Buddhahood* means that the mind becomes Buddha; *this mind is itself Buddha* means that there is no Buddha apart from the mind. This is like the relationship of fire and wood: fire arises from wood; it cannot exist apart from the wood. Because it cannot exist apart from the wood, it consumes the wood. The wood, on the other hand, is consumed by the fire; it becomes the fire. (*CWS, Kyogyoshinsho*, I, p. 113, III:68)

Tao-ch'o
-575- The Pure Land teaching is abstruse and extensive and its scriptures have explicit and hidden meanings. If we allow our ordinary people's con-

jectures to guess the meanings, we will perhaps take the holy words as false and wavering jargon; we will then cling to distorted views like blind people and, confused and ignorant, create hindrances to birth in the Pure Land. . . .

. . . The Buddha's exposition of the *Dharma* is based on two causes: 1) it is dependent on the principle of reality of the *Dharma*-nature and 2) it should accord with the two-fold truth. You presuppose that no-thought in the Mahayana is solely in accord with the *Dharma*-nature and unjustifiably reject seeking salvation through causal relationships. In so doing, you run counter to the twofold truth. . . . Although the principle of reality is that nothing really comes into existence, in view of the twofold truth, it does not follow that aspiration for birth in terms of causal relationships is impossible. All beings, therefore, can attain birth. (Hisao Inagaki, trans., "Tao-ch'o's *An-le-chi* Part 2," *The Pure Land*, New Series 22 [December 2006], pp. 191-192, adapted)

Shan-tao

-576- I take refuge in and prostrate myself with sincerity of heart to Amida Buddha in the Western Quarter.

Amida Buddha's land has come into existence as the due recompense (for his Vows and practices);

The Western Land of Utmost Bliss is inconceivable.

Avidly listening to the teaching of *Prajna*, one has no desire for drink;

Being fed with mindfulness of non-arising, one quenches hunger.

All the glorious adornments proclaim the *Dharma*;

One perceives it without conscious mind and understands it spontaneously.

One enters the flower-pond of the seven factors of enlightenment as one wishes;

With a mind of concentration, one sees the eight *samadhis* of emancipation congealed in a twig.

Innumerable *bodhisattvas* become one's fellow-students.

(Hisao Inagaki, trans., *Shan-tao's Liturgy for Birth* [*Ojoraisan*], 43, http://www12.canvas.ne.jp/horai/raisan.htm)

Shan-tao

-577- This mind attains Buddhahood. This mind is itself Buddha. There is no Buddha apart from this mind. (*CWS*, *Kyogyoshinsho*, I, p. 113, III:69)

Zonkaku

—**Non-Duality**

-578- The perfection of the Buddha's enlightenment hinges on the birth of the sentient beings, and the perfection of the birth of the sentient beings hinges on the Buddha's enlightenment—in this configuration of unity of seeker and *Dharma* (*ki-ho ittai*), and non-duality of savior and saved, the life force of the Buddha and the life force of the sentient beings merge as one, and thus with impermanence eliminated and the state of permanence gained, no gradient of difference exists between savior and saved. (W.S. Yokoyama, Suzuki Hiroshi, eds., *Zonkaku's Sermons*, #2d-1, unpublished translation; see also -042-; -053-; -119-; -353-)

## —Refuting Opposition

Shan-tao

-579- The teachings and practices of the Buddhas exceed in number the grains of sand. They are different for each sentient being according to the respective conditions of their endowment and understanding. For instance, the eyes of people in the world have the ability to see and to believe that light breaks darkness; empty space contains [a variety of] beings; earth sustains and nourishes; water produces moisture; fire destroys. All these things are called *dharmas* of relations and although they are visible to the eye, there is an enormous difference between them. How far more then do the inconceivable powers of the Buddha's *dharma* possess all kinds of benefits! If someone accordingly leaves one school of thought, he leaves a school of delusion; if someone accordingly enters a school, he enters a school of wisdom toward emancipation. Therefore, each person follows a course of action which is favorable to himself, with the final aim of emancipation in view. Why then do you take up this irrelevant practice to confuse and hinder me? Indeed, the practice I like, that is the one relevant to me; it is not the one you look for. The practice you like, that is the one relevant to you, and is not what I look for. Therefore everyone cultivates a practice to his own liking, and will certainly soon obtain emancipation.

[However] the practitioner should know, that if he wants to apply himself to [the way, method of] understanding, he must acquire an all-pervasive knowledge from [the stage of] ordinary being up to that of holy being and finally up to Buddha fruit. If [on the other hand] he wants to apply himself to practice, he must necessarily rely on the methods that are relevant; then although the efforts are less demanding, the obtained benefits are more numerous. (Julian F. Pas, *Visions of Sukhavati: Shan-Tao's Commentary on the Kuan-wu-Liang-Shou-Fo-Ching* [Albany, NY: State University of New York Press, 1995), pp. 246-247)

## K. Pure Land Tradition

Shinran

-580- Relying on the teacher of the sutras and turning to the commentaries of the masters, I find that, with regard to the teaching of sutras, there are five kinds, distinguished in terms of their expositors: first, the Buddha's exposition; second, the exposition of holy disciples; third, the exposition of heavenly beings and hermit-sages; fourth, the exposition of demigods; and fifth, the exposition of miraculous spirits. Thus, [the latter] four kinds of exposition are not to be relied upon. The three [Pure Land] sutras are the Great Sage's own exposition. (*CWS, Kyogyoshinsho*, I, p. 241, VI:70)

Shinran
-581- Hymn of True *Shinjin* and the *Nembutsu*
    I take refuge in the *Tathagata* of Immeasurable Life!
    I entrust myself to the Buddha of Inconceivable Light!
    *Bodhisattva* Dharmakara, in his causal stage,
    Under the guidance of Lokesvararaja Buddha,
    Searched into the origins of the Buddhas' pure lands,
    And the qualities of those lands and their men and *devas*;
    He then established the supreme, incomparable Vow;
    He made the great Vow rare and all-encompassing.
    In five *kalpas* of profound thought, he embraced this Vow,
    Then resolved again that his Name be heard throughout the ten quarters.
    Everywhere he casts light immeasurable, boundless,
    Unhindered, unequaled, light—lord of all brilliance,
    Pure light, joyful light, the light of wisdom,
    Light constant, inconceivable, light beyond speaking,
    Light excelling sun and moon he sends forth, illumining countless
        worlds;
    The multitudes of beings all receive the radiance.
    The Name embodying the Primal Vow is the act of true settlement,
    The Vow of entrusting with sincere mind is the cause of birth;
    We realize the equal of enlightenment and supreme *nirvana*
    Through the fulfillment of the Vow of attaining *nirvana* without fail.
    Sakyamuni *Tathagata* appeared in this world
    Solely to teach the ocean-like Primal Vow of Amida;
    We, an ocean of beings in an evil age of five defilements,
    Should entrust ourselves to the *Tathagata*'s words of truth.
    When the one thought-moment of joy arises,
    *Nirvana* is attained without severing blind passions;
    When ignorant and wise, even grave offenders and slanderers of the
        *dharma*, all alike turn and enter *shinjin*,
    They are like waters that, on entering the ocean, become one in taste
        with it.
    The light of compassion that grasps us illumines and protects us always;
    The darkness of our ignorance is already broken through;

Still the clouds and mists of greed and desire, anger and hatred,
Cover as always the sky of true and real *shinjin*.
But though light of the sun is veiled by clouds and mists,
Beneath the clouds and mists there is brightness, not dark.
When one realizes *shinjin*, seeing and revering and attaining great joy,
One immediately leaps crosswise, closing off the five evil courses.
All foolish beings, whether good or evil,
When they hear and entrust to Amida's universal Vow,
Are praised by the Buddha as people of vast and excellent understanding;
Such a person is called a pure white lotus.
For evil sentient beings of wrong views and arrogance,
The *nembutsu* that embodies Amida's Primal Vow
Is hard to accept in *shinjin*;
This most difficult of difficulties, nothing surpasses.
The masters of India in the west, who explained the teaching in treatises,
And the eminent monks of China and Japan,
Clarified the Great Sage's true intent in appearing in the world,
And revealed that Amida's Primal Vow accords with the nature of beings.
Sakyamuni *Tathagata*, on Mount Lanka,
Prophesied to the multitudes that in south India
The *mahasattva* Nagarjuna would appear in this world
To crush the views of being and non-being;
Proclaiming the unexcelled Mahayana teaching,
He would attain the stage of joy and be born in the land of happiness.
Nagarjuna clarifies the hardship on the overland path of difficult practice,
And leads us to entrust to the pleasure on the waterway of easy practice.
He teaches that the moment one thinks on Amida's Primal Vow,
One is naturally brought to enter the stage of the definitely settled;
Solely saying the *Tathagata*'s Name constantly,
One should respond with gratitude to the universal vow of great com-
passion.
*Bodhisattva* Vasubandhu, composing a treatise, declares
That he takes refuge in the *Tathagata* of unhindered light,
And that relying on the sutras, he will reveal the true and real virtues,
And make widely known the great vow by which we leap crosswise
beyond birth-and-death.
He discloses the mind that is single so that all beings be saved
By Amida's directing of virtue through the power of the Primal Vow.
When a person turns and enters the great treasure ocean of virtue,
Necessarily he joins Amida's assembly;
And when he reaches that lotus-held world,
He immediately realizes the body of suchness or *dharma*-nature.

Then sporting in the forests of blind passions, he manifests transcendent
    powers;
Entering the garden of birth-and-death, he assumes various forms to
    guide others.
Turning toward the dwelling of Master T'an-luan, the Emperor of Liang
Always paid homage to him as a *bodhisattva*.
Bodhiruci, master of the *Tripitaka*, gave T'an-luan the Pure Land teach-
    ings,
And T'an-luan, burning his Taoist scriptures, took refuge in the land of
    bliss.
In his commentary on the treatise of *Bodhisattva* Vasubandhu,
He shows that the cause and attainment of birth in the fulfilled land lie
    in the Vow.
Our going and returning, directed to us by Amida, come about through
    Other Power;
The truly decisive cause is *shinjin*.
When a foolish being of delusion and defilement awakens *shinjin*,
He realizes that birth-and-death is itself *nirvana*;
Without fail he reaches the land of immeasurable light
And universally guides sentient beings to enlightenment.
Tao-ch'o determined how difficult it is to fulfill the Path of Sages,
And reveals that only passage through the Pure Land gate is possible
    for us.
He criticizes self-power endeavor in the myriad good practices,
And encourages us solely to say the fulfilled Name embodying true
    virtue.
With kind concern he teaches the three characteristics of entrusting and
    non-entrusting,
Compassionately guiding all identically, whether they live when the
    *dharma* survives as but form, when in its last stage, or when it has
    become extinct.
Though a person has committed evil all his life, when he encounters the
    Primal Vow,
He will reach the world of peace and realize the perfect fruit of enlight-
    enment.
Shan-tao alone in his time clarified the Buddha's true intent;
Sorrowing at the plight of meditative and non-meditative practicers and
    people of grave evil,
He reveals that Amida's light and Name are the causes of birth.
When the practicer enters the great ocean of wisdom, the Primal Vow,
He receives the diamond-like mind
And accords with the one thought-moment of joy; whereupon,

Equally with Vaidehi, he acquires the threefold wisdom
And is immediately brought to attain the eternal bliss of *dharma*-nature.
Genshin, having broadly elucidated the teachings of Sakyamuni's life-
    time,
Wholeheartedly took refuge in the land of peace and urges all to do so;
Ascertaining that minds devoted to single practice are profound, to
    sundry practice, shallow,
He sets forth truly the difference between the fulfilled land and the
    transformed land.
The person burdened with extreme evil should simply say the Name:
Although I too am within Amida's grasp,
Passions obstruct my eyes and I cannot see him;
Nevertheless, great compassion is untiring and illumines me always.
Master Genku, well-versed in the Buddha's teaching,
Turned compassionately to foolish people, both good and evil;
Establishing in this remote land the teaching and realization that are the
    true essence of the Pure Land way,
He transmits the selected Primal Vow to us of the defiled world:
Return to this house of transmigration, of birth-and death,
Is decidedly caused by doubt.
Swift entrance into the city of tranquility, the uncreated,
Is necessarily brought about by *shinjin*.
The *mahasattvas* and masters who spread the sutras
Save the countless beings of utter defilement and evil.
With the same mind, all people of the present, whether monk or lay,
Should rely wholly on the teachings of these venerable masters.
(*CWS*, *Kyogyoshinsho*, I, p. 69, II:102)

### L. Society and Ethics

Honen
-582- One with filial piety who desires to respect and be dutiful to his parents should rely on the compassion of Amida Buddha first. He then should
think: To have been given life as a human being and to be able to recite *nembutsu* in aspiration for birth in the Pure Land is due entirely to nurturing by
his parents.

   Therefore, if you ask Buddha Amida to take mercy on your merit cul-
tivated through the practice of *nembutsu*, to welcome your parents into
His Land of Ultimate Bliss, and to eliminate their unwholesome karma
there, Amida Buddha will, with certainty, welcome your parents into the
Pure Land. (Yoko Hayashi, Joji Atone, trans., *The Teachings of Honen* [Los
Angeles: Bukkyo University-Los Angeles Extension, 2007 rev.], p. 92)

Honen

-583- Nevertheless, knowing that birth in the Pure Land is possible through *nembutsu* and yet indulging in non-virtuous acts, neglecting compassionate deeds, and not devoting oneself to *nembutsu* violates the teachings of Buddha Sakyamuni. It is like parents who compassionately nurture all of their children, whether they are good or bad, yet rejoice in good children and grieve for the bad children. Amida Buddha extends his mercy equally to all beings and saves both the good and bad, but he finds joy in the good and feels sorrow for the bad. Elation over the good is analogous to the good seed sown in fertile soil resulting in a good crop. Still, even the good should recite *nembutsu*. They are then, in the true sense, the follower of the teachings of Buddha Sakyamuni. (Joji Atone, Yoko Hayashi, trans., *The Promise of Amida Buddha: Honen's Path to Bliss* [Boston: Wisdom Publications, 2011], p. 365)

Shinran

-584- In contrast, how lamentable that people who have not fully awakened from drunkenness are urged to more drunkenness and those still in the grips of poison encouraged to take yet more poison. It is indeed sorrowful to give way to impulses with the excuse that one is by nature possessed of blind passions—excusing acts that should not be committed, words that should not be said, and thoughts that should not be harbored—and to say that one may follow one's desires in any way whatever. It is like offering more wine before the person has become sober or urging him to take even more poison before the poison has abated. "Here's some medicine, so drink all the poison you like"—words like these should never be said.

In people who have long heard the Buddha's Name and said the *nembutsu*, surely there are signs of rejecting the evil of this world and signs of their desire to cast off the evil in themselves. When people first begin to hear the Buddha's vow, they wonder, having become thoroughly aware of the karmic evil in their hearts and minds, how they will ever attain birth as they are. To such people we teach that since we are possessed of blind passions, the Buddha receives us without judging whether our hearts are good or bad.

When, upon hearing this, a person's trust in the Buddha has grown deep, he or she comes to abhor such a self and to lament continued existence in birth-and-death; and such a person then joyfully says the Name of Amida Buddha deeply entrusting himself to the vow. That people seek to stop doing wrong as the heart moves them, although earlier they gave thought to such things and committed them as their minds dictated, is surely a sign of having rejected this world.

Moreover, since *shinjin* that aspires for attainment of birth arises through the encouragement of Sakyamuni and Amida, once the true and real mind is made to arise in us, how can we remain as we were, possessed of blind passions?

There are reports of wrongdoing even of some among you. I have heard of their slandering the master, holding their true teachers in contempt, and belittling their fellow-practicers—all of which is deeply saddening. They are already guilty of slandering the *dharma* and committing the five grave offenses. Do not associate with them. The *Treatise on the Pure Land* states that such thoughts arise because they fail to entrust themselves to the Buddha *dharma*. Moreover, in explaining the sincere mind it teaches that one should keep a respectful distance and not become familiar with those who give themselves to such wrongdoing. It teaches us rather to draw close to and become companions of our teachers and fellow-practicers. As for becoming friends with those who are given to wrongdoing, it is only after we go to the Pure Land and return to benefit sentient beings that we can become close to and friendly with them. That, however, is not our own design; only by being saved by Amida's vow can we act as we want. But at this moment, as we are, what can we possibly do? Please consider this very carefully. Since the diamond-like mind that aspires for birth is awakened through the Buddha's working, persons who realize the diamond-like mind will surely not slander their master or be contemptuous of their true teachers. (*CWS, Lamp for the Latter Ages*, #20, I, pp. 553-554)

Kakunyo

-585- On the fact that even if you are aware that the persons with the [great] sins of the five transgressions and slander of the *dharma* are born (into the Pure Land), [all the same] we should not make small sins:

In the same vein, as our late teacher Nyoshin Shonin told us, the Shonin (Shinran) once said that people always think: "While small sins are one thing, we should think sins fearful and think not to commit them by deciding in our heart to stop them; [likewise,] if we set our mind on cultivating the roots of good karma and put this plan into action, by storing up [good karma] we will be able to receive great benefit, and surely this will become the means by which we can make our escape [from transmigration]." This claim turns its back on the essential point of the true teaching and contradicts what was heard from our late teacher. First of all, with regard to doing bad deeds and sins, this has absolutely nothing to do with whether one holds to the regulations of the other schools or has a mind based in the Buddha-*dharma*; the *bombu* of evil karma is drawn by karmic causes that lie in their past which cause them to commit grave sins, and as such these sins are virtually impossible to stop or prevent. Also, if we say that even a small sin should not be committed, that sounds as if the matter should be left up to the mind of the *bombu*, and if there is a sin, he ought to be able to put a stop to it or deter it. However, as the *bombu* is a body of sin from the ground up, it is not a matter of great sin or small sin when there is nothing in their three actions (what they do, think, and say) that is not sin. Moreover, if we claim that even a small sin should not be committed, and that even if you repent, you will not be born since you have already committed it, can that serve as the bottom line (for *Shinshu*)? If we think about this claim and examine it further, is this not, rather, the thinking of those who hold to deterrence as a means? [While] deterrence is a form of compassionate means (*upaya*) for Shakyamuni, the bottom line in *Shinshu* is to be exacted [instead] in Amida's true Vow. Further, whether it is a small sin or a great sin, if we discuss the problem of sin and investigate how to put a stop to it, we come to the general conclusion that there is indeed no way to stop or deter it; this should make us realize that, indeed, the person who entrusts themselves to Amida's true Vow [has to be our basic model]. If, again, we see the slander of the *Dharma* as arising from the lack of a heart that believes in the Buddha-*dharma*, that means there is no receptacle (for the Buddha-*dharma*) in such a person from the very beginning; [but] if they repent, then they are born. Therefore, it is explained in a commentary (Shan-tao's *Hojisan*) that, "The slanderer of the *Dharma* and the unreceptive (Jap.: *sendai*; Skt.: *icchantika*) undergo a conversion; hence all of them are born." (W.S. Yokoyama, trans., *Kakunyo's What Shinran Taught* [*Kudensho*], #20, unpublished translation)

Kakunyo

-586- . . . we should never choose to make ourselves stand out by donning a pleatless robe and owning a black *kesa* (Skt.: *kasaya*) in the manner of those who retire from the world [to live as a Buddhist reclusive life]. . . . But I have heard strange rumors carried on the wind to the effect that [once one renounces the world] "we can forget all about worldly law and put our Buddhist identity first." In this view, then, are we to assume the role of those who scoff at worldly law when they put on the pleatless robe and own a black *kesa*; but let me answer this with a resounding "No!". . . In town and country there are drifts of people who call themselves *tonseisha*, "world evaders," many of them, it seems, affiliated with Ippen-bo and Ta Amidabutsu.[11] Their league passes themselves off as those who solely live by the creed of the *goseisha*, "after-worlders," and they have sworn to make it a point to look and conduct themselves in every way like *bupposha*, "Buddhists," [their entire existence] revolving around it. The way of thinking of our great master (Shinran) Shonin is opposed to theirs. One of his favorite sayings was, "Herein I aspire to model myself after Kyoshin *shami* of Kako." [This *shami* (Skt.: *sramana*, or

---

[11] Ta Amidabutsu (1237-1319) was the successor of Ippen, the founder of the *Jishu* branch of Pure Land Buddhism.

Buddhist layman) is referred to in Zenrin no Yokan's *Ojojuin*.] . . . However, in the turn of events that resulted from the *Senju Nembutsu* prohibition, when the exclusive *nembutsu* movement was banned from the capital, and [Shinran] was ordered by the authorities to go to Sasen (Echigo), from that time on he used the name Gutoku for his signature. In the use of this name is expressed the dimension of his being neither a monastic nor a layman, as was the case with Kyoshin *shami*. From this experience he was heard to say, "It's one thing if people accuse you of being a cow thief, but it's inexcusable if you go around putting on airs of being a good man, or an after-worlder, or a Buddhist; that you should never do!" In this case the thoughts and actions of this league [of Buddhist after-worlders] who ply the pleatless robe and black *kesa* are as far apart as the clouds above and the mud below. While [our school] may well go beyond the teachings and methods of the hidden and revealed schools of the larger and smaller vehicle, shut away the cardinal point of Amida's Other-Power in the depths of your heart and to all outward appearances keep that merit hidden from view. (W.S. Yokoyama, trans., *Kakunyo's Setting the Record Straight* [*Gaijasho*], #3, unpublished translation)

Rennyo

-587- These days, as in the past, it seems that many of those who call themselves followers of the Buddha-*dharma* and extol and proclaim the teaching in various places in the provinces are themselves not truly rounded in the right teaching of our tradition. When we ask the reason for this, [the answer is that], in the first place, although they act as if they knew the Buddha-*dharma* in depth, no part of their understanding has been gained from authentic sources. Some have heard the teaching quite by chance, from the edge of a veranda or from outside a sliding door. . . . They simply ingratiate themselves with people, make up lies, and take things [from them], saying that they are sent from the head temple when they are carrying out personal matters. How can these people be called good followers of the Buddha-*dharma* or readers of scripture? This is utterly deplorable. It is the one thing we should lament above all else. Those who want to present our tradition's teaching and instruct others must therefore, first of all, be fully aware of the steps in instruction. When we consider presenting our tradition's Other-Power faith, we must first distinguish between the people who have good from the past and those who lack good from the past. For, however long ago a person may have listed his name as a participant in this [tradition], it will be difficult for one who lacks good from the past to attain faith. Indeed, faith (*shin*) will of itself be decisively settled in the person for whom past good has unfolded. And so, when we discuss the two [kinds of] practice—right and sundry—in the presence of people who lack good from the past, this may lay the foundation for slander, contrary to what one would expect. To teach extensively in the presence of ordinary people without understanding this principle of the presence or absence of good from the past is in total opposition to our tradition's rules of conduct. . . .

. . . In particular, first of all, take the laws of the state as fundamental and, giving priority to [the principles of] humanity and justice, follow the generally accepted customs; deep within yourself, maintain the settled mind of our tradition; and, outwardly, conduct yourself in such a way that the transmission of the *dharma* you have received will not be evident to those of other sects and other schools. This distinguishes the person who fully knows our tradition's right teaching, which is true and real. (Minor L. Rogers and Ann T. Rogers, trans., *Rennyo: The Second Founder of Shin Buddhism* [Berkeley, CA: Asian Humanities Press, 1991], pp. 214-215, fascicle III-12)

Rennyo
-588- When Rennyo Shonin spotted a scrap of paper on the corridor, he said, "How dare you waste something that is given by the Buddha!" So saying, he held it up with both his hands with a bow of gratitude. Since he considered everything, down to a piece of paper, to be the Buddha's gift, Rennyo never wasted anything. So said the former abbot (Jitsunyo). (Hisao Inagaki, trans., *Thus Have I Heard From Rennyo Shonin* [*Rennyo Shonin's Goichidaikikigaki*] [Judet Dolj, Romania: Dharma Lion Publications, 2008], #308, p. 131)

Rennyo
-589- "Uphold the state laws and keep the Buddhist laws deep in the mind," so said the Shonin. "Morality—that is to say, benevolence and justice— should also be faithfully observed," he added. (Hisao Inagaki, trans., *Thus Have I Heard From Rennyo Shonin* [*Rennyo Shonin's Goichidaikikigaki*] [Judet Dolj, Romania: Dharma Lion Publications, 2008], #141, p. 77; see also -029-; -030-; -043-; -045-; -046-; -049-; -052-; -063-; -118-; -188-; -266-; -287-; -326-; -327-)

—Other Religions
Shinran
-590- To begin with, it should never happen under any circumstances that the Buddhas and *bodhisattvas* be thought of lightly or that the gods and deities be despised and neglected. In the course of countless lives in many states of existence, through the benefit of innumerable, incalculable Buddhas and *bodhisattvas*, we have practiced all the various good acts, but we were unable to gain freedom from birth-and-death through such self-power practice. Accordingly, through the encouragement of the Buddhas and *bodhisattvas* for countless *kalpas* and innumerable lives, we now encounter Amida's vow, which is difficult to encounter. To speak slightingly of the Buddhas and *bod-*

*hisattvas* out of ignorance of our indebtedness to them is to be totally lacking in gratitude for their profound benevolence.

Those who deeply entrust themselves to the Buddha's teaching are protected by all the gods of the heavens and earth, who accompany them just as shadows do things; hence, people who have entrusted themselves to the *nembutsu* should never think of neglecting the gods of the heavens and the earth. Even the gods and deities do not abandon us; hence, as for the Buddhas and *bodhisattvas*, how could we speak disparagingly or think slightingly of them? If one speaks slightingly of the Buddhas, then one is surely a person who does not entrust oneself to the *nembutsu* and who does not say Amida's Name. (*CWS, A Collection of Letters*, #4, I, p. 563)

Rennyo

-591- Followers of our tradition should be aware of the significance of the provisions of the six items [below] and, inwardly entrusting themselves deeply to the Buddha-*dharma*, should act in such a way as to give no outward sign of it. Therefore, it is a serious error that, these days, *nembutsu* people in our tradition deliberately make known to those of other sects the way things are in our school. To put it briefly: from now on you must follow the Buddha-*dharma*, observing the intent of these provisions. Those who go against these rules will no longer be counted among the followers [of our tradition].

Item: Do not make light of shrines.

Item: Do not make light of the Buddhas, *bodhisattvas*, or temples [enshrining deities].

Item: Do not slander other sects or other teachings.

Item: Do not slight the provincial military governors or local land stewards.

Item: The interpretation of the Buddha-*dharma* in this province is wrong; therefore, turn to the right teaching.

Item: Other-Power faith as established in our tradition must be decisively settled deep in our hearts and minds. (Minor L. Rogers and Ann T. Rogers, trans., *Rennyo: The Second Founder of Shin Buddhism* [Berkeley, CA: Asian Humanities Press, 1991], pp. 209-210, fascicle III-10)

Rennyo

-592- Within the school of teaching propagated by our tradition's founding master, there have been discrepancies in what everyone has preached. From now on, therefore—from the priests in charge of the lodgings on this mountain on down to those [priests] who read [but] a single volume of the scriptures—each of the people who assemble [here], and each of those who want to be enrolled as followers of this school—[all] must know the provisions of these three items and, henceforth, be governed accordingly.

Item: Do not slander other teachings and other sects.

Item: Do not belittle the various *kami* and Buddhas and the *bodhisattvas*.

Item: Receive faith and attain birth in the fulfilled land.

Those who do not observe the points in the above three items and take them as fundamental, storing them deep in their hearts, are to be forbidden access to this mountain [community]. . . .

. . . Therefore, if you honor [the items], knowing their significance, this will indeed accomplish my fundamental intent in staying in this region for these months and years.

Item: By *kami* manifestations, we mean [Buddhas and *bodhisattvas*] appear provisionally as *kami* to save sentient beings in whatever way possible; they lament that those who lack faith in the Buddha-*dharma* fall helplessly into hell. Relying on even the slightest of [related past] conditions, they appear provisionally as *kami* through the compassionate means to lead [sentient beings] at last into the Buddha-*dharma*.

Therefore, sentient beings of the present time [should realize that] if they rely on Amida and, undergoing a decisive settling of faith, repeat the *nembutsu* and are to be born in the land of utmost bliss, then all the *kami* [in their various] manifestations, recognizing this as [the fulfillment of] their fundamental purpose, will rejoice and protect *nembutsu* practicers. Consequently, even if we do not worship the *kami* in particular, since all are encompassed when we rely solely on the one Buddha, Amida, we give credence [to them] even though we do not rely on them in particular.

Item: Within our tradition, there must be no slandering of other teachings and other sects. As the teachings were all given by Sakyamuni during his lifetime, they should be fruitful if they are practiced just as they were expounded. In this last age, however, lay people like ourselves are not equal to the teachings of the various sects of the Path of Sages; therefore, we simply do not rely on them or entrust ourselves to them.

Item: Because the Buddhas and *bodhisattvas* are discrete manifestations of Amida *Tathagata*, [Amida] is the original teacher and the original Buddha for the Buddhas of the ten directions. For this reason, when we take refuge in Amida, the one Buddha, we take refuge in all the Buddhas and *bodhisattvas*; hence the Buddhas and *bodhisattvas* are all encompassed within the one body of Amida.

Item: Amida *Tathagata*'s true and real Other-Power faith, taught by our founder Master Shinran, is formalized in our entrusting ourselves to the Primal Vow by discarding all the sundry practices and steadfastly and single-heartedly taking refuge in Amida through the single practice [of the *nembutsu*] and single-mindedness. . . .

Therefore, in accord with what we have heard from our predecessors—bearing in mind continually that Amida *Tathagata*'s true and real faith is the inconceivable [working] and having determined that the [awakening of the] one thought-moment [of faith] is the time when birth [in the Pure Land] is assured—[we realize that] it is a matter of course that if one's life continues on after that, there will naturally be many utterances [of the *nembutsu*]. Accordingly, we are taught that the many utterances, the [many] callings of the Name, are in grateful return for Buddha's benevolence, birth [in the Pure Land] being assured in ordinary life with [the awakening of] a single thought-moment [of faith]. (Minor L. Rogers and Ann T. Rogers, trans., *Rennyo: The Second Founder of Shin Buddhism* [Berkeley, CA: Asian Humanities Press, 1991], pp. 175-176, fascicle II-3; see also -050-; -060-; -062-; -266-; -287-; -312-)

Shinran
-593- And has not Sakyamuni *Tathagata* taught such people to be "people lacking eyes" and "people lacking ears"? Those people, described here as such, perform deeds that will bring about the suppression of the *nembutsu* and act out of malice toward people of the *nembutsu*. In this regard, without bearing any ill will toward such persons, you should keep in mind the thought that, saying the *nembutsu*, you are to help them. (*CWS, A Collection of Letters*, #5, I, p. 566)

Shinran
-594- In relation to this, your understanding of the *nembutsu* has now been confirmed. While holding the *nembutsu* in your heart and saying it always, please pray for the present life and also the next life of those who slander it.

With the understanding of the people there, what more is necessary now regarding the *nembutsu*? But if you simply pray for the people in society who are in error and desire to lead them into Amida's Vow, it will be a response out of gratitude for the Buddha's benevolence. (*CWS, A Collection of Letters*, #8, I, p. 570)

# Selected Glossary

**Amitayus, Amitabha** (Sanskrit): two interchangeable names for the central Buddha of Pure Land tradition. The former means Eternal Life, while the latter is Infinite Light. In East Asian Buddhism, the name is shortened to Amida/Amita Buddha (Chinese: Omitofu, Korean: Amit'a bul).

**Anagamin** (Pali): a non-returner from transmigration; in Theravada Buddhism, the final stage before *nirvana.*

**Anjin** (Japanese): tranquil mind, peace of mind; in Shin Buddhism equivalent of *shinjin*, true entrusting. Used mainly by Rennyo, the Eighth Abbot.

**Anuttara-Samyak-Sambodhi** (Skt.): supreme enlightenment.

**Arhat** (Pali): a Hinayana Buddhist saint; the highest level of attainment before enlightenment.

**Asura** (Skt.): angry spirit.

**Avalokitesvara** (Skt.): the Bodhisattva of Compassion (Jpn. Kannon); an attendant of Amida, symbolizing his quality of compassion, comprising a triad with Mahashtamaprapta (Jpn. Daiseishi or Seishi), who symbolizes wisdom.

**Great Avici Hell** (Jpn. Abijigoku): the Hell of No-Interval; lowest of eight great hells in Buddhist cosmology.

**Bhiksu** (Pali): the term for a monk in Hinayana Buddhism.

**Bodhi** (Skt.): enlightenment.

**Bodhicitta** (Skt.): mind aspiring for enlightenment.

**Bodhisattva** (Skt.): aspirant to become Buddha; a Buddha to be.

**Bombu** (Jpn.): foolish being; a common mortal, ordinary person.

**Borderland**: sphere in the Pure Land where doubters and self-power devotees are born. It is also termed embryonic birth, the realm of indolence and pride, the womb-palace, or the city of doubt.

**Chakravartin** (Skt.): a universal wheel-turning king. Chariot wheels crush enemy.

**Chie** (Jpn.): wisdom.

**Crosswise Leap**: a term in Shinran's critical classification of doctrines, representing sudden, absolute Other-Power. Other terms are *oshutsu*: crosswise going out, gradual method of general Pure Land, gradually piling up merit of *nembutsu* recitation; *jucho*, vertical transcendence found in Zen, Tendai, and Shingon; and *jushutsu*, vertical going out, the gradual practice of Theravada, taking numerous rebirths.

**Dana** (Skt.): selfless giving. Consists of three forms: the giving of goods, *dharma*, and fearlessness.

**Dharani** (Skt.): protective, ritual speech; a spell.

**Dharma** (Skt.): Truth, teaching.

**Dharmadhatu** (Skt.): literally "realm of *Dharma*"; the universe, ultimate reality.

**Dharmakaya** (Skt.): the body of truth, distinguished as the truth body as ultimate truth and the body of truth as compassionate means; As ultimate truth, the Buddha is formless, inconceivable and inexpressible. As compassionate means, it assumes form for human understanding. They represent the metaphysical and mythic dimensions of religious thought.

**Directing of Virtue**: two aspects of Amida's working: directing of virtue for going to the Pure Land, and for our return to this world. Originally an aspect of the devotee's effort to attain birth and enlightenment by transferring merit for that purpose; in Shin Buddhism, the transfer is only from Amida.

**Eight Sufferings**: birth, illness, old age, death, loss of loved ones (the five sufferings), plus to meet what you dislike, not to obtain what you seek, and attachment to the elements that make up one's environment (*skhanda*).

**Eightfold Noble Path**: consists of right view, right thoughts, right speech, right acts, right living, right effort, right mindfulness, right meditation.

**Emma-O** (Jpn.): the king of the dead, or god of the dead (Skt. Yama), in Buddhist mythology of the afterlife. He keeps the record book of one's good or bad deeds and determines the form of one's next rebirth in transmigration.

**Exclusive Practice**: sole practice of *nembutsu* recitation, devoted to Amida Buddha, taught by Honen, and transmitted by his disciples. No other practice is required for birth in the Pure Land; *see also* Miscellaneous Practice

**Five Defilements**: pollutions appear at the end of a *kalpa* cycle. They include defilement of the age (famine, plagues, wars), defilement of views, defilement of evil passions, defilement of sentient beings (breakdown of moral law), defilement of life (shortened lifespan).

**Five Grave Offenses**: the five damning acts include matricide, patricide, killing an *arhat* (Hinayana adept), injuring a Buddha, and creating divisions in the *sangha*.

**Five Powers**: faith in the Buddha, great effort, mindfulness, concentration, and deep wisdom.

**Five Roots of Goodness**: consist of faith in Buddha, *Dharma*, and *Sangha*, the practice of good deeds, mindfulness of Buddha-*dharma*, concentration, and insight into the true nature of existence.

**Five Sufferings**: birth, illness, old age, death, loss of loved ones.

**Four Perverse Views**: Ignorant people take impermanence as permanent, displeasure as pleasure, non-self as self, impure as pure.

**Four Streams**: desire, existence, ideation, and ignorance.

**Four Truths**: the truth of suffering, the cause of suffering, the extinction of suffering, the path to *nirvana*.

**Gandhara** (Skt.): divine musician and protector of Buddhism.

**Gatha** (Skt.): verse.

**Heizei Gojo** (Jpn.): a major principle of Shin Buddhism, referring to the arising of true entrusting in our ordinary mind which assures birth in the Pure Land.

**Higan** (Jpn.): the other shore of enlightenment; *see also* Shigan

**Hinayana** (Skt.): the small narrow vehicle viewed from the standpoint of Mahayana Buddhism, which signifies a broad spacious vehicle of universal salvation. Mahayana sutras depict conceited monks who think they have all the truth the Buddha had to offer.

**Hoben** (Jpn.): compassionate, tactful device to convey the deeper, inexpressible truth of Buddhism, according to one's capacity to understand.

**Hoon Kansha** (Jpn.): the Shin way of life of true entrusting, expressed by grateful recitation of *nembutsu*.

**Jambudvipa:** a continent in ancient Buddhist mythic geography where Buddhism is taught.

**Jihi** (Jpn.): compassion.

**Jinen Honi** (Jpn.): a major concept of Shin Buddhism, the principle of naturalism, spontaneity, things as they really are, ultimate reality; refers to the working of Amida's vow power, which is self-caused, in perfect freedom.

**Jishu** (Jpn.): Time sect; the name for the sect initiated by Ippen, which designated certain specific times for the recitation of *nembutsu*. Ippen also taught that one should recite *nembutsu* as though it were the last moment.

**Jodo Shinshu** (Jpn.): originally a term denoting the "true essence (teaching) of the Pure Land." Used by Shinran, it later came to designate the sect reputedly founded by Shinran.

**Kalpa** (Skt.): an enormously long period of time, an aeon, in the millions of years' duration.

**Kami** (Jpn.): "god" or "spirit" in the native Japanese tradition of Shinto.

**Karma** (Skt.): act or action, deed. One's future birth or transmigration is determined by one's good or bad deeds.

**Koti** (Skt.): extremely large number, typically given as 100 million.

**Ksatriya** (Skt.): Indian caste, including kings, nobles, and warriors.

**Lokeshvararaja** (Skt.): the Buddha under whom Dharmakara *Bodhisattva* made his vows to create the Pure Land and gain enlightenment as Amida Buddha, thereby establishing the Pure Land path to enlightenment and Buddhahood for all sentient beings.

**Mahasattvas** (Skt.): an honorific title meaning "great being."

**Mahayana** (Skt.): great, large, spacious vehicle; inclusive in comparison to the Hinayana or small and narrow vehicle.

**Mani** (Skt.): efficacious, magical gem, jewel.

**Mappo** (Jpn.): one of three stages in the decline of Buddhist teaching after the passing of Sakyamuni Buddha. The first stage, true *Dharma* (500-1000 years' duration), is when Buddhist ideals are fulfilled through teaching, practice, and realization; the second stage is semblance *Dharma* (also 500-1000 years' duration) where there is teaching and practice, but no realization; and finally the last age, which lasts 10,000 years, where there is only teaching, with no practice or realization. During the last stage the Pure Land teaching becomes applicable to all people, monks or lay.

**Mara** (Skt.): a demon, devil; symbol of the passions and obstruction to Buddhism.

**Merit Transference**: a fundamental principle underlying Pure Land teaching which evolved with the development of the teaching. The merit of the *Bodhisattva* establishes the Name of Amida as the infinite resource for salvation. The recitation of the Name of Amida yields merit to the devotee toward the purification of their defilements, which enables birth in the Pure Land. In Shin Buddhism, the merit of the *Bodhisattva*/Amida expresses itself as true entrusting (*shinjin*), assuring birth in the Pure Land. All merit is provided by Amida, no merit being transferred by the devotee.

**Middle Path Philosophy**: expounded by Nagarjuna, deducing the voidness (emptiness) of all things through the logic of cause and effect and contingency implied in the 12 link chain of dependent co-origination. Later within Mahayana the Consciousness-Only school of thought developed, based on a concept of store-consciousness from which all things are manifest. It is a form of psychological idealism.

**Miscellaneous Practice**: refers to all practices, other than the *nembutsu*, employed to attain enlightenment.

**Nayuta(s)** (Skt.): a large number from 100,000 to 10 million.

**Nembutsu** (Jpn.): originally the term meant "to think on the Buddha," meditative practice. In Pure Land tradition it came to mean the recitation of Amida Buddha's Name. In Shin Buddhism, it was interpreted by Shinran as faith or true entrusting. Recitation is not for salvation but to express gratitude for the salvation assured through trust in Amida's vow.

**Nirmanakaya** (Skt.): *see* Three Bodies of the Buddha

**Non-Meditative Practices**: the practices of morality, filial piety, and all good deeds which enable birth in the Pure Land.

**Non-Retrogression**: the seventh stage in the *bodhisattva* path, from which he does not fall back; a condition of those born into the Pure Land. For Shinran, when true entrusting arises, devotees are in the stage of non-retrogression.

**One Vehicle**: the one path to enlightenment among the two or three vehicles; taught in the *Lotus Sutra*. Emphasized by Shinran as the ultimate teaching of Buddhism.

**Paramita** (Skt.): means going to the other shore (*higan*) of spiritual perfection; the six virtues in Mahayana Buddhism: selfless giving, patience-endurance, energy-endeavor, morality-precepts, meditation-concentration, and wisdom. Also an additional four: adaptability, vows, strength of purpose, knowledge.

**Pratyekabuddha** (Skt.): a devotee who gains enlightenment without a teacher; one who contemplates the twelve links of dependent causation.

**Primal Vow** (also Original Vow, Fundamental Vow): generally refers to the eighteenth vow of Amida, the vow of salvation; also used to represent the forty-eight vows of Amida which establish the Pure Land.

**Pure Land Teaching** (Gate, Path): *contra* Saintly Path (Holy Path, Sage Path). A distinction made by Tao-ch'o to highlight the significance of Pure Land teaching in the *mappo* age. The Pure Land way is the easy path of *nembutsu*, while the Saintly Path is the way of difficult practices.

**Raigo, Raiko** (Jpn.): The descent or coming of the Buddha and his retinue from the Pure Land to welcome faithful devotees at their death, according to the nineteenth vow.

**Recompensed Land**: *see* Three Bodies of the Buddha

**Response-Body of Visualization**: visualizing the body of the Buddha in human form with worldly features.

**Rightly Established State**: the stage of being certain to attain enlightenment and Buddhahood expressed in the eleventh vow of Amida Buddha. In general Mahayana, attained in the Pure Land; in Shinran's thought, gained in the moment one receives true entrusting (*shinjin*) in this life.

**Saha** (Skt.): the world of pain and suffering.

**Saintly Path** (Holy Path, Sage Path): *see* Pure Land Teaching

**Samadhi** (Skt.): the practice of meditation and concentration.

**Samantabhadra** (Skt.): a *Bodhisattva*, "universally gracious," symbolizing the practice of meditation in Buddhism. Represented sitting on a white elephant and as an attendant of Sakyamuni Buddha.

**Samatha, Shamatha** (Skt.): the process of calming the mind in meditation. Paired with vipasyana (also vipassana): exploring, contemplating reality. In Pure Land contemplating the 29 features of the Land.

**Samsara** (Skt.): the wheel of births and deaths; the realm of finitude.

**Sangha** (Skt.): the community of monks; later it came to represent all Buddhists, monk or lay, male or female.

**Sanron** (Jpn.): the Three Treatise school, teaching the Middle Path philosophy of Nagarjuna.

**Satori** (Jpn.): enlightenment, insight.

**Seishi** (Jpn.): *see* Avalokitesvara

**Seizan** (Jpn.): a sect in the Japanese Pure Land tradition, initiated by Shoku (1177-1247).

**Seven Practices Leading to Enlightenment**: (1) distinguishing the true teaching from the false, (2) making efforts to practice the true teaching, (3) rejoicing in the true teaching, (4) eliminating indolence and attaining comfort and relaxation, (5) being mindful so as to keep the balance between concentration and insight, (6) concentration, and (7) detaching one's thoughts from external objects, thereby securing serenity of mind.

**Shaba** (Jpn.): *see* Saha

**Shigan** (Jpn.): this world of suffering and transmigration.

**Shinjin** (Jpn.): in Shin Buddhism, true entrusting; the mind of faith in Amida's vow aroused through the working of Amida Buddha.

**Shingon** (Jpn.): mantra, true word, a mystically endowed word or phrase. Also the name of a sect established by Kukai (774-835).

**Shinshu** (Jpn.): *see* Jodo Shinshu

**Shravaka** (Skt.): a disciple of Buddha in the Hinayana tradition.

**Sramana** (Skt.): a Buddhist monk.

**Stage of Becoming a Buddha After One More Life**: the highest stage of the *bodhisttva* in the process of becoming Buddha. The *bodhisattva* returns once more to the suffering world to work for the salvation of all beings. The fifth gate of going out in Vasubandhu's five gates of practice, in which the devotee transfers the merit of practice to all beings.

**Stage of the Definitely Settled**: *see* Rightly Established State

**Sukhavati** (Skt.): the land of highest bliss, the Pure Land.

**Sunyata** (Skt.): emptiness, voidness. In Mahayana, things and concepts are void. Emptiness means nothing has its own, independent self-nature or is self-explanatory; everything is the result of dependent co-origination, and without intrinsic value.

**Tathagata** (Skt.): a title of the Buddha, "thus come from suchness, thus gone to suchness."

**Ten Bodhisattva Stages**: the highest among the fifty-two stages in the process of becoming Buddha.

**Tendai** (Skt.): a sect in Japanese Buddhism, and the background for teachers such as Honen and Shinran, who all studied on Mount Hiei near Kyoto, the Tendai center in Japan.

**Ten Transgressions**: they include: killing, stealing, adultery, lying, using harsh language, causing enmity, idle talk, greed, anger, wrong views.

**Theravada** (Skt.): a major division of Buddhism meaning the "Way of the Elders." Largely present in South and Southeast Asia, its teaching traces back to what Mahayanists called Hinayana Buddhism.

**Thirty-Two Physical Characteristics and Eighty Secondary Marks**: the features of either a Universal King or a Buddha in ancient Buddhist thought marking the excellence and superiority of a Buddha, particularly.

**Three Bodies of the Buddha**: there are concepts of two bodies of the Buddha (*dharma*-nature body and body of compassionate means) and three bodies of the Buddha (*dharmakaya*, the body of truth, *sambhogakaya*, the reward, recompense, or fulfilled body, and *nirmanakaya*, the transformed body) along with their corresponding lands. These distinctions arose to account for the variety of Buddha concepts in Buddhist texts. The three bodies represent the Buddha in history, in myth in the sutras receiving rewards for his deeds, and as ultimate truth.

**Three Defilements**: greed, anger, and ignorance.

**Three Evil Realms**: lowest levels of the six paths of transmigration: hells, hungry ghosts, animals, angry spirits, humans, gods.

**Threefold Devotional Heart**: the genuine heart (sincerity), the heart of profound faith (which includes our passion-ridden nature and Amida's embrace), and the turning over of merit for birth in the Pure Land.

**Threefold Discipline**: ethical conduct, meditation, and wisdom (*sila*-precepts, *samadhi*-concentration, and *prajna*-wisdom).

**Threefold Shinjin**: the three minds of the eighteenth vow; sincerity, joyous faith, and desire for birth in the Pure Land; in Shin Buddhism, endowed by Amida Buddha.

**Threefold Wisdom**: wisdom of the Hinayana, general knowledge of things; the bodhisattva, discriminating knowledge; and the Buddha, complete general and discriminating knowledge.

**Three Holy Ones**: Amida Buddha and his two attendants, Avalokitesvara (right) and Mahasthamaprapta (left).

**Three Minds**: in the *Contemplation Sutra*, sincerity, deep faith, and mind to transfer merit for birth in the Pure Land; in Shin Buddhism regarded as self-powered faith.

**Three Obediences**: Confucian concept for wives obedient to father, husband, and eldest son.

**Three Treasures**: Buddha, *Dharma*, and *Sangha*.

**Three Worlds**: sentient, non-sentient, and world of five *skhandas* (elements making up beings).

**Transformed Buddhas**: *see* Three Bodies of the Buddha

**Tripitaka** (Skt.): three baskets of scriptures: sutra, teachings of Buddha; *vinaya*, rules of discipline and precepts; and *abhidhamma*, commentaries.

**Tusita Heaven**: the realm where Maitreya is believed to have resided while waiting to become Buddha.

**Twelvefold Causation**: twelve links in the chain of dependent co-origination: ignorance, blind volition, consciousness, mental functions, six sense organs, contact (with external objects), sensations, desire for pleasure, grasping, state of existing, birth, and old age and death.

**Two Vehicles**: *shravakas* and *pratyekabuddhas*.

**Upadesa** (Skt.): discourse, discussion of doctrine often in dialogic form.

**Upaya** (Skt.): a tactful, compassion device.

**Vipashyana** (Skt.): *see* Samatha

**Worldly Merits**: these include filiality, respect for teachers, compassion, and the ten good actions: no killing, no stealing, no adultery, no lying, no harsh words, no words causing enmity, no idle talk, no greed, no anger, no wrong views.

**Yama Heaven**: third heaven in the world of desire; the Heaven of Good Time.

**Yojana** (Skt.): term of distance, one *yojana* is said to be about 30-40 Chinese *li* or about 9 miles.

**Zenchishiki** (Jpn.): a good friend or good teacher who leads one in the Buddhist way.

**Zojo-en** (Jpn.): a dominant or promotive cause, bringing something into existence.

# Bibliography

Atone, Joji and Yoko Hayashi, trans. *Teachings of Honen*. Los Angeles: Bukkyo University-Los Angeles Extension, 2007, rev.

————. *The Promise of Amida Buddha: Honen's Path to Bliss*. Boston: Wisdom Publications, 2011.

Coates, H.H. and R. Ishizuka, trans. *Honen the Buddhist Saint: His Life and Teaching*. Kyoto: Chion' in, 1925.

Hakeda, Yoshito, trans. *Awakening of Faith*. New York: Columbia University Press, 1967.

Hirota, Dennis, trans. *No Abode: The Record of Ippen*. Honolulu: The University of Hawai' i Press, 1997, rev.

Inagaki, Hisao, trans. *Dharma Words at Yokawa*. http://www12.canvas.ne.jp/horai/yokawa-hogo.htm.

————. *Discourse on the Ten Stages, Easy Practice Section*. http://www12.canvas.ne.jp/horai/igyohon.htm.

————. *Kannenbomon: The Method of Contemplation on Amida*. Kyoto: Nagata Bunshodo, 2005.

————. *Liturgy for Birth*. http://www12.canvas.ne.jp/horai/raisan.htm.

————. Nagarjuna's *Junirai Twelve Adorations*. http://www12.canvas.ne.jp/horai/larger-sutra-1.htm.

————. *One Sheet Profession of Faith*. http://www12.canvas.ne.jp/horai/ichimai-kishomon.htm.

————. *T'an-luan's Commentary on Vasubandhu's Discourse on the Pure Land*. Kyoto: Nagata Bunshodo, 1998.

————. "Tao-ch'o's *An-le-chi* (Part I)." *The Pure Land*. New Series 21, December 2004.

————. "Tao-ch'o's *An-le-chi* (Part II)." *The Pure Land*. New Series 22, December 2006.

————. "Tao ch'o's *An-le-chi* (Part III)." *The Pure Land*. New Series 23, December 2007.

————. "Tao-ch'o's *An-le-chi* (Part IV)." *The Pure Land*. New Series 24, December 2008.

————. *The Three Pure Land Sutras*. Kyoto: Nagata Bunshodo, 1994.

————. *Three Refuges.* http://www12.canvas.ne.jp/horai/kisamboge.htm.

————. *Thus Have I Heard from Rennyo Shonin.* Judet Dolj, Romania: Dharma Lion Publications, 2008.

————. Vasubandhu's *Treatise on the Pure Land.* http://www12.canvas. ne.jp/horai/jodoron.htm.

Matsunaga, Daigan and Alicia Matsunaga. *Foundation of Japanese Buddhism, Vol. I: The Aristocratic Age.* Los Angeles, Tokyo: Buddhist Books International, 1974.

————. *Foundation of Japanese Buddhism, Vol. II: The Mass Movement (Kamakura and Muromachi Periods).* Los Angeles, Tokyo: Buddhist Books International, 1976.

Pas, Julian F. *Visions of Sukhavati: Shan-tao's Commentary on the Kuan Wu-Liang-Shou-Fo Ching.* Albany, NY: State University of New York Press, 1995.

Reischauer, A. K., trans. "Genshin's *Ojoyoshu:* Collected Essays on Birth into Paradise." *The Transactions of the Asiatic Society of Japan* (December 1930), 2nd Series, Vol. VII.

Rogers, Minor L. and Ann T. Rogers, trans. *Rennyo: The Second Founder of Shin Buddhism.* Berkeley, CA: Asian Humanities Press, 1991.

Rhodes, Robert F. "The Beginning of Pure Land Buddhism in Japan: From its Introduction through the Nara Period." *Japanese Journal of Religion* (January 2006), Vol. 31, No. 1.

Senchakushu English Translation Project. *Honen's Senchakushu: Passages on the Selection of the Nembutsu in the Original Vow.* Honolulu, HI: University of Hawaii Press, 1998.

Shinshu Shogyo Zensho, I. Kyoto: Kokyo Shoin, 1953.

Tanaka, Kenneth K. *Pure Land Buddhism: Historical Development and Contemporary Manifestation.* Bangalore, India: Dharmaram Publications, 2004.

————. trans. *The Dawn of Chinese Pure Land Buddhism: Ching-ying Hui-yuan's Commentary on the Visualization Sutra.* Albany, NY: State University of New York Press, 1990.

Watts, Jonathan and Yoshiharu Tomatsu, eds. *Traversing the Pure Land Way: A Lifetime of Encounters with Honen Shonin.* Tokyo: Jodo-shu Press, 2005.

Won Hyo. http://www.newworldencyclopedia.org/entry/Wonhyo#Thought_
and_Works.

Yokoyama, W.S., trans. *A Collection of Statements to Live By*. Unpublished
translation.

―――. *Embracing the Name*. Unpublished translation.

―――. *How to Be at Peace with Yourself: In the Spirit of the Anjinketsujosho*.
Unpublished partial translation.

―――. *The Life of Shinran*. Unpublished translation.

―――. *Liturgy for a Gathering to Express Gratitude to Shinran*. Unpublished
translation.

―――. *On the Redemption of Women by Birth* [*in the Pure Land*]. Unpublished translation.

―――. *Setting the Claims Straight*. Unpublished translation.

―――. *What Shinran Taught*. Unpublished translation.

―――. & Suzuki Hiroshi, eds. *Zonkaku hogo*. Unpublished translation.

# Index of Quoted Sources

Kakunyo
*Embracing the Name*: -406-; -532-; -546-

*Setting the Record Straight (Gaijasho)*: -333-; -334-; -414-; -458-; -459-; -549-; -550-; -563-; -564-; -565-; -566-; -567-; -586-

*What Shinran Taught (Kudensho)*: -413-; -504-; -505-; -506-; -507-; -524-; -548-; -585-

Kuya: -376-

Nagarjuna
*Commentary on the Mahaprajnaparamita Sutra*: -572-

*Easy Practice Chapter in the Sutra on the Ten Stages of the Bodhisattva*: -318-; -319-; -329-

*Fundamentals of the Middle Way (Madhyamaka karikas)*: -571-

*Twelve Personal Dedications (Twelve Adorations, Junirai)*: -330-

*Rakuho monrui (Collection of Passages on the Land of Bliss)*: -490-

Rennyo
*Letters (Gobunsho)*: -462-; -511-; -512-; -513-; -518-; -519-; -587-; -591-; -592-

*Thus I Have Heard from Rennyo Shonin (Rennyo goichidai kikigaki)*: -435-; -461-; -463-; -464-; -465-; -466-; -467-; -471-; -472-; -473-; -477-; -516-; -517-; -551-; -552-; -562-; -568-; -569-; -588-

Ryonin: -378-

Ryukan
*Clarification of Once-Calling and Many-Calling*: -394-

Seikaku
*Essentials of Faith Alone*: -392; -393-; -446-; -475-; -542-; -543-

Shan-tao
*Commentary on the Contemplation Sutra*: -326-; -353-; -470-; -579-

*Kannenbomon*: -349-; -350-; -351-; -362-; -363-; -364-; -430-; -431-; -438-; -482-; -554-

*Three Refuges (Kisamboge)*: -337-

*Liturgy for Birth (Ojoraisan)*: -323-; -324-; -325-; -332-; -338-; -339-; -340-; -352-; -365-; -366-; -367-; -368-; -426-; -427-; -429-; -439-; -440-; -526-; -576-

Shinran

 *Collection of Letters*: -402-; -590-; -593-; -594-

 *Gutoku's Notes*: -500-

 *Hymns of the Dharma Ages*: -396-; -397-; -433-; -434-; -528-; -529-; -531-; -544-; -559-; -561-

 *Hymns of the Pure Land*: -395-; -420-; -421-; -476-

 *Hymns of the Pure Land Masters*: -422-

 *Lamp for the Latter Ages*: -401-; -403-; -404-; -405-; -451-; -452-; -453-; -454-; -455-; -520-; -521-; -584-

 *Notes on Essentials of Faith Alone*: -398-; -447-; -448-; -497-; -514-; -515-; -545-

 *Notes on Inscriptions on Sacred Scrolls*: -399-; -400-; -424-; -425-; -450-; -556-

 *Notes on Once-Calling and Many-Calling*: -423-; -449-; -498-

 *Kyogyoshinsho* (Miscellaneous texts and writers): -374- Beob-wi; -371- Chang-jun; -369- Shan-tao; -370- Shan-tao; -428- Shan-tao; -481- Shan-tao; -483- Shan-tao; -484- Shan-tao; -485- Shan-tao; -486- Shan-tao; -487- Shan-tao; -488- Shan-tao; -489- Shan-tao; -557- Shan-tao; -577- Shan-tao; -479- T'an-luan; -525- T'an-luan; -574- T'an-luan; [Shinran -580-; -581- Shoshinge]; -372- Yuan-chao; -373- Yuan-chao

 *Record in Lament of Divergences (Tannisho)*: -457-; -501-; -522-; -523-; -530-

 *The Virtue of the Name of Amida Tathagata*: -456-

Shoku: -407-; -547-

T'an-luan

 *Commentary on Vasubandhu's Discourse on the Pure Land (Ojoronchu)*: -321-; -322-; -336-; -347-; -348-; -355-; -436-; -437-; -442-; -468-; -469-; -478-; -533-; -534-; -553-; -573-

 *Gathas in Praise of Amida Buddha*: -331-

Tao-ch'o

 *An-le-chi*: -356-; -357-; -358-; -359-; -360-; -361-; -443-; -535-; -536-; -575-

Vasubandhu

 *Commentary on the Larger Pure Land Sutra (Jodoron)*: -320-; -335-; -344-

Zonkaku

 *Shinyosho*: -415-

 *Zonkaku's Sermons (Zonkaku hogo)*: -508-; -509-; -510-; -578-

# Biographical Notes

**ALFRED BLOOM** was born in Philadelphia. After enlisting in the US Army in 1944, he had the opportunity to study Japanese. Greatly influenced by his Christian background, this occasion motivated his decision to become a missionary. However, an encounter with Buddhism stimulated his interest in other religions. After graduating from a seminary, Bloom began his study of Buddhism. Upon receiving a Fulbright grant, he traveled to Japan where he studied the life and thought of Shinran (1173-1263), the founder of Shin Buddhism. In 1963, he completed his doctoral studies at Harvard University.

Dr. Bloom has since taught at a number of universities, including the University of Oregon and the University of Hawaii. After retiring from the University of Hawaii, Bloom became the Dean of the Institute of Buddhist Studies in Berkeley, California, a seminary and graduate school sponsored by the Buddhist Churches of America and affiliated with the Christian Graduate Theological Union.

Throughout his 40-year career, Bloom has participated in the research and study of world religions and in the Buddhist-Christian dialogue. He was ordained as a Shin minister and presently lives in Hawaii, where he is a member of the Honpa Hongwanji Mission and is active in ecumenical Buddhist activities.

Dr. Bloom is the author and editor of numerous books and articles, the most important of which are *Shinran's Gospel of Pure Grace*, which has been translated into both Japanese and Korean, *Living in Amida's Universal Vow: Essays in Shin Buddhism* (World Wisdom, 2004), *The Essential Shinran: A Buddhist Path of True Entrusting* (World Wisdom, 2007), and *The Shin Buddhist Classical Tradition: A Reader in Pure Land Teaching, Vol. 1* (World Wisdom, 2013).

**KENNETH K. TANAKA** was born in 1947 in Yamaguchi, Japan, but moved to California as a child with his Japanese American parents. He was introduced to Buddhism at the Mt. View Buddhist Temple, where he attended Sunday school and the Young Buddhist Association (YBA).

After graduating from Stanford University in 1970 with a degree in Cultural Anthropology, he took a year-long journey around the world that included a stint as a monk in a Buddhist monastery in Thailand. He then entered the M.A. program at the Institute of Buddhist Studies. In Japan, he studied at Tokyo University where he earned an M.A. in Indian Philosophy, followed by his ordination in 1978 as a Jodo Shinshu priest. Returning to the US, he earned a Ph.D. in Buddhist Studies at University of California, Berkeley.

Dr. Tanaka's first professional position was at the Institute of Buddhist Studies, where he spent 11 years on its staff. He then took a leave for 3 years to become the resident minister at the Southern Alameda County Buddhist Church. In 1998, he was appointed professor at Musashino University. He has also taught courses at Tokyo University, Ryukoku University (Kyoto), Renmin University (Beijing), and Dharmaram College (Bangalore).

He currently serves as president of two academic associations: the International Association of Shin Buddhist Studies and the Japanese Association for the Study of Buddhism and Psychology, and is a board member of the Association of Buddhist Christian Studies. His publications include *The Dawn of Chinese Pure Land Buddhist Doctrine*, *Ocean: An Introduction to Jodo Shinshu Buddhism in America*, and *Amerika bukkyo* (American Buddhism).

# Other World Wisdom Titles on Buddhism

*The Buddha Eye:*
*An Anthology of the Kyoto School and Its Contemporaries,*
edited by Frederick Franck, 2004

*A Buddhist Spectrum: Contributions to Buddhist-Christian Dialogue,*
by Marco Pallis, 2004

*The Essential Shinran: A Buddhist Path of True Entrusting,*
edited by Alfred Bloom, 2007

*The Golden Age of Zen: Zen Masters of the T'ang Dynasty,*
by John C.H. Wu, 2004

*Honen the Buddhist Saint: Essential Writings and Official Biography,*
edited by Joseph A. Fitzgerald, 2006

*An Illustrated Outline of Buddhism: The Essentials of Buddhist Spirituality,*
by William Stoddart, 2013

*The Laughing Buddha of Tofukuji: The Life of Zen Master Keido Fukushima,*
by Ishwar Harris, 2004

*Living in Amida's Universal Vow: Essays in Shin Buddhism,*
edited by Alfred Bloom, 2004

*Master of Zen: Extraordinary Teachings from Hui-Neng's Altar Sutra,*
translated and adapted by Tze-si Huang, illustrated by Demi, 2012

*Naturalness: A Classic of Shin Buddhism,*
by Kenryo Kanamatsu, 2002

*Samdhong Rinpoche: Uncompromising Truth for a*
*Compromised World: Tibetan Buddhism and Today's World,*
edited by Donovan Roebert, 2006

*Treasures of Buddhism,*
by Frithjof Schuon, 1993

*The Way and the Mountain: Tibet, Buddhism, and Tradition,*
by Marco Pallis, 2008

*Zen Buddhism: A History, Vol. 1: India and China,*
by Heinrich Dumoulin, 2005

*Zen Buddhism: A History, Vol. 2: Japan,*
by Heinrich Dumoulin, 2005